# A CULTURAL HISTORY
# OF FOOD

VOLUME 4

**A Cultural History of Food**

*General Editors: Fabio Parasecoli and Peter Scholliers*

**Volume 1**
A Cultural History of Food in Antiquity
*Edited by Paul Erdkamp*

**Volume 2**
A Cultural History of Food in the Medieval Age
*Edited by Massimo Montanari*

**Volume 3**
A Cultural History of Food in the Renaissance
*Edited by Ken Albala*

**Volume 4**
A Cultural History of Food in the Early Modern Age
*Edited by Beat Kümin*

**Volume 5**
A Cultural History of Food in the Age of Empire
*Edited by Martin Bruegel*

**Volume 6**
A Cultural History of Food in the Modern Age
*Edited by Amy Bentley*

# A CULTURAL HISTORY
## OF FOOD

# IN THE EARLY
# MODERN AGE

### VOLUME 4

*Edited by Beat Kümin*

Bloomsbury Academic
An imprint of Bloomsbury Publishing Plc

BLOOMSBURY
LONDON · OXFORD · NEW YORK · NEW DELHI · SYDNEY

**Bloomsbury Academic**
An imprint of Bloomsbury Publishing Plc

50 Bedford Square          1385 Broadway
London                     New York
WC1B 3DP                   NY 10018
UK                         USA

www.bloomsbury.com

**BLOOMSBURY and the Diana logo are trademarks of
Bloomsbury Publishing Plc**

Hardback edition first published in 2012 by Berg Publishers,
an imprint of Bloomsbury Academic
Paperback edition first published in 2016 by Bloomsbury Academic

**British Library Cataloguing-in-Publication Data**
A catalogue record for this book is available from the British Library.

ISBN: HB:      978-0-8578-5026-3
      HB set: 978-1-8478-8355-1
      PB:      978-1-4742-6999-5
      PB set:  978-1-4742-7075-5

**Library of Congress Cataloging-in-Publication Data**
A catalog record for this book is available from the Library of Congress.

Typeset by Apex CoVantage, LLC

# CONTENTS

# SERIES PREFACE

GENERAL EDITORS, FABIO PARASECOLI
AND PETER SCHOLLIERS

*A Cultural History of Food* presents an authoritative survey from ancient times to the present. This set of six volumes covers nearly 3,000 years of food and its physical, spiritual, social, and cultural dimensions. Volume editors and authors, representing different nationalities and cultural traditions, constitute the cutting edge in historical research on food and offer an overview of the field that reflects the state of the art of the discipline. While the volumes focus mostly on the West (Europe in its broadest sense and North America), they also draw in comparative material and each volume concludes with a brief final chapter on contemporaneous developments in food ideas and practices outside the West. These works will contribute to the expansion of the food history research in Asia, Africa, Oceania, and South America, which is already growing at an increasingly fast pace.

The six volumes, which follow the traditional approach to examining the past in Western cultures, divide the history of food as follows:

Volume 1: A Cultural History of Food in Antiquity (800 BCE–500 CE)
Volume 2: A Cultural History of Food in the Medieval Age (500–1300)
Volume 3: A Cultural History of Food in the Renaissance (1300–1600)
Volume 4: A Cultural History of Food in the Early Modern Age (1600–1800)
Volume 5: A Cultural History of Food in the Age of Empire (1800–1900)
Volume 6: A Cultural History of Food in the Modern Age (1920–2000)

This periodization does not necessarily reflect the realities and the historical dynamics of non-Western regions, but the relevance of cultural and material exchanges among different civilizations in each period is emphasized.

Each volume discusses the same themes in its chapters:

1. *Food Production.* These chapters examine agriculture, husbandry, fishing, hunting, and foraging at any given period, considering the environmental impact of technological and social innovations, and the adaptation to the climate and environment changes.

2. *Food Systems.* These chapters explore the whole range of the transportation, distribution, marketing, advertising, and retailing of food, emphasizing trade, commerce, and the international routes that have crisscrossed the world since antiquity.

3. *Food Security, Safety, and Crises.* We cannot have a complete picture of the history of food without discussing how societies dealt with moments of crisis and disruption of food production and distribution, such as wars, famines, shortages, and epidemics. These essays reflect on the cultural, institutional, economic, and social ways of coping with such crises.

4. *Food and Politics.* These chapters focus on the political aspects of public food consumption: food aspects of public ceremonies and feasts, the impact on public life, regulations, controls, and taxation over food and alcohol production, exchange, and consumption.

5. *Eating Out.* The communal and public aspects of eating constitute the main focus of these essays. Authors consider hospitality for guests, at home and in public spaces (banquets and celebrations), and discuss public places to eat and drink in urban and rural environments, including street food, marketplaces, and fairs.

6. *Professional Cooking, Kitchens, and Service Work.* These chapters look at the various roles involved in food preparation outside the family nucleus: slaves, cooks, servants, waiters, *maitre d'hotel* etc., investigating also the most relevant cooking techniques, technologies, and tools for each period, giving special consideration to innovations.

7. *Family and Domesticity.* The acquisition, shopping and storage, preparation, consumption, and disposal of food in a domestic setting

are among the most important aspects of food culture. These chapters analyze family habits in different periods of time, paying particular attention to gender roles and the material culture of the domestic kitchen.

8. *Body and Soul*. These chapters examine fundamental material aspects such as nutritional patterns, food constituents, and food-related diseases. Furthermore, spiritual and cultural aspects of thinking about and consuming food are highlighted, including religion, philosophy, as well as health and diet theories.

9. *Food Representations*. These essays analyze cultural and discursive reflections about food, which not only contributed to the way people conceive of food, but also to the social and geographical diffusion of techniques and behavior.

10. *World Developments*. These brief chapters overview developments, dynamics, products, food-related behaviors, social structures, and concepts in cultural environments that often found themselves at the margins of Western modernity.

Rather than embracing the encyclopedic model, the authors apply a broad multidisciplinary framework to examine the production, distribution, and consumption of food, as grounded in the cultural experiences of the six historical periods. This structure allows readers to obtain a broad overview of a period by reading a volume, or to follow a theme through history by reading the relevant chapter in each volume.

Highly illustrated, the full six-volume set combines to present the most authoritative and comprehensive survey available on food through history.

# Introduction

BEAT KÜMIN

For the visit of a group of patricians in the mid-seventeenth century, the innkeeper of Jegenstorf (in the Swiss canton of Bern) received advance orders for a lavish banquet, involving the loan of luxury crockery and cutlery and even the hiring of additional cooks and *traiteurs*. The instructions specified three courses including: 1. Good soups with boiled and roast meat; 2. A range of fish-, chicken- and dove-pies; 3. Cakes and other baked dishes; olives; boiled and baked fish and crabs; boiled and roast poultry and doves; roast porkling; glazed roast pig; well-made sausages. Also salad and the like and finally confectionery appropriate for such "noble" company.[1]

During his journeys through the Bavarian countryside in the 1780s, travel writer Philipp Wilhelm Gercken found "nothing but Sauerkraut, cow's meat and pork or sausages. Who cannot face such fare, has to bring along some cold roast from the towns. Meat soups are available as early as 8 o'clock in the morning, they are not too bad…and good beer is always served. People with a healthy stomach find life here terrific."[2]

Visiting the village of Grindelwald in the Alps at about the same time, J.W.F. von Reinach was not impressed: "At last our host served the meal...The meat was prepared in a fashion which made it bearable only in an emergency, the drink was even worse (with the white wine having a foul smell and the red hardly an improvement). The only alternative was—fortunately good—fountain water. Dessert turned out a little better: cheese and cherries, which helped to fill our stomach. We soon left this miserable table."[3]

These three snapshots provide some initial impressions of the range and variety of food provision between the Renaissance and the modern age. Many of the dishes sound familiar to modern consumers, but dining contexts and preferences were naturally very distinct. The fourth volume of the series *A Cultural History of Food* sets out to examine alimentary practices and meanings in the period from the late sixteenth to the late eighteenth centuries. As indicated by the book's title, the main emphasis is on food, albeit with consideration of closely related topics such as drink, material culture, and socio-economic conditions.

The chronological framework for this collection broadly corresponds to Europe's so-called "early modernity." While there is much debate about boundaries (at both ends), defining features, and long-term legacies, most scholars accept the term as a pragmatic label for the time between the Reformation and French Revolution.[4] Some, particularly in the Anglophone world, tend to detach the eighteenth-century Enlightenment as a distinct entity, pointing to the latter's innovatory emphasis on reason, critical reflection, and cultural innovation, but there are equally good reasons—such as the resilience of feudal relationships and princely powers—to embed the 1700s in the early modern tradition.

To situate and connect the following contributions, the introductory remarks are structured in three parts: (1) a general historical overview, (2) ways in which early modern developments interacted with the culture of food, and (3) the themes and emphases of this volume. The argument concludes with (4) an outline of research perspectives and preliminary conclusions.

## EARLY MODERN EUROPE

As in any other historical period, the early modern centuries were characterized by a complex blend of continuities and transformations.[5] Legacies from the Middle Ages included the hierarchical and patriarchal structure of European society. Lineage and birth right still determined lifestyles and personal opportunities to a large extent, although the traditional division into three estates (those who fought, prayed, and worked) became inadequate for a growing and ever more differentiated population. Women were subject to men, regardless of the fact that many made essential contributions to their families' livelihoods. Politically, the vast majority of Europeans lived in monarchical regimes granting a disproportionate share of influence to members of the nobility. Republics such as those of the Dutch, Swiss, and Venetians were exceptions and not immune to the oligarchic tendencies of the period. Religion played a towering role in all polities (including, until at least the late seventeenth century, international relations), with regular church attendance and adherence to Christian values expected from all subjects. Socio-economically, feudalism remained operational: peasants (who made up the vast majority of the population) owed various combinations of rents, dues, and services to their lords. Where serfdom had survived, as in Eastern Europe, nobles also exercised local jurisdiction and extensive control over their tenants' personal lives. At the same time, participation in urban, rural, and parochial communities provided the common people with some social and political powers of their own.[6]

Numerous dynamic forces, however, gave the early modern period a distinct profile. A cluster of transformations between 1450 and 1550 marked the emergence of a new era: the invention of print (and thus Europe's first instrument of mass communication), the beginnings of transatlantic expansion, the scientific revolution (including, most startlingly, the shift from a geo- to a heliocentric model of the universe), and the fragmentation of the Christian Church into rival confessions (Catholic, Lutheran, Reformed).[7] Politically, rulers embarked on the consolidation of their territories, aiming not only for the acquisition of new dominions, but also the greater penetration and subordination of existing possessions. This process of state formation involved increasing levels of legislation, administration, and taxation, culminating—in areas such as France, Brandenburg-Prussia, and Russia—into regimes of an absolutist nature, where previous checks on princely powers (by the Church, nobles, and representative assemblies) were eroded to a greater or lesser extent. This centralizing trend found symbolic expression in the personality cult of monarchs and the rise of princely courts as nodal points of political life. Yet none of these regimes acquired total or even despotic powers, since they remained limited by natural or divine law, dependent on provincial brokers and threatened by popular resistance against excessive demands.[8]

Religious division, dynastic ambitions, and the struggle over colonial resources turned warfare into an almost permanent feature of early modern politics. Innovations in military tactics and weaponry (especially the growing reliance on gunpowder and artillery) boosted army sizes, creating an ensuing need for greater discipline, bureaucracy, and financial revenues. This so-called military revolution—whose exact parameters remain contested—allowed longer and more ambitious campaigns, albeit at enormous monetary and social cost. The Thirty Years' War (1618–1648) in particular devastated many parts of Central Europe, causing population losses of over fifty percent in some cases. While religion still mattered greatly in this conflict, the Seven Years' War (1756–1763) exemplified the increasingly global repercussions of European politics and the essential role of naval resources. By that point, both troop numbers and casualties could approach the one million mark—a far cry from the modest dimensions of late medieval encounters.[9]

Regional variety was a key feature of early modern experience. Overseas expansions benefitted, above all, areas and cities along the Atlantic seaboard, with Spain and Portugal at the forefront of trading activities in the sixteenth century, and the Dutch and British obtaining pre-eminence from the seventeenth century onward. North-western Europe was most heavily urbanized and differentiated, while agriculture—in numerous forms of arable husbandry and pastoral regimes—dominated most other areas of the continent. There were pockets of early industry (as in the mines of the Austrian Tyrol or the English Midlands), and manufacturing, too, could be increasingly co-ordinated, especially in the decentralized *putting out* system under which rural laborers produced textiles for marketing by urban merchants. After the harsh decades of the late 1500s, when population increases, climatic deterioration, and harvest failures caused serious hardship for the European poor, conditions mostly stabilized in the seventeenth century. Moderate levels of dispensable income allowed members of the middling sort to become consumers, purchasing goods in line with personal tastes and changing fashions. This was most conspicuous in large cities such as London, Paris, Vienna, and Amsterdam, where colonial imports and new standards of (court-inspired) manners nurtured a civil society versed in the fine arts, critical reasoning, and polite sociability in salons and coffee houses, but even prosperous peasants invested in luxury items such as porcelain and plate with which to embellish their domestic environments.[10]

Culturally speaking, Europe moved from reliance on given authorities (especially scholastic theology and classical philosophy) towards individual education and observation—personified in astronomers such as Kepler, anatomists such as Vesalius, and physicists such as Newton. Personal merits and professional qualifications, most notably studies of law in one of the growing number of universities, provided new routes for social advancement, be it in the service of a prince or one of the established Churches. The Renaissance had fostered more critical attitudes to ancient texts and religious practices, the Confessional Age brought campaigns for greater social discipline (including clampdowns on traditional popular culture), and the Enlightenment set new priorities for human endeavors in all spheres of life—principally the pursuit of reason, social utility, and general happiness. There was no linear process of secularization in early modern Europe, but the devastation of religious wars and the experience of pragmatic coexistence promoted a grudging realization that Christian unity had been lost for good, and that there was little alternative to the acceptance of other faiths.[11] By around 1700, Europe was also in the midst of a communication revolution. The postal network, first developed for letters and diplomatic correspondence in the sixteenth century, had diversified into comprehensive transport services. Thanks to the introduction of regular and reliable stagecoach routes (and widespread investment in better public highways during the eighteenth century), long-distance mobility increased dramatically. The growth in pleasure trips—both mass pilgrimages in Catholic areas and early forms of tourism in the Alps—manifested itself in a flood of travel literature and practical guides.[12]

## DEVELOPMENTS IN EARLY MODERN FOOD CULTURE

By the close of the Middle Ages, the European diet could already be seen as rather impressive, at least among the elites. Cultural leadership was provided

by the Renaissance courts and cities of the Italian peninsula, where celebrated cooks such as Bartolomeo Scappi (who worked for Rome's prelates
and, in 1570, published a cookbook with over 1,000 recipes) acquired
good reputations and where Humanists engaged in culinary debates.[13]
Banquets had to be as opulent as possible, with a rich variety of dishes,
large quantities of food, and extravagant use of spices—the latter obtained
through the merchants' extensive trading networks with Asia. Further
north and among the common people, of course, everyday fare was much
more modest, cereal-based, and heavily dependent on location and season,
but it is widely accepted that the golden age of European peasants and
laborers (when low population levels following the Black Death resulted in
relatively high wages and favorable terms of tenure) allowed even humble
people to consume remarkable volumes of meat.[14] Excavations of late medieval inn locations, too, reveal that meals served on the premises featured
a surprising range of victuals. At Villingen in South Germany, for example,
archaeologists discovered a "wide range of animal bones" and beneath
the drinking hall of Munich's town council, they found various types of
fish (including Mediterranean seafood), nuts, as well as cherries, plums,
peaches, apples, figs, and strawberries.[15]

Many of the general early modern trends outlined above affected
European food culture very directly. According to Ken Albala's pioneering
overview, change occurred, above all, in towns and among social elites,
whose lifestyles were most likely to be affected by the growth of the market, colonial imports, and more refined dining cultures.[16] The latter included more civil table manners and an increasing preference for simpler,
more elegant menus in the fashion of the French court, rather than the
heavy and elaborate banquets which had characterized Renaissance tables
of the fifteenth and sixteenth centuries.[17]

The single most striking development, of course, was the enrichment
of diets and the introduction of new crops through the Columbian exchange (addressed in chapter 10).[18] Yet immediate large-scale adoptions—
as documented for maize in Northern Italy—were the exception rather
than the rule. After a great deal of initial skepticism, the take-off of potato
cultivation only occurred in the late eighteenth and nineteenth centuries.
Compared to the volume of petty, inner-continental trade, furthermore,
the extent of overseas exchange with the New World remained relatively

modest well into the 1700s: "Indeed, overseas expansion was less spectacularly significant in reality than contemporary propagandists and some historians might lead us to expect."[19] European state building manifested itself at least as visibly, for instance by a growing volume of central "police" legislation on the production and marketing of victuals from the late Middle Ages, high indirect taxes levied on salt or alcohol in the age of absolutism, and official encouragement of higher-yield crops—especially potatoes—in the Age of Enlightenment.[20] The new print technology allowed a more extensive dissemination of cookery books and dietetic literature, with Platina's *De honesta voluptate* one of the most influential early publications (see Figure 0.1).[21] Religious change associated with the Reformation(s) led to the abolition of traditional fasting rules in Protestant areas of the continent, albeit in combination with intense campaigns against immoderate eating and drinking.[22] The growing purchasing power of the middling sort, in turn, boosted differentiation in agricultural production, exemplified by the rise of market gardening—cultivation of fruit and vegetables (alongside fashionable flowers such as tulips) for prosperous urban consumers—in the Dutch Republic and parts of France, as well as the rise of strong (brandy, gin) and hot beverages (tea, coffee, chocolate) over the course of the early modern centuries.[23]

Regional variation in climate, topography, socio-economic structures, and crops, emphasized throughout this volume, makes it difficult to speak of an *overall* European food culture. Travellers routinely commented on the differences in culinary regimes encountered on their journeys. With regard to the Swiss, Fynes Moryson remarked in 1617: "For foode, they abound with Hony, Butter, and Milke, and haue plenty of Venson found in the wilde *Alpes,* and especially of excellent sorts of fish, by reason of their frequent lakes," while eighteenth-century Bavarian countryfolk, according to Johann Pezzl, "enjoy meat only on Sun- and feast days; during the week, they live on dishes made with flour, vegetables and cooked fruit."[24] Social status was another obvious factor affecting the availability or choice of food and drink. At the lowest end of the scale, harvest and distribution problems could lead to deprivation, and reactions ranging from begging via humble petitions to frequent food riots (as in the case of the hard-pressed French peasantry of the Ancien Régime).[25] At the top of the hierarchy, quality wine imported from—depending on the political situation—France,

FIGURE 0.1: Print technology allowed unprecedented dissemination of culinary information in early modern Europe. This picture shows the "New Cook = Book from Salzburg / for princely and other noble households / monasteries / manor houses / court = and house = masters / cooks and purchasers...With over 2,500 dishes / and 318 beautiful copperplate illustrations / compiled from long-standing personal practice / so that one can most delicately provide the tables...for large banquets and common meals with the most pleasant varieties.../ by Conrad Hagger / Cook of the Town and Land of the High = Princely territory of Salzburg. With gracious permission of his Roman Imperial Majesty. Augsburg / printed and distributed by Johann Jacob Lotter / 1719." Reproduced with kind permission of Ludwig Weiß sen., keeper of the archive of the "Hotel zur Post" at Fürstenfeldbruck in Bavaria.

Spain, or Portugal appeared on the tables of English elites as a matter of course, while poorer compatriots had to make do (at best) with beer brewed at home, or fetched from an alehouse.[26] Religious mentalities exercised influence, too: while Mediterranean Baroque Catholicism—in diets as well as other walks of life—celebrated ostentatious display and copious consumption, some pious women renounced food for long periods of time. Motivated by a quest for spiritual purity, but perhaps also by a desire for more worldly gains, their miraculous stories fascinated medics and members of the public alike.[27] Conventional gender roles provided early modern Europeans with further points of reference: an ability to hold copious amounts of drink enhanced male reputations, but was strongly frowned upon for women. According to medical theory, the female constitution was naturally weaker and thus less suited to cope with the effects of alcohol, but just as important was the patriarchal desire to keep women away from anything that might make them unruly and prone to dissolute behavior.[28]

Among the continuities, in contrast, were the modest yields of agricultural crops, caused by a combination of traditional cultivation techniques and extra-economic constraints on the peasantry. With the exception of highly commercialized regions such as England and the Netherlands, dearth and famine remained threats for the continent until the agricultural revolution of the eighteenth century (see chapters 1 and 3). Furthermore, even in years with satisfactory harvests, most contemporaries experienced an idiosyncratic rhythm of want and plenty, depending on the seasons, religious feasts/fasts, and the rites of passage (baptisms, weddings, funerals) that punctuated early modern lives.

## STRUCTURE AND CONTENT OF THIS VOLUME

In accordance with the general pattern of *A Cultural History of Food*, the volume opens with a survey of *production*. Govind Sreenivasan discusses a dazzling variety of landscapes and agricultural regimes. Grain remained the single most important crop (the author, in fact, observes a further cerealization of European diets), but colonial imports, the so-called new husbandry and—at least in more commercialized regions such as England and the Low Countries—greater labor efficiency highlight the ways in which productivity ceilings could be expanded. The second essay addresses *systems of food distribution*. Anne Radeff emphasizes the predominance of petty exchange over bulk trade and the significant role of the "periphery." Simple models of centrality fail to capture the complexity of early modern networks, where commercial routes could bypass major cities, and where petty traders were remarkably mobile and entrepreneurial (for example, with regard to the marketing of their goods).

In most contexts, therefore, European peasants did not starve. As Pier Paolo Viazzo explains, mortality rates reflected epidemics rather than widespread famine (although *food crises* such as that of the 1590s brought extreme hardship). Variations in demographic development, degree of commercialization, and government action account for significant regional differences.[29] *Food politics* in this period, according to Victor Magagna, cannot be understood as a mere function of power relations and economic priorities; the negotiation of interests between producers, distributors, consumers, and regulators—in forms ranging from paternal appeals to violent risings—reflected widely-shared cultural norms such as the dignity of customs, the preservation of livelihoods, and the operation of a moral market.

Economic differentiation and growing spatial mobility enhanced the frequency of *eating out* in this period. Large sections of the laboring population depended on catering at work or access to ready-made meals, while elite travellers and the emerging leisure industry boosted the range and sophistication of services in early modern dining establishments. In the field of *professional cooking,* guild restrictions loosened and—in an intriguing contrast to other occupational fields such as brewing—female participation increased. Prominent chefs acquired celebrity status, while others specialized in new areas such as the preparation of desserts. Sara Pennell stresses the impact of cultural innovations such as the advent of print and changing food tastes. Within the *domestic sphere,* kitchens (or rather spaces used for food-preparation activities) served as household hubs, and the smooth provision of meals was of fundamental importance for the state of marital and family relations. Over the course of the early modern period, Pennell notes greater attention to sociable dining, increased access to new victuals, and a multiplication of food service goods.

Charting the evolving relationship between *body and soul,* David Gentilcore detects an almost circular journey from (partly religiously-motivated) moderation via Baroque elaboration towards a new kind of natural simplicity. Medical and dietetic literature reveals a gradual superseding of Galenic theories with contemporary mathematical and chemical ideas. Artistic *representations* continued to carry moral and symbolic messages, but Brian Cowan finds growing interest in food per se (for example, in new genres such as still-life images and the emerging culinary discourse). In contrast to the appreciation of large volumes and strong flavors in the Italian Renaissance, early modern tastes put much greater emphasis on elegance and lightness *à la française.*

The volume concludes with a sketch of *global developments.* Fabio Parasecoli stresses the role of commodities such as sugar, coffee, and spices in the rise of the Western European empires and the emergence of hybrid colonial cuisines in India, as well as in the Americas. The early modern period, however, was equally characterized by fierce power struggles, the cultural resilience of China and Japan, and the ruthless exploitation of human labor in the transatlantic slave trade.

## OUTLOOK

Food history has come a long way over the last few decades. Calls to supplement the long-standing concentration on production and distribution with wider cultural approaches have certainly been heeded.[30] And yet, much remains to be discovered (if not permanently elusive), particularly for the relatively scarcely documented pre-modern period. When we move from general trends to personal experience, the sheer diversity of individuals, contexts, and factors confronts historians with almost impossible challenges. While official early modern discourse was heavily biased toward greater discipline, moderation, and rational behavior, there is certainly evidence for Bacchanalian excess, drinking rituals, and food- (or deprivation-) induced hallucination.[31] The symbolic meaning of victuals—exemplified by the striking religious connotations of bread and wine—forms another fascinating topic awaiting further scrutiny. Why exactly did early modern people choose certain foods or drinks for specific occasions and what did this signal to those who shared in these meals? Protestants who served Catholics meat on fast days might have been ignorant or negligent, but the possibility of a deliberate confessional provocation should not be discounted. No less demanding is the task to reconstruct developments in individual and collective taste over the *longue durée*. How can we explain that white or wheat beer became enormously popular in seventeenth-century Bavaria, but very difficult to sell only a few decades later?[32] Last but not least: while food and drink consumption was a physiological necessity and a cultural practice invested with multiple meanings (including—as the oyster eater on the cover suggests[33]—sensual pleasure[34]), it could simply be a source of enjoyment, too.

Some preliminary conclusions can be drawn. Expansion, lightness, elegance, refinement, and innovation—many themes and findings within this volume reinforce the ongoing reassessment of the centuries under investigation. Following recent work on aspects as diverse as human rights, communication structures, leisure pursuits, material culture, and consumer demand,[35] the dynamic and innovatory potential of the early modern period appears in much sharper focus. Europe in general—and people's diet in particular—became more differentiated, commercialized, and globally embedded.[36] Yet, even in 1800 neither was modern, of course, as dramatic transformations such as mechanization, refrigeration, rail, and air transport, international-aid programs, and genetically modified crops (to name just a few) still lay in the future. It is this kind of enhanced awareness of the distinct profile of each era that the long-term comparative series *A Cultural History of Food* hopes to facilitate.

## ACKNOWLEDGMENTS

I am grateful to the series editors for their invitation to take charge of this volume and for their support throughout the production process. I am also indebted to the copyright holders of the illustrations reproduced in this book, to Anne McBride for translating chapter 2, to Louise Butler and Agnes Upshall at Berg Publishers, to Emily Johnston of Apex Publishing, to Nina Kümin for her help with indexing, and, above all, to the authors who kindly agreed to write chapters on their areas of special expertise.

## CHAPTER ONE

# Food Production

GOVIND SREENIVASAN

Food production was the central process of the early modern European economy. This is true not simply in the sense that adequate nutrition is the logical precondition of all economic activity, but also in terms of the dominant position of food production both as a generator of economic value, and as an employer of labor. At the height of the late-sixteenth-century European trading boom, the annual value of spice imports from Asia (equivalent to c. 137 tons of silver) and treasure imports from the Americas (c. 309 tons) was of about the same order as the European international grain trade (c. 450–c. 600 tons), and all of these were dwarfed by the value of the European domestic grain trade (c. 14,000 tons).[1] And as late as the mid-nineteenth century, the proportion of the European labor force engaged in agriculture ranged from 45–55 percent (France, Germany, and the Low Countries) to 60–75 percent (Scandinavia, Eastern, and Mediterranean Europe), with Great Britain (22% in 1851) showing the only significant divergence from this pattern.[2] This chapter accordingly divides its efforts between a consideration of food as a *product* and an analysis of food production as the paramount socio-economic *process* in early modern Europe.

## LANDSCAPES OF FOOD PRODUCTION

As remains the case in the present, early modern food production was profoundly shaped by the constraints of the physical environment. While it may seem obvious that basic geography should predispose the individual regions of Europe to produce (and trade, and consume) food portfolios of varied composition, it is worth remembering that these portfolios further differed in terms of their volume, value, risk, cost, and social and legal regimes of production. We must therefore begin with a discussion of the different landscapes of early modern food production.

Perhaps the most familiar geographic distinction—often replicated in political and cultural history—is the large-scale divide between southern and northern Europe. With respect to food production in particular, the contrast between lighter Mediterranean soils and heavier northern soils has become something of a commonplace differentiator in general literature on social and economic history. More specialized research evinces an acute sensitivity to the fine-grained characteristics of much smaller, individual farming regions, and highlights the imprecise, and limited nature of the standard north–south contrast: imprecise because meaningful soil classification requires more than two categories (the recent *European Soil Atlas* works with no fewer than twenty-three main types of soil),[3] and limited because soil composition turns out be only one of several important geographic variables.

Three kinds of geographic variables are of greatest importance for our purposes. The first of these is the simple fact that some soil types are considerably more fertile than others, with predictable consequences for crop yields in arable agriculture. In this regard, it is worth emphasizing that northern and Central Europe has a much more favorable distribution of soils suitable for agriculture than either the southern Mediterranean or the Near East (despite the fact that agriculture is actually much older in these less-favored zones). Even within the European continent, it can be no coincidence that those regions blessed with the highest concentrations of soil types most suitable for agriculture (for example, cambisols [brown forest soils, *Braunerde*] and luvisols [alluvial soils]) are the same regions that were economic leaders for so much of European history: southern England, northeastern France, the Low Countries, the Rhineland, and northern

Italy. Equally noteworthy is the prevalence of much less fertile soil types—calcisols, regosols, and leptisols—in the Mediterranean and Turkey.[4] The gradual northern and northwestern shift in Europe's economic center of gravity during the early modern period almost certainly had some geological basis. Even so, there was clearly no automatic relationship between soil fertility and economic prosperity in these centuries. The chernozem soils of the southern Ukraine are arguably the most fertile soils in all of Europe, but they were not brought into full-scale cultivation until well after the early modern period.

Two less frequently commented upon, but still extremely important, geographic variables in food production are temperature and precipitation. As with soil fertility, there is no simple north–south relationship with these variables in Europe. It is certainly true that the Mediterranean tends to have higher temperatures than northern Europe, but the Atlantic Ocean powerfully mitigates winter temperatures along the coasts, giving Normandy and Brittany, for example, a much longer frost-free season than Bohemia and eastern Bavaria. Precipitation varies still more widely. The southern Mediterranean as a whole receives less rain than northern Europe as a whole, but the area all around the Adriatic Sea is much wetter, making Italy the most favored of all Mediterranean regions, and certainly comparable to most of the north. Much of north-central and southern Spain, by contrast, is extremely dry, with parts of Old Castile receiving significantly less precipitation than northern Morocco. Again, as with temperature, an extended favored region runs along the Atlantic coastline from Galicia through the western British Isles and Normandy, all the way up to coastal Norway; this region has some of the highest annual rainfall in all of Europe.[5]

The combined effects of regional differences in soil types, temperatures, and precipitation are complicated, and are not simply reducible to the observation that some areas were endowed by nature to produce more food than others (although that is certainly also true). Some of the most important consequences pertain to the kinds of crop mixes that were possible in arable agriculture. The olive tree and the grape vine, both of which produce high-value but also extremely labor-intensive crops, were largely (though not entirely) confined to the warmer Mediterranean. Temperature differentials also help to explain why the New World crop maize, which requires a long growing season (140+ days) and extended summer highs of over twenty degrees Celsius, was only transferable to the Mediterranean, and not to northern Europe. A similar explanation accounts for the place of rye (a hardier, but generally lower yield crop than wheat) as the predominant bread grain in Central and Eastern Europe, while the milder winters of Atlantic Europe permitted English and French farmers to concentrate on growing wheat.

Regional variation in crop mixes had ramifications far beyond the type of grain from which bread was made. These differences exerted considerable influence on field systems, on the possibilities for animal husbandry, on the energy available for agricultural work, and on the kinds of responses available to cultivators when faced with economic adversity. Most fundamentally, the classic spring-sown grains of the European continent—above all oats—have moisture requirements which make them harder to grow outside of northern and Atlantic Europe. This constraint helps to explain the much greater popularity of barley (which requires less precipitation) in the Mediterranean and Near East.[6] More importantly, it also helps to explain the persistence of two-course rotation (that is, alternating winter-sown grains with fallow courses in the fields) in much of the Mediterranean, when more efficient three-course rotations (that is, sequencing winter-sown grains, spring-sown grains, and fallow courses) become the norm in regions blessed by greater rainfall. Finally, the long, dry summer which characterized much of the Mediterranean also created acute shortages of winter fodder for livestock. This represented a major constraint on the possibilities for intensive livestock husbandry by comparison with Atlantic Europe. Down into the nineteenth (and, indeed, the twentieth) century, therefore, food production in the Mediterranean was marked by a substantially smaller share of animal as opposed to plant products, and significantly less animal power for the actual work of production.[7]

## FOOD AS A PRODUCT

As was the case in virtually every other contemporary, sedentary society, the caloric bulk (75–80%) of the early modern European diet came from grain. The most important of these grains were wheat, rye, spelt, oats, and barley, most of which were consumed as both bread, and porridge. There was considerable local variation in crop mixes, but as noted above, differences in humidity, temperature, and soil chemistry made wheat and barley the most common grains in the Mediterranean, wheat and oats in Atlantic Europe, and rye and oats in Central and Eastern Europe.

From a historical global perspective, the most prominent characteristic of these rain-fed European grains was their relatively low yield (in terms of edible calories per hectare) by comparison to other crops grown in settled agricultural societies elsewhere in the early modern world, in particular, when compared to rice yields in Southern and Eastern Asia, and maize in Central and South America. Originally emphasized by Fernand Braudel, and since confirmed by subsequent research, this disparity was twofold. First of all, both rice and maize yielded vastly (50–100%) more calories per acre than wheat (which, in turn, yielded more than rye or spelt), and also required much less processing and energy than was required to produce bread. Second, when grown in irrigated fields, both rice and maize could be double-cropped, yielding two harvests in a single year. Irrigated rice also seems to have returned more nutrients to the soil than dry-farmed wheat, making fewer subsequent demands for either fallow periods or fertilizer.[8]

The foregoing gains particular importance in light of current scholarly controversies over the so-called rise of the West during the eighteenth and nineteenth centuries. Recent research has provided an overdue corrective to earlier triumphalist portrayals of early modern Europe as enjoying a long-term lead in material prosperity over non-Western civilizations. That this was not the case is now beyond dispute. Instead, it seems clear that living standards in the wealthiest parts of Eastern (and possibly Southern) Asia were at least as high as in the most advanced parts of Europe until the late eighteenth century. It was only during the nineteenth century that Western and Central Europe (and their extensions in Anglo North America) became the wealthiest parts of the world.[9] Debate on these issues is certain to continue; the point here is that even early modern Europe's *parity* with the great Asian civilizations appears a considerable accomplishment given the structural disadvantages of Europe's food-production systems.

Over the course of the early modern period, the traditional European grains were supplemented with a series of new arrivals. Rice had been known since the early Middle Ages through contact with the Islamic world; by the fifteenth century it was grown in southern Spain and especially in northern Italy, where it could be grown under irrigated conditions in the

Po valley. Maize was introduced to the Iberian Peninsula from the New World in the sixteenth century, and over the next two centuries spread to southern France, Italy, and the Balkans. An American (more specifically, Peruvian) import of even greater significance was the potato, which was grown in Spain by the 1570s, and it had spread not only throughout the Mediterranean, but all over northern and Central Europe by the eighteenth century. All told, these new grain and grain substitutes had only a modest impact on total food production. Due to its temperature and humidity requirements, rice was narrowly confined to a few especially favorable regions, and even in Italy, made up only a small proportion of the overall cereal harvest (only 8% of total value as late as 1914). By contrast, maize had, by the seventeenth century, become part of the ordinary diet in Spain at least, while the potato seems to have constituted fully a third of carbohydrate intake of the Belgian population by 1800.[10] Be that as it may, in most of early modern Europe the traditional grains continued to dominate food production. It thus seems fair to conclude that outside of a few atypical regions, there was no fundamental transformation of the European diet between the late fifteenth and late eighteenth centuries, even if by the end of the period the rise of the potato was clearly underway.

Of course, early modern Europeans did not live by bread (or porridge) alone, and field crops were always supplemented with gathered and gardened plant foods (often directly through the addition of greens and roots to gruel to make pottage). Forests and fields were important sources for the collection of wild nuts, berries, fruits, roots, greens, and herbs, while vegetables and fruit trees were planted in gardens and orchards.

Assessing the overall place of these plants in food production is complicated by the scarcity of evidence, even though gardens were, just as grain fields were, subject to the ecclesiastical tithe. In 1695 Gregory King estimated that gardens accounted for 9 percent of the total value of English agricultural production, although this figure included industrial crops such as hemp, flax, and woad, along with fruit, vegetables, and "garden stuff."[11] However modest their caloric share may have been, non-grain plants were essential supplements to the nutritional content and flavor of an overwhelmingly farinaceous diet, and held a place of particular importance for the poor. In mountainous regions the chestnut was an important grain substitute, and has been estimated as constituting one-sixth of carbohydrate intake in mid-eighteenth-century Piedmont.[12] Root vegetables had the particular virtue of keeping well in cellars or when pickled. The German physician Walter Ryff's *Kurtze aber vast eigentliche Beschreibung der Natur* (1549) specifically designates cabbage, chestnuts, beans, and turnips as the staples of the poor, while the English gentleman Sir Hugh Platt's *Sundrie Remedies against Famine* (1596) similarly recommended beans, peas, chestnuts, acorns, and vetches as stopgaps in times of dearth.[13]

Fruits and vegetables were, of course, also consumed by (and produced for) more affluent populations. The concentrated demand provided by cities was an important stimulus for market gardening, particularly in the Low Countries, and all modern Western varietals of the familiar orange carrot (purple, yellow, and white strains also exist) descend from lines developed by late-sixteenth-century Dutch gardeners.[14] The grape (strictly speaking, wine) was by far the most valuable horticultural product, and although no longer planted as far north as in the later Middle Ages,[15] when vineyards could be found in Flanders, East Prussia, and southern Norway, grapes were still widely cultivated in early modern Europe, with small vineyards still found in places like Saxony and Hertfordshire.[16]

Animal products in general, and meat in particular were the most expensive, and prestigious elements in the early modern European diet, but the majority of the population ate relatively little meat. Although estimates of average consumption vary widely, most fall between 22 and 66 pounds per annum. Within this range, wealthy, urban, and northern European populations tended to consume more, and poorer, rural, and Mediterranean populations less. Some meat was procured by hunting and trapping, but these forms of production did not represent a significant proportion of meat calories, even for the aristocracy. Fishing, both riverine and oceanic, was more important, especially with the expansion of old, open-sea fisheries (the North Sea and Iceland) and the discovery of new ones (the Grand Banks of Newfoundland) during the sixteenth century. Even so, overall estimates (on the basis of admittedly rather fragmentary data) suggest that fish also represented only a very small proportion of total meat calories.[17]

Most meat in the early modern diet came, therefore, from livestock husbandry, and here we may helpfully distinguish intensive from extensive regimes of production. Intensive regimes stocked the animals in meadows within the confines of human settlements and usually focused on cattle, though sometimes on sheep. Animals were certainly eaten under these intensive regimes, but dairying was of considerable, and occasionally of primary, importance. Most dairy production seems to have ended up as cheese, which was much more easily preserved and transported than fresh milk; salted, liquid (and, one suspects, often rancid) butter occupied an intermediate position in terms of these qualities, and hence also in terms of volume of production. Under extensive animal-husbandry regimes, the livestock were raised in large, sparsely populated, and economically peripheral regions: Russia, Poland, Hungary, Scandinavia, northern England, and Scotland, the central European Alps, Spain, and southern Italy. Raised for their meat, hides, and wool, the animals moved back and forth between widely separated highland summer, and lowland winter pasturages in a pattern known as transhumance. Their final journeys to market also often involved very long distances, with huge herds of tens of thousands of animals journeying hundreds of miles to the (usually urban) point of sale.[18]

## FOOD PRODUCTION AS A PROCESS

Evaluating the adequacy of European food production is one of the central problems (and arguably *the* central problem) of the continent's early modern economic history, and adequacy evaluations are often framed in terms of questions about when, where, and especially how the European food supply (and more specifically the grain supply) finally grew large enough to sustain a significant non-agricultural (that is, urban, and later industrial) population. Provisional answers to these questions are offered below, and some aspects of the adequacy issue are also further discussed in chapter 3. It must, however, first be emphasized that grain production is not a unitary process whose performance can be expressed in a single metric. Rather, the labor processes associated with grain production entailed a whole series of considerations, many of which had to be balanced against each other. To understand fully both the nature of the constraints on the early modern food supply and the ways in which these constraints could, and could not be overcome, thus requires a more detailed look at the actual tasks entailed in food production.

The most well-known constraint was the problem of maintaining soil fertility to guard against the exhaustion of arable lands. To be sure, there were a few thinly-populated areas (for example, the Upper Volga, the

moraine lands of eastern Finland) where swidden agriculture was still practiced in the early modern period, but west of Russia most of the continent
was too densely settled to permit fields to be slashed and burned out of
the forest, cultivated for a year or two, and then abandoned, and allowed
to revert to tree cover. Grain was instead grown in permanent, or at least
semi-permanent fields whose nutrients (most critically nitrogen) would be
steadily depleted by uninterrupted cultivation.[19]

The two most significant measures to restore soil fertility, both well-
known since classical Antiquity, were (1) the direct replenishment of nutrients through the addition of animal manure or (where urban supplies
were available) human nightsoil, and (2) the interspersing of fallow periods
between cropping cycles to allow the land to recover through the action of
soil bacteria. Fertilizing thus entailed the keeping of livestock to produce
manure, and maintaining livestock in turn entailed keeping land under pasture in order to provide fodder.[20]

Maintaining the balance of arable and pasture land was relatively easy in
contexts of land abundance, as in the aftermath of the great pestilence-driven
collapse of the European population during the fourteenth and fifteenth centuries. Over the course of the sixteenth century, however, virtually all of
Europe experienced massive demographic growth. The attendant increase
in the demand for food was at first met through the traditional response of
reclaiming land for cultivation from forests, wastes, marshes, and even the
sea, but demand clearly outpaced supply, and cereal prices increased between two and a half and four times across Europe between 1500 and 1600.
Tensions had always existed between feeding people and feeding animals, as
reflected in the widespread tradition of slaughtering animals on St Martin's
Day (November 11) so as not to have to maintain them over the winter.
However, as grain prices rose much faster than the prices of animal or industrial products, meadows, and even vineyards were increasingly ploughed
up, and sown with grain. The result was not only a significant cerealization
of the early modern European diet (especially at the expense of animal products), but a declining ability to fertilize the grain fields themselves.[21]

Yet the management of soil fertility was hardly the only structural constraint on early modern agriculture; at least as important (if not more so)
were the energy demands of food production. These demands were particularly pressing with respect to ploughing—a process whose significance

extended far beyond the task of simply opening the soil for seeding. Ploughing was a vital means of moisture management. In drier regions such as the Mediterranean, ploughing served to conserve water by leveling and breaking up the topsoil, and thereby impeding moisture from rising to the surface by capillary action, and being lost to evaporation. In wetter Atlantic and northern Europe, by contrast, ploughing was needed for the opposite reason—to drain excess water from the land. Here the fields were ploughed in a ridge-and-furrow pattern (German *Hochacker,* Dutch *hoogakker*) to promote surface drainage from the high backs of the long, parallel ridges.[22] Ploughing was also essential to keep the fields free from weeds that would otherwise compete with the crops for soil nutrients.[23] Learned commentators recommended that fields be ploughed at least three, preferably four, and in some cases as many as six times per year. Actual practice varied, but plough-ing a field two to four times in the fallow year, and at least once each other year seems to have been a common arrangement.[24] Altogether then, plough-ing operations constituted a considerable demand for hauling power. When one considers that an ox generated roughly four times and a horse something like six times the mechanical energy of a human being,[25] it becomes clear that early modern food production necessitated a set of complex calculations to balance the multiplier effects of animal labor against its greater costs.

An additional kind of balancing act governed the myriad of human labor tasks in agriculture, tasks which even in the eighteenth century were only negligibly affected by the first stirrings of agricultural mechanization. Not only was there an obvious positive relationship between crop yields and the effort expended on the preparation and cleaning of the tilth (spad-ing, weeding, etc.), but overall labor demand varied considerably over the course of the year, with a peak demand at harvest time (above all for mow-ing, winnowing, and threshing) of something like three to four times the demand in the mid-winter trough.[26] This seasonality represented a con-siderable socio-economic challenge, as the very nature of food production regularly created a pressing, but only temporary demand for large amounts of labor, which at other times was a burden.

## THE ADEQUACY OF EARLY MODERN FOOD PRODUCTION

Did early modern Europeans produce enough food to feed themselves? The question is forcibly posed by two suggestive patterns that emerged all over the continent at the end of the sixteenth century: (1) an end to the population growth that had characterized the previous century and a half, while the buying power of wages settled at the lowest level ever measured in Europe between the twelfth and twenty-first centuries; and (2) the multiplication of subsistence crises—sudden spikes in the price of grain accompanied by surges in mortality. Subsistence crises would punctuate the early modern period with alarming frequency, erupting across most of Europe every 20 to 30 years between the 1570s and the 1810s.

The widespread impression that a failure of food production left early modern Europe teetering on the brink of a Malthusian collapse is reinforced by the evidence of long-term stability (often seen as stagnation) of agricultural productivity in these centuries. Decades of research have confirmed that the best medieval levels of grain output per unit area were not exceeded anywhere in Europe—including the successful regions of England and the Low Countries—before the second half of the eighteenth century at the earliest.[27] An ancien régime of food production would prevail in most of Europe until the development of chemical fertilizers and concentrated animal feeds in the second half of the nineteenth century.

It is incontrovertible that many early modern Europeans lacked adequate nutrition. The contrast between modest and often only temporary improvement in material living conditions between the sixteenth and eighteenth centuries, and the onset of sustained economic growth in the nineteenth and twentieth centuries, further suggests that the early modern European economy was subject to some kind of structural constraint (that these are separate propositions is demonstrated by the case of modern India, where per capita GDP tripled between 1989 and 2006 while almost half of India's children continue to suffer from malnutrition).[28] Yet while greater food production clearly would have eased (and later did ease) the amply documented adversity of daily life, this does not mean that an incapacity to produce food was itself the most important obstacle confronting the early modern economy. The place of food production in the wider economy thus requires more careful specification, which is less a matter of fuller description than an interpretive task essential for the understanding of how the constraints on the early modern European economy were ultimately eased.

We must resist the seductive image of early modern Europe as a full world, living at some kind of saturation point, and operating at the brink of its productive capacities. In the first place, the demographic evidence usually adduced to prove this claim is much more ambiguous than is commonly acknowledged. Mortality from subsistence crises was only a small percentage of overall mortality in early modern Europe. Moreover, before the mid-eighteenth century, social elites with ample access to calories (the English peerage is a classic case) did not have significantly higher life expectancies than the population as a whole. The balance of evidence suggests that infectious disease was a much more important cause of mortality than malnutrition, and while there are some infective processes (cholera, intestinal parasites, tuberculosis) which are clearly aggravated by undernourishment, there are many others where the relationship is either uncertain (influenza, diphtheria, typhus), or non-existent (plague, smallpox).[29]

Furthermore, subsistence crises themselves do not admit of simple interpretation. Research into the much better-documented famines of the twentieth century, above all the work of Amartya Sen, has drawn attention to the difference between deficits of food entitlement (the condition of people not *having* enough to eat) and deficits of food availability (the situation of there not *being* enough food to eat). The latter is only one of many possible causes of the former.[30]

The point is not that early modern European famines were totally artificial; they were clearly linked with documentable harvest failures. The question, rather, is the degree to which mortality surges were directly proportional to the production shortfall. The French case is particularly suggestive. Before about 1630, harvest failures in France tended to be followed by grain price increases of 40–80 percent. Thereafter, and until about 1710, by contrast, price surges of 300–450 percent became common during harvest failures. There is no indication of any change in food-production processes in this period; the dynamic element was instead the rising, predatory power of Parisian demand in a context of poorly integrated, regional grain markets.[31] The English experience complicates the picture in a different way. Here, the mortality increase attendant upon harvest failure eased substantially after the mid-seventeenth century, again in the absence of any compelling evidence of a transformation in the realm of production, but with compelling evidence of the establishment of an integrated national market for grain.[32] All in all, it is difficult to avoid the conclusion that mortality during subsistence crises was shaped not only by patterns of production, but also, and possibly even more so, by patterns of circulation.[33]

The relationship between population movements and food production was thus quite complex, and the demographic consequences of any particular level of food production varied widely on the basis of other features of the economy. The fact that putatively economically stagnant regions such as Italy, Spain, France, and Germany ultimately experienced population increases of 35–60 percent between 1600 and 1800 further undermines the vision of early modern European society as a society only barely able to feed itself.[34]

The second main limitation of the concept of an early modern Malthusian ceiling is that it seriously understates the flexibility of European food-production systems. The fact that medieval grain yields were not decisively exceeded until the late eighteenth or nineteenth centuries does not mean that yields were invariant. Ever since the pioneering work of B. H. Slicher van Bath in the 1950s, it has been clear that early modern Europe fell into four zones of differential agricultural productivity: an eastern zone (Bohemia, Moravia, Hungary, Poland, and Russia) where farmers harvested 3.5 to 4.7 grains for each grain sown, a central zone (Germany, Switzerland, and Scandinavia) with yield ratios between 4.0 and 5.1 to 1, a western and Mediterranean zone (France, Spain, and Italy) with yield ratios between 6.2 and 7.0 to 1, and finally, a northwestern zone (England and the Low Countries), with yield ratios between 6.7 and 10.1 to 1.[35] Far from being dictated by physical geography, these productivity differentials were more obviously influenced by (if not reducible to) differences in human geography and social property regimes. Thus, yields tended to be higher in more densely settled regions, while at the same time the heavy labor-service obligations and closer seigneurial control of the peasantry characteristic of Eastern Europe depressed productivity there by comparison with Western Europe, where peasants had more robust personal and property rights.[36] The range of regional variation thus illustrates at least the possibility of adaptation in agricultural productivity.

The possibility was not merely theoretical, and before the end of the agricultural ancien régime there is clear evidence of the growing productivity of land in many parts of Europe. The best-known mechanism of improvement was the spread of the so-called new husbandry where more complicated crop rotations involving the planting of legumes (above all clover, but also lucerne [alfalfa], sainfoin, and turnips) and pulses (peas, beans, vetches) in fields which would otherwise have lain fallow took place. These plants supplied nitrogen to the soil through the action of symbiotic bacteria in their root systems, thereby restoring the fertility of the arable land. At the same time, they enabled the production of more fodder for animals and, in the case of turnips, peas, and beans, more food for people.[37]

Although the new husbandry only became widespread in the nineteenth century, it did not represent the discovery of new information. The classical Roman agronomists had been well-acquainted with the rejuvenating properties of legumes, and much of their knowledge was preserved by medieval commentators such as Pietro Crescenzi, and then diffused via the printing press by humanist botanists in the later sixteenth century.[38] Differential agricultural productivity in early modern Europe was thus less a matter of whether or not farmers knew how to increase productivity, and more a matter of whether or not it was economically rational for them to do so.

Attention to the wider economic context of agricultural decision making is especially important if we are to avoid misleading categorizations of early modern European food-production systems as successes (typically England and the Low Countries) and failures (typically France, Germany, and especially the Mediterranean and Eastern Europe). In the first place, it is important to distinguish between the different ways of measuring agricultural productivity. England has a time-honored status as a region of unusually productive agriculture during the early modern period, and deservedly so. Yet late-eighteenth-century English crop yields per unit area were not much higher than in contemporary northern France, Ireland, or western Germany, and over the course of the following century England actually fell behind the rest of Europe in this respect.[39] By 1890, English agricultural output per unit area was significantly lower in value than in Italy, Germany, France, Denmark, and (especially) the Netherlands.[40] The real advantage of English agriculture was in *labor* productivity: whereas about three-quarters of English adult males worked in agriculture in 1500, by 1750 the proportion had fallen to about 45 percent, and by 1820 to about 38 percent.[41] Elsewhere in Europe, as noted above, agriculture continued to absorb the majority of the labor force until the early (in the Netherlands) or later nineteenth century (France, Germany, Belgium), or even the twentieth century (Italy, Spain, Sweden, Finland, Hungary).[42]

There were several reasons for these variations in labor productivity. By 1800, the average English agricultural worker disposed of 50 percent more mechanical energy than his French counterpart due to a more plentiful supply of draught animals and the scale of this energy advantage closely matched the proportional difference in agricultural labor productivity.[43] Also noteworthy are differences in the composition of food production. Thanks to a physical environment more favorable for livestock husbandry, northern European agriculture in general (and English agriculture in particular) was marked by a much higher share of animal products (which tend to have greater value) than was the case in the Mediterranean.[44]

Most important of all, however, was the articulation between food production and the rest of the economy. It is often tacitly (and sometimes explicitly) assumed that early modern Europe was in some sense waiting for food production to reach the critical volume to allow for a significant population to devote itself to other pursuits. This is an unhelpful way to look at the problem. Careful research by George Grantham has established that at yields of 11.5–13.8 bushels of grain per hectare, which were commonly attained all over (if not everywhere in) medieval and early modern Europe, the share of the labor force needed in agriculture to sustain the population as a whole was at most 40 percent, and possibly as little as 25 percent.[45] That most parts of early modern Europe retained much larger agricultural labor forces for much longer than was strictly necessary underscores the significance of risks, constraints, and lack of opportunities outside the realm of food production itself. Where agriculturalists faced inefficient or volatile factor markets, shortages of capital, and a lack of alternative sources of income, it made perfect sense to adopt labor-intensive strategies of diversified production. In the absence of these constraints, specialized and labor-efficient forms of production were more likely to appear.[46]

It is difficult to specify precisely the optimal matrix of social and commercial relations for the release of labor from food production in the early modern period. It is clear that the English experience is of limited use in explaining developments in the rest of Europe, since many of the factors traditionally invoked to account for England's precocious economic growth—enclosures, very large farms, the replacement of household servants with wage workers—were only faintly echoed on the continent, even after the onset of industrialization.[47] Indeed, even where a seemingly

English pattern of large farms worked by wage labor did emerge elsewhere in Europe (for example, in southern Spain), it did not achieve the same kinds of labor efficiencies in food production.[48] It does seem that effectively co-ordinated urban demand was a more broadly important motor of specialization and enhanced labor productivity. Cities represented the most concentrated markets for large-scale trade in agricultural produce, and it is now recognized that the urban network of industrial Europe, and in particular the organization of that network around metropolises, took basic shape during the seventeenth and eighteenth centuries.[49] Yet cities did not always have the same impact on their hinterlands; while the growth of London is credited with stimulating commercialization and specialization in southern England, Madrid's expansion is held to have contributed to the stagnation of Castile.[50] The spread of rural textile production (or proto-industrialization) was once seen as an essential stepping stone to the emergence of regional specializations in agriculture and industry. This was true in some regions, but in others cottage industry served primarily as a support for underemployed agriculturalists, and thus contributed to strategies of diversification and intensifying (rather than specializing and making more efficient) the labor of rural households.[51]

More careful investigations into the rural household's economic decision-making processes and their social context must therefore head the list of requirements for a better understanding of the wider importance of early modern food production. Closer attention to an historical product returns us, in the end, to the people who actually produced it.

## CHAPTER TWO

# Food Systems: Central–Decentral Networks

ANNE RADEFF

*Translated by Anne E. McBride*

## CENTRAL REPRESENTATIONS

From the 1960s, specialist socioeconomic studies have demonstrated that large-scale, international trade, favored by previous generations of scholars, only affected a minority of exchanges in the early modern period. The majority of exchanges, particularly for foodstuffs, took place on a regional and local scale.[1] Yet these works have done little to influence cultural historians, whose interests focus on material uses and symbolic representations of food, rather than on the ways it reached the consumers' tables.[2]

To move beyond the opposition between economic and cultural approaches, this chapter offers an economic, social, and cultural critique of so-called central representations. The metaphor of the center does indeed play a major role in food exchanges and networks. In the Ancien Régime, distance-measuring tables used Paris as their midpoint (*poinct milieu*) or represented London as a "radiant sun" surrounded by English towns.[3] In 1621, Robert Burton wrote that London grew by contracting other towns: "sola crescit decrescentibus aliis."[4] In 1724, Daniel Defoe attempted to prove "how this whole kingdom, as well the people as the land, and even the sea, in every part of it, are employed to furnish something, and I may add, the best of everything, to supply the City of London with provisions; I mean by provisions, corn, flesh, fish, butter, cheese, salt."[5] According to François Marlin, at the end of the eighteenth century, "we take good care of [Paris], this voracious beast; all the provinces work for it."[6] This central focus appears in the work of numerous historians, for whom food went from the villages to the large towns, passing through small towns on the way.[7] To feed itself, it is claimed, London had spun "a veritable spider's web, linking to itself and to each other scattered centres of production," where the "magnetic attraction" it exerted on its surrounding areas justified the use of a dual model to understand its role.[8]

Not all representations of food circuits are center-focused, however. Joan Thirsk discovered reciprocal relationships between the metropolis and supposedly isolated hamlets—the former not being the only engine of change.[9] Initiatives were launched far away from big cities, even in the mountains, and numerous commercial food practices in the Ancien Régime took place outside of a strictly hierarchical, spatial organization.[10] Peasants could exchange their goods without the mediation of urban merchants (point one emerges from the examination of central–decentral food *trade* conducted below); they could travel great distances to exchange products of low value without passing through nearby towns (point two is substantiated by the study of central–decentral *networks*); and finally, promotional efforts focused not only on luxury products made in the big centers, but also on low-value goods sold in the localities (point three results from a closer look at central–decentral *marketing*). Women, it will be seen, also played active roles in many of these central–decentral exchanges.

Rather than providing a general overview, I will proceed by comparative analysis of contrasting examples: the two largest European cities of the time period (Paris and London) on the one hand, and regions between the Alps and the Jura (Switzerland, Franche-Comté, Savoy) located at great distance from any metropolis, on the other hand.

## EARLY MODERN FOOD TRADE

The central–decentral organization of food procurement functioned on various complementary scales (from local to global), which interacted with each other in the "global economy of the Ancien Régime."[11] Autarchy did not exist anywhere; all economic agents had to obtain varying shares of the foodstuffs they consumed. While self-consumption and gift exchange played important roles, they only represent a small share of overall food procurement. Most people either owned no land or not enough to secure year-round subsistence, while the wealthy complemented their diet with imported victuals. Many indispensable products, such as salt, had to be purchased by everyone.

Most food commerce was not cash-based. The poorest traded their labor. From the transcontinental (such as in the triangular exchange of African slaves, New World foodstuffs, and European goods) to the regional and local scale, barter was omnipresent: in the Bernese Alps, for example, muleteers illegally bartered butter for salt. Credit also played an essential role: obligations and *I owe you* pledges for small amounts, as well as bills of exchange for larger sums. Private bankers operated within trading sites, which multiplied to the detriment of large fairs.[12] Two banks profited most from financial transactions at the highest (inter-)continental levels: the Bank of Amsterdam, created in 1609, and the Bank of England, established in London in 1694. No similar institution existed in France.

Over the course of the last century, numerous historians have studied long-term trends in agricultural production and prices.[13] Many observed a correlation (which should not be mistaken for causality) with demographic evolution: high growth in the sixteenth century, leading to a crisis that began in the 1570s. The economic recovery that followed remained weak and uneven, and at times there was stagnation. With slight exaggeration, some historians have talked of an agricultural crisis in some regions in the seventeenth century, in stark contrast to the perceived agricultural revolution of the eighteenth century. Prices and production rose again after the 1750s.

It is, however, difficult (if not impossible) to know if these trends reflect the reality of foodstuff circulation, since they derive from sources privileging exports on the one hand, and wholesale commerce on the other, while small-scale trade in local and regional markets accounted for the majority of exchanges. Its volume, undocumented in any statistics, must have been vastly superior to that of wholesale exports. Moreover, prices of foodstuffs that were relatively unaffected by macroeconomic trends, but were important components of early modern diets (such as leguminous

plants, chestnuts, fish, game, and gathered wild fruits) cannot be extrapo-
lated from surviving serial data (typically relating to heads of cattle, wine
barrels, tons of cereals, and similar products).

Food trade took place in urban as well as rural locations. The largest
European fairs catered for wholesale merchants and bankers rather than
food retailers (except those concentrating on luxury goods such as spices).
Regular markets and small fairs were more strongly focused on food procurement, with cereals typically traded at the former, and cattle at the latter. Fairs abounded in the spring, when stockbreeders bought cattle for
fattening or transport to alpine summer quarters, and in the autumn, when
they sold them on.

The distinction between wholesale and retail trade remained "rather
fuzzy in this period." Theoretically, wholesale commerce took place at
large fairs and retail trade at smaller fairs and markets. In the biggest
cities, market halls catered primarily to wholesale trade (which grew particularly strongly in eighteenth-century London).[14] While fairs took place
outdoors, markets were sometimes located in covered halls protected from
sun or rain. Such venues could serve representational purposes, especially
when linked to town halls. Some were combined with granaries, where the
authorities stocked grain reserves for periods of high prices. Together, they
formed the heart of a city's commercial district. In Paris, a lively neigh-
borhood surrounded the wheat market (*Les Halles*), consisting of seven
covered, and five open-air markets. In London, "market houses, piazzas,
arcades, quadrangles, common slaughterhouses, coffeehouses or taverns,
residential accommodation, enclosed and numbered shops" multiplied
around marketplaces.[15] While increasing numbers of markets and halls
came under private ownership in the biggest cities, in 1704 the Venetian
Senate attempted to regain control by creating four new *fondachi* for the
sale of flour.[16]

The spatial organization of markets and fairs remained uneven; no integrated pyramid structure seems to have emerged anywhere. In our case
studies of the Swiss Confederation, Franche-Comté, and Savoy in the eighteenth century, a third of the markets were situated in villages with few
administrative and political functions.[17] In France, the time–space organization of periodic trade failed to abide by a "rigorous economic ratio-
nality."[18] In England, the distance between one market town and another

varied from 1 to more than 100 miles, without clearly defined, mutually exclusive territorial demarcations.[19] True, "a ring of market towns which acted as collecting points for London dealers" existed around Paris or London,[20] but decentral uses competed with centralizing forces. "From a political, administrative, and juridical perspective, Paris was undeniably at the 'centre' of the kingdom. In terms of food procurement, however, the pretences of the capital to be the 'central market' of the country were not rationally institutionalized. Paris had to obtain its food from very scattered places," and around Paris, "the markets were in fierce competition to gain hegemony at the local and extra-local levels. In parallel, they nearly all shared a rather ambivalent attitude toward the capital's imperialism."[21] This decentrality manifested itself not only in regional commercial networks but also more locally. In London after 1650, "a spatially decentralized marketing framework emerged" when markets multiplied outside of the City.[22]

In large towns, intense and constant trading took place in the river ports: around twenty operated in both Paris were and London. London's ports tended to be polyvalent, while those in Paris were rather more specialized, with "heavy duty items upstream, more elaborate, higher-value products downstream." Colonial products were concentrated in St Nicholas, by the Louvre, where "oil, soaps, oranges, pepper, coffee, cod, herring, oysters, ciders, wines, spirits, and liqueurs" could be found in the late eighteenth century. Alongside wholesale commerce, some retailing for daily consumption is also documented. The port constituted "a favored meeting place of the Parisian society."[23]

Foodstuffs could also be purchased in shops, albeit in small quantities. Luxury and diversity prevailed in large towns. From the beginning of the seventeenth century, thanks to its shops, "London well deserves to beare the name of the choicest storehouse in the world."[24] In Paris, the Duke of Coigny's cook purchased macaroni and chocolate at the Italian grocer Bovelly, and chocolate, dragées, jams, syrups, Italian pastas, and Bayonne ham at the French grocer Perrot.[25] Shops also multiplied in villages, often run by women in small rooms in their farmhouses. Around London, the number of markets—particularly for products such as rice, brandy, and sugar—decreased because of the competition from shops in smaller towns and villages.[26]

Agricultural traders came from a variety of social backgrounds. Everywhere, from isolated hamlets to capitals, private individuals complemented (or competed with) official food-procurement systems. There is no evidence for neat pyramid structures, in which rural producers delivered their goods exclusively to urban merchants, although the latter gained most from food commerce, especially as far as grain, cattle, and fruit were concerned. In England, the growth of London and the enclosure movement (that is, the changing of common land into private property, or of open-field systems into enclosed fields owned by individuals) weakened grain producers to the benefit of merchants. Wholesalers and middlemen—composed of "gentlemen, yeomen, brewers, maltsters, millers" rather than "peasants or labourers"—prospered from the beginning of the seventeenth century. They turned into a small, but powerful professional elite that controlled local suppliers through the allocation of funds and credit.[27] By 1760, the grain and cattle trades—albeit still highly competitive—were largely dominated by these men.[28]

Wheat came to Paris thanks to great merchants, such as the wheat factors (*blatiers*), who "took hold of grain in small quantities in lands rather far away, and moved them closer to central locations," as well as rich ploughmen (*laboureurs*) and other agents, often women, who would "sort the goods, stock them, transport them, and of course sell them for the best possible price." Decentrality in the villages competed against the centralizing intentions of the Parisian authorities. "When they could not reach a satisfying price, ploughmen and merchants removed their goods from the public marketplace and invited buyers to visit them at home or in their granaries."[29] Seventeenth-century producers from the Ile-de-France, in fact, became rich by no longer attending Parisian markets, but by using intermediaries and selling wholesale instead.[30]

The prosperity of breeders also increased. In the Alps of the canton of Vaud around 1785, young shepherds had the resources to own harpsichords and books written in French and German. Merchants—sometimes former breeders—established long-distance connections on the basis of their extended contact networks. In the Alsace, the intermediaries were often Jewish; they connected producers with consumers, and Christians with Jews.[31] In London, "[s]mall-scale producers were connected with the consumer through a pair of major middlemen, with a rather less powerful

drover in between."[32] "Wholesale butchers" competed with "cattle factors" who sold goods produced by others for a fixed commission.[33]

Great merchants did not participate much in the trade of fruits and vegetables, even in the largest towns. Fruit-tree growers from the Ile-de-France
sold their peaches, cherries, and cellar fruits directly in the Halles—a situation contrasting with "a town-country relationship merely resembling
one of economic domination." Fruit farmer-merchants had a "capacity of
adaptation" and were "dynamic enough to respond to urban demand."[34]
Direct contacts between producers and consumers are also documented
for London, where "[t]he consumer market in greenstuffs built on, and
exploited, an existing tradition."[35] With regard to spirits, different systems
operated in the Swiss Confederation and the Franche-Comté: while distillers' brokers purchased unripe cherries in bulk to make *Kirsch* in the former,
growers in the latter distilled and sold to customers, or to nearby markets
directly.[36]

One type of merchant was always on the road, whether on a local scale
(for example, cries in large towns) or over long distances (such as peddlers). In large towns, "cries of London" or "itinerant food traders"—
often women, such as the "oyster girls" at the entrances of taverns—helped
to meet the rising demand for "eating out".[37] In Paris, hucksters (*regrat-
tiers*) and leftover sellers (female *revendeuses de restes*) retailed "vegetables, eggs, fish or meats, but also cheese, salt, and fruits. Above all, some
of them passed the leftovers of high society's meals on to the starving commoners."[38] Far from the capitals, foodstuffs made up only a small share of
the stock haberdashers offered across Bernese territory in 1785. Coming
down from the Alps, small traders from Glarus sold a local specialty, green
*Schabzieger* cheese, as well as Swiss tea (herbal teas), along with writing
pads, umbrellas, and various kinds of cloth, while haberdashers from the
French Jura retailed lemons—perhaps preserves—silk, the latest fabrics,
umbrellas, beautiful kitchenware, blankets, and baskets.[39]

In military camps, soldiers exchanged their loot for food supplies on the
black market. During peacetime, state authorities used various systems to
supply troops with food, including distribution at staging posts (*étapes*)
to purchases on credit. *Vivandières* (female victuallers) sold bread, meat,
and wine to those who could afford them. On a larger scale, provisioning officials (*munitionnaires*) bought large amounts of wheat abroad—at

times, even in enemy countries. Some became extremely wealthy, others ended up bankrupt—as did the Jewish banker and Austrian army provider Samuel Oppenheimer in 1703—while fraudulent subcontractors reduced bread prices by increasing the proportion of water, bran, or glume.[40]

In the seventeenth and eighteenth centuries, the differentiation of trade became ever more pronounced, particularly in the largest towns. Villages, however, did not lag far behind: many agricultural producers no longer needed to visit towns to purchase supplies or sell their goods. Turnovers of small shops or minor fairs may seem derisory compared to the biggest enterprises, but a local commercial infrastructure had come into being. Towards the end of the Ancien Régime, a large majority of the population participated in an exchange economy, be it regularly, or occasionally. It had taken much time and effort to establish trading networks, since they emerged "from below,"[41] but as a result, the global economy had far-reaching social, cultural, and political repercussions.

The wealthiest producers, with access to surplus goods and extensive networks, had excellent prospects in this system. The poorer ones traded their labor or foraged products (such as the snails poor Bernese children gathered for Capuchin monks south of the Alps). Smallholders, in turn, faced ruin, especially when they came to depend on credit from agricultural brokers between harvests.[42]

## CENTRAL–DECENTRAL NETWORKS

Foodstuffs transported over long distances often became very expensive. This was especially true of colonial goods carried over hundreds, if not thousands of miles to reach their consumers. Circulation in this area was predominantly central, as exemplified by the coffee imported by the merchants of Nantes: the best mocha came from Yemen; yellow coffee from the island of Bourbon; and green coffee from the Antilles. Following an initial sea journey of several weeks, goods were redistributed at Nantes, from where boats carried the coffee onward to Hamburg and Amsterdam. After a second reloading, loads entered the Holy Roman Empire and Poland via land or river routes.[43] Far up the Rhine River, the goods reached small towns on Swiss lakes, from where merchants sold it on to inn- and shopkeepers for distribution all the way to the Alps.

Yet distance-related hierarchies could be undermined: smaller settlements relied not just on the nearest port, but on several competing providers. At eighteenth-century Yverdon (a town of 2,500 inhabitants on Lake
Neuchâtel, connected to the Rhine by the river Aare), the Mandrot firm
obtained goods in several ports before distributing them throughout the
Swiss Confederation, including larger towns such as Geneva. Sugar arrived
from Hamburg, tea from Amsterdam, coffee from England, and cocoa
from Spain (via Italy, Rotterdam, or England). Dutch ports dominated the
spice trade, including that of nutmegs from the Maluku Islands, pepper
from England or Amsterdam, and turmeric (for mustard) from England.[44]

The European cattle trade involved participants at all levels, from peasants selling cows at nearby fairs, to entrepreneurs transporting hundreds of
animals from the Hungarian lowlands or the Alps to Milan and Paris.[45]
Centrality dominated in large-scale operations. In seventeenth-century
Venice, the Zrinyi family imported fattened oxen by sea from more than
495 miles away in Central Europe.[46] In eighteenth-century England, herds
of cattle, sheep, horses, pigs, and even poultry made their way to London.
Geese and turkeys could walk 100 miles in three months![47] For resting and
feeding, the drovers leading the herds had access to meadows, often located
near inns.[48] On their shorter circuits, peddlers from Brabant (*Teuten*) practiced numerous nomadic activities from the sixteenth century onwards:
retailing of various objects, castration or shearing of animals, and so on.
In the eighteenth century, they specialized in the trading of pigs (bought
in neighboring towns and villages to sell at markets in larger towns). This
strengthened—relatively speaking—the economy of their villages of origin.[49] In France in 1803, the Parisian entrepreneur Lavauverte offered to
deliver hundreds of oxen to the markets of Sceaux and Poissy each week.
The men he entrusted with the purchase of animals lived in Basle, Karlsruhe,
and Landau, and visited fairs throughout the Swiss Confederation and the
Empire. Oxen could travel more than 370 miles from east to west, driven
onward by herders and their dogs. Buyers, however, who did not speak
local patois, struggled to find enough cattle, and funds took time to reach
them from the capital.[50] Such problems illustrate the limits of centrality,
and the decentral resistance of local breeders and merchants.

On a smaller geographic scale, decentral circulation patterns strengthened local centralities. In the autumn of 1800, a dozen cattle merchants

(some probably breeders, too) from the Swiss Alps crossed the Gotthard pass "to sell cows." Some travelled with servants, such as Johann Vanzin, who led a herd of thirty cows with three assistants to Milan (a journey of more than 124 miles). Within the logic of regional centrality, they should have stopped at the nearest cattle fairs to sell their herd on to intermediaries, who would then take them onward to large towns. By going to Milan, they bypassed those intermediaries, regardless of several months' absence, and covering large distances for small gains.[51] Decentralities were even more striking when buyers travelled: in the eighteenth century, loud-mouthed butchers, with their servants and dogs, left Italian, Swiss, French, and German towns to attend cattle fairs in the Swiss Alps. In the Jura, Parisian purchasers competed with Genevans, and Highland villages, too, attracted people from several hundred miles away.[52]

With its naturally smaller reach, fresh-fruit distribution was mainly centered round large towns. Fruit merchants from the valley of Montmorency visited Paris every day during the cherry season. They travelled, "either on foot with a hood on their back or with a packhorse," more than 18 miles to avoid the cost of overnight stays, and set out at night "to reach the Halles between one and two in the morning" (while their "women and children continued picking cherries"). Thus, "the network of peddlers [was] complemented by that of merchant-farmers whose fruit trade provides only one example which, at least in the northern Ile-de-France, lace merchants, baker-merchants, and ploughman-merchants (*marchands laboureurs*) could follow."[53]

Distribution of dried fruits and preserves could be more extensive, despite their low value: here, price was no longer linked to distance. These networks followed more decentral patterns than those for fresh fruits: farmer-merchants did not go to the nearest towns, but travelled dozens, if not hundreds of miles between their villages and the final destination. In the eighteenth century, farmers from Gottschee (Slovenia) with their packhorses undertook journeys of more than 620 miles—to Austria, Hungary, southern Germany, Moldavia, and Valachia—to sell lemons, bitter oranges, olives, almonds, dates, and so on, along with olive oil and wine. On the road from October to spring, some became wealthy. The same applies to German orange merchants (*Pomeranzhändler*) trading in lemons, limes, bitter oranges, pomegranates, capers, and olives, later also in spices, and accessories (*galanteries*) such as belts and stockings. Originally from around the lakes of Lombardy, they crossed mountain passes to reach the Rhine and the Main valleys, and cities such as Frankfurt, Mainz, Cologne, Bonn, Trier, and Heidelberg, all more than 370 miles away. Some even settled in those regions.[54] In 1799, Johann-Peter Pons, a Piedmont lemon merchant resident in Lausanne, crossed the Alps to buy fruits, and returned to sell them in the Swiss Confederation.[55]

Seafood networks were more limited due to the obvious problems of preservation. In France, they stretched from the coasts of the Channel to Paris, which exerted a strong pull of centrality. Sea products were purchased from fishermen and packaged in baskets by women (*les emballeuses*); porters then tied them "on pack animals or on carriages" for transport by wagon, with numerous changes of horses at "inns alongside the road to Paris, which served in a way as private relay stations for the coach drivers." "Its weight makes fresh fish difficult to transport on bad roads and requires a strong pulling force; its perishable nature precludes long detours and places extreme demands on horses; being fragile, it is lost if climatic conditions change suddenly and drastically; its fragmented character makes it an ideal target for dishonest store clerks or skillful thieves." Sales took place in the Halles, where wagons arrived at night, just as in the case of fresh fruit. Buyers were often women, who had exclusive fish-retailing rights in Paris. Among the female fishmongers (*poissonnières*) and "retailers" (*détailleresses*) who "will sell the goods in the four corners of the capital," the only male buyers were officers of the major Parisian households and religious establishments.[56]

Some foodstuffs did not circulate at all. In England, large fish from the Essex seaboard were indeed sent to London, but small ones were consumed locally. Decentral sales occurred because the wealthiest city consumers showed no interest in these products. The seaboard was "full of small fisher-boats in very great numbers, belonging to the villages and towns on the coast, who come in every tide with what they take; and selling the smaller fish in the country, send the best and largest away upon horses, which go night and day to London market."[57]

In the Swiss Confederation, the local population purchased lesser quality cattle at lower prices, which increased the region's decentrality in relation to the major towns, and increased its local centrality. In the eighteenth-century Alps, the internationally acclaimed fattened oxen of the

Pays-d'Enhaut were sold "to butchers with high sales volumes, while small town butchers obtain their stock, less fattened and cheaper than the former, at lower costs and in small numbers from local breeders, according to their needs." The same was true of cheeses. The greatest and fattest ones, produced in Saanen, bore the name *gruyères,* renowned for their production on the most bountiful alps and for weighing between 40 and 100 pounds. Merchants did not accept anything below 40 pounds; those cheeses were destined for local consumption.[58]

Foodstuffs did not only flow in one direction, from deep in the countryside and mountain areas via smaller towns towards large cities. The networks were both central and decentral, and the logic of exchange extended beyond the minimization of travel. Producers and merchants had no hesitation in embarking on long journeys for moderate profits. "The country merchant sometimes travelled with his barley to Flushing, his oats to Brittany, his malt to Galway, his butter to La Rochelle, and his wheat to St Sebastian and the Canaries."[59]

This coexistence of centrality and decentrality can be partly explained by the fact that the largest towns (of more than 500,000 inhabitants) represented just 1 percent of the total urban population—and still fewer than 3 percent when those with 100,000 to 500,000 residents are factored in. Towns with a population over 2,000 inhabitants did account for about one-third of the population, but many little towns were smaller than that. The vast majority of the population lived in small towns and villages.[60] While modest in both quality and quantity on an individual basis, the combined consumption of these people thus greatly surpassed that of burghers in large towns.

## MARKETING: A GLOBAL, RURAL, AND URBAN PHENOMENON

Promotion campaigns often emanated from large cities to small towns along a centrality circuit. For the marketing of luxury products, "Paris is [...] an omnipresent reference."[61] Parisian merchants even used foreign languages to showcase their international reach and compete with other European capitals: around 1790–1810, a merchant from Rue St Antoine offered a wine and spirits list in German and English.[62] Many merchants, such as the Queen's confectioner (*confiseur de la Reine*), Ravoisié, offered to "ship abroad."[63] Some Parisians produced goods originally imported from the Antilles: Robin, distiller at the military café of the *Tour du Pin* (Pine Tower), supposedly made Barbados cream.[64] Several shop signs reflected the capital's colonial centrality, such as the *Tête Noire* (Black Head) in the Faubourg St Antoine or the palm tree of a pharmacy. Less distant regions were equally present: alongside the Louvre quay, the wine merchant *Au petit Suisse* (the Little Swiss) appealed to the Swiss guards of the Tuileries; he might have been a former soldier himself.[65]

The interrelation of centrality–decentrality became more complex in provincial towns. In Nancy (with 30,000 inhabitants at the end of the eighteenth century), Paris did not figure on the long list of prices charged by Demoiselle Clomeny, merchant of spirits and elixirs from England, to be paid with "silver money having currency in Lorraine." The centrality of grocer and confectioner Géry Dupont in Valencienne (with 17,000 inhabitants) appears to be mainly regional: he sold "Verdun dragees, spices from Provence, candles from the Mans, etc.,"[66] but foodstuffs could come from much further away, as in Lausanne (with 9,000 inhabitants). In 1800–1801, the *Feuille d'Avis* featured goods from all of Europe. In spite of the existence of vineyards near the fortified walls of the town and the production of more prestigious white wines a mere 12 miles away, advertisements offered a large selection of French denominations (Claret, Champagne, Burgundy, Beaujolais, Mâcon, Languedoc, Roussillon, and so on), along with fortified wines from Malaga, French spirits (*eaux-de-vies*), liquors from Turin, and English whisky. Fruits could also come from afar: figs from Marseille and Provence, hazelnuts from Piedmont, sweet oranges from Portugal, plums from Tours, and prunes from Brignoles in Provence.[67]

Everywhere, inns promoted their services to potential customers. Marketing techniques varied greatly: printed materials, oral communication—including "appeals to passers-by to enter the premises"—and, particularly, "the visual appearance of an establishment": panels, street-facing walls, and signs. Large inns, found mostly in towns, were adorned with a hanging sign, such as those of the Croix-Blanche, Lyon d'Or, Ange, and Quatre-Cantons in Coppet (Swiss Confederation), which advertised the name of the inn and "good accommodations on foot or horseback." But village inns used similar instruments, signaling the availability of food, drink, and lodging via a plank or a simple assortment of leaves. In some Bernese localities, the messages could be very explicit: "'In here for cool wine' visitors have read on the sign of the *Hart* at Matten near Interlaken ever since 1666, 'here you find good red/white wine' on that of the *Fir Tree* at Trachselwald (Emmental) since 1759 and 'Drop in here at the Little Horse where you often find good wine' at nearby Zollbrück since 1772."[68]

Promotion of foodstuffs thus took on different forms depending on the location and the audience it sought to reach. It was not only an urban phenomenon radiating out of the largest towns. It is inscribed in a central–decentral logic that affected all settlements, from hamlets to capitals, and the whole population, from commoners to high nobility.

## GLOBAL ECONOMY OF THE ANCIEN RÉGIME: CENTRALITIES–DECENTRALITIES

The value of goods is not always related to the distance between producer and consumer. When historians or contemporaries envisage the circulation of foodstuffs as a flow from villages to very large cities, they adopt the perspective of centrality. The reality differs: the metaphor of the center conveys a biased image of trade, circuits, and marketing of foodstuffs.

In the seventeenth and eighteenth centuries, the main pillars of the commercial infrastructure (large banks, stock exchanges) were indeed located in very large towns, together with imposing market halls, port infrastructures, multiple daily markets, and specialized shops. However, the fairs had lost their importance in these cities, and the two main banks emerged in Amsterdam and London, rather than in Paris or Naples, despite the latter's extremely large population. Medium-size towns hosted fairs, weekly markets, and shops, and, at times, so did small ports. However, their markets sometimes faltered, market halls might be absent, and villages provided stiff competition. Indeed, fairs, shops, and markets multiplied in rural settings. There were thus commercial activities—wrongly termed *central* rather than *central–decentral* by many historians—in thousands of locations, rural and urban alike.

The mobility of traders was just as much central–decentral. Farmers and middlemen did go to the largest cities, looking for an abundant and wealthy clientele. However, many also circumvented medium-size towns, despite them being closer: central hierarchies, in other words, were not always respected. Foodstuffs could be exchanged directly between villages, while inhabitants of large towns travelled far into the countryside (such as the butchers who purchased cattle in the highlands).

The relationship between localities reflected a similar mixture of centralities and decentralities. Villages exerted their pull on neighboring hamlets and competed not only with other villages, but also with nearby, medium-sized towns. Some of the latter were weakened by rural dynamism, as well as, at times, the proximity of a large city—but others achieved a local hegemony to the detriment of centers such as Paris. Metropolitan cities exercised a strong appeal over their surrounding areas, but without complete domination. Moreover, they also competed against one another.

Finally, centralities–decentralities depended on scale. The multiplication of London's markets increased the centrality of the capital, but their distance from the heart of the city reduced centrality at the level of its suburbs. When the ports of medium-size towns rivaled each other in obtaining colonial foods, they boosted decentralities at the European scale, while strengthening local centralities. The spirits merchant from Nancy simultaneously enhanced *local* centrality (when she demanded payment in local Lorraine currency) and *European* decentrality (by listing England rather than Paris on her price list). The *Teuten* of Brabant, who led pigs from villages to larger towns, fostered regional centrality, but equally fostered the local centrality of their own villages. When towns intended as relay stations for the Parisian marketplace started to behave in hegemonic fashion, they increased both their local centrality and regional decentrality in relation to Paris. Alpine merchants and breeders who went to Milan to sell their herds reinforced the centrality of the Lombard capital (on the international scale) and, through the profits of their sales, that of their villages (on the local scale). At the same time, they strengthened their decentrality in relation to neighboring medium-size towns.

The centralities–decentralities observed in the circulation of food contradict many established theories. Contrary to Christaller's system of central places,[69] the localization of commerce sites did not resemble a pattern of regular hexagons, and trading functions were not organized according to hierarchical pyramids with villages at the bottom, regional towns in the middle, and the largest cities at the top. Contrary to the center–periphery model of spatial organization devised by Fernand Braudel and Immanuel Wallerstein for early modern Europe,[70] neither countryside nor mountains represented truly peripheral regions. The emergence of a dense, rural commercial network, built for and by the local population, demonstrates that their economies were not at the mercy of hegemonic countries such as England, or metropolitan cities such as Paris. Furthermore, closer engagement with the complexities of centralities–decentralities casts doubt on the spatial conceptions of economists, geographers, and historians who reject ideas of a regular geometric distribution of sites, but continue to work with the concept of center(s), looking for one, or several sites that they can interpret as such.[71]

Figures 2.1 and 2.2, charting central and central–decentral circuits of food circulation, summarize the conclusions of this chapter. When historians or observers living in the Ancien Régime imagine the circulation of foodstuffs as a flow going from lowland or highland villages to big cities through medium-size towns (figure 2.1), according to a logic of distance reduction, they adopt the perspective of urban authorities—that of centrality. However, the metaphor of the center presents a skewed image of the actual pattern of trade, circulation, and marketing shown in figure 2.2. Several locations had a reciprocal relationship of centrality–decentrality: between towns, foodstuffs travelled mostly from smaller to larger towns (dominant centrality), but a reverse circulation also took place, since residents of the former purchased food in the latter (centrality–decentrality). Villages maintained several distinct types of relationships with towns. In the mountains, some (case 1) exported foodstuffs to the large towns without purchasing anything in exchange (centrality), but sold and bought in small towns at the same time (centrality–decentrality); other villages (case 2) had centrality relationships with small towns and centrality–decentrality interactions with large cities. In the lowlands, some villages (case 5) maintained centrality–decentrality relationships with all locations, urban or rural, while others (case 6) forged central ties with large cities, and central–decentral ones with small towns. Finally, some localities privileged rural exchanges (cases 3 and 4), prioritizing centrality–decentrality relationships with both high- and lowland villages without trading directly with towns of any size. Distance did not play a major role, since the type of relationship between the locations (central or central–decentral) appears unrelated to the distance between them.

Awareness of the tensions between centrality and decentrality is essential for a proper understanding of the global economy of the Ancien Régime,

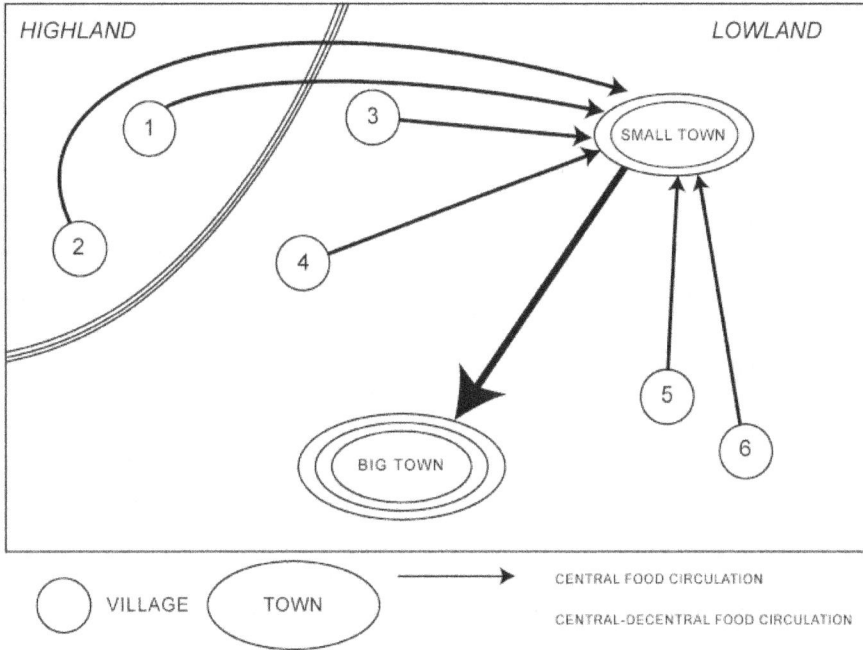

FIGURE 2.1: Central food circulation. Graph by Georges Nicolas.

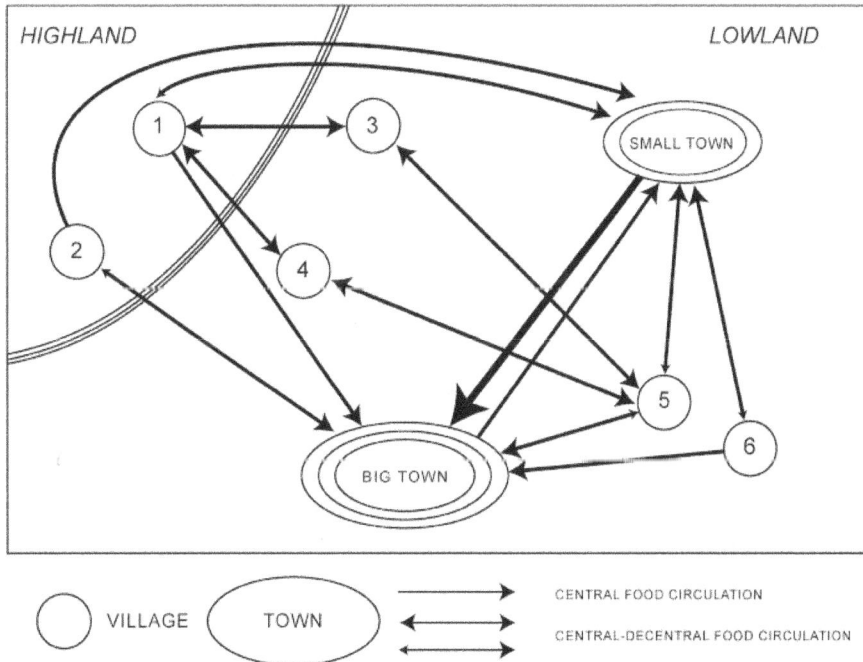

FIGURE 2.2: Central–decentral food circulation. Graph by Georges Nicolas.

which combined production, self-consumption, exchange, and various degrees of market integration. The global economy encompassed all possible goods (common or rare) on all scales, from local to global. It involved the entire population (rich or poor, rural and urban), albeit to different degrees, with regard to international exchange.[72] Barter and credit remained much more common than cash-based payments and most exchanges fell outside of regulations. It differed from twenty-first-century globalization in the sense that it linked different levels (local, regional, national, and so on) rather than fusing them into one in which the same foodstuffs were consumed throughout the world.

These conclusions converge with the current concerns of economists who suggest a global—not only economic—consideration of spatial phenomena, getting close to the notion of a global economy.[73] They no longer think only in terms of centrality, but in complementary patterns of centrifugal–centripetal processes or centralization–decentralization.[74] In the dialectic logic between locations, centrality is an ideal type dreamt up by certain ideologies (religious, philosophical, and political). However, centrality and decentrality cannot be separated, with each taking turns at being dominant.

## CHAPTER THREE

# Food Security, Safety, and Crises

PIER PAOLO VIAZZO

## THE BLACK HORSE OF FAMINE

Did the peasants really starve? This is the classic and still provocative question Peter Laslett raised over forty years ago in his famous book *The World We Have Lost*. "'The starving peasantry,'" he observed, "is a common phrase, especially in popular literature": besides evoking images of men and women badly fed and clothed, and wretchedly housed in hovels, it conveys the idea that from time immemorial up to the arrival of industry, most people all over Europe were always and everywhere on the brink of starvation.[1] Laslett believed that one of the duties of the new sociological history he was trying to establish was "to decide how far famine was an endemic feature of the world we have lost." Investigating whether the inhabitants of early modern Europe were actually besieged by hunger (and, indeed, whether they really died of lack of food) remains a difficult and important task today.

There can be little doubt that in medieval times famines were deeply feared: when people prayed to God to deliver them from the three evils of hunger, pestilence, and war (*a fame, peste et bello libera nos, Domine*), it was hunger that took pole position. At the end of the Middle Ages, these scourges were represented by Albrecht Dürer as three of the four horsemen of the Apocalypse, in the most celebrated of the fifteen illustrations he produced for a Latin and German edition of the *Book of Revelation* published in Nuremberg in 1498. Historians Andrew Cunningham and Ole Peter Grell have recently suggested that this famous woodcut best encapsulates the sense of apocalyptic dread that permeated early modern Europe from the 1490s to the middle of the seventeenth century.[2] This period, they argue, was an age of crises in Europe: there was, of course, religious crisis, which ignited an increase in warfare; but there was also crisis in the economy and, crucially, in demography, as in the late fifteenth century, for the first time since before the Black Death of 1348, the European population began to expand inexorably, putting stresses on the food supply, "causing intense famines," and eventually creating "the crisis mentality which made the 'Four horsemen of the Apocalypse' the popular image of the age."[3] The third horseman, the one riding the Black Horse of famine, would thus appear to have been the most calamitous of all. Cunningham and Grell maintain, on the other hand, that after the mid-seventeenth century, when the end of the Thirty Years' War brought about a more stabilized society, the fear of the coming of the four horsemen rapidly diminished, not least because demographic growth began to level out around 1650, and the frequency and severity of famines declined markedly. Yet, exactly three centuries after Dürer published his text of the *Book of Revelation* with its woodcut illustrations, Thomas Malthus still had no hesitation in naming famine, along with war and pestilence, as one of the three "positive checks" which were bound to brutally curb population growth. Indeed, he defines famine as "the last and most dreadful mode by which nature represses a redundant population."[4] One of the aims of this chapter will be to assess whether the 150 years between 1498 and 1648 were actually different from the century and a half that separates the end of the Thirty Years' War from the publication of Malthus' *Essay on the Principle of Population*.

Before doing that, however, it will be useful—for two different reasons—to go back to Laslett's question: "Did the peasants really starve?" The first reason is that it is advisable to pause on the ambiguities of the very term *starvation*—a powerfully evocative word which condenses at least three meanings, namely (according to the *Oxford English Dictionary*): (1) dying of hunger, (2) suffering from lack of food, and (3) suffering extreme poverty. Other dictionaries may slightly change the sequence, but the three basic meanings are always there to suggest both an intimate relation and an implicit causal sequence: people in dire need are bound to suffer lack of nourishment and eventually to die of hunger. This link between impoverishment, famine, and mortality lies at the heart of Malthus' reasoning and, in more recent years, of several other models that have been put forward to encompass the relations between population and resources in pre-industrial times, although some scholars have seen heightened mortality as resulting from acute subsistence crises, while others have explained exceptionally high mortality as due proximately to epidemic diseases, but ultimately to endemic dearth. As we shall see, there are grounds for doubting that some of the relations between poverty, famine, and mortality that have long been taken for granted actually obtain.

The second reason is that the adverb *really* in Laslett's sentence directs our attention to a possible gap between the representations of the starving peasantry in folk tales and popular culture, and the harder evidence uncovered by historical demographers, and economic and medical historians. As we have seen, it is generally assumed that our ancestors lived in a "land of hunger," to cite the title of Piero Camporesi's well-known journey into the folk culture of early modern Europe.[5] However, as John Walter noted two decades ago, the repertoire of folk tales in which peasant families face the dilemma of too many mouths to feed is not the same, and not equally rich, everywhere in Europe: indeed, he noticed a remarkable "absence of English Hansels and Gretels wandering in a Malthusian world,"[6] a surprising finding, which took added meaning in the light of then recent research suggesting that by the mid-seventeenth century England had slipped the shadow of famine, in sharp contrast to the continuing vulnerability of most other European countries. Since ancien régime Europe appears not to have been a homogeneous land of hunger, another aim of this chapter will be to explore the historical geography of dearth and famines in order to pinpoint differences in both space and time, and see which countries or regions were more famine-prone than others, and why.

In view of the role Cunningham and Grell grant to population growth as the key factor "underlying all the crises of the age,"[7] it seems sensible to start from demography and verify whether the overall scenario they outline is supported by available estimates. This is all the more necessary since a very different picture has been proposed by Massimo Livi-Bacci in a book on population and nutrition of special relevance to us. Although he agrees that there was "strong recovery from mid-fifteenth to the end of the sixteenth century," he believes that from approximately 1600, this phase of growth was "followed by crisis, or stagnation, until the beginning of the eighteenth century, at which point the forces of modern expansion began to gather momentum."[8]

## EUROPEAN PATTERNS OF POPULATION GROWTH, 1500–1800

Estimating the size of historical populations has not been a popular endeavor for some decades. This explains why our most precious sources on the evolution of Europe's population as a whole remain two works published thirty years ago, namely Colin McEvedy and Richard Jones' *Atlas of World Population History* and a brisk article by Jean-Nöel Biraben.[9] As shown by table 3.1, the two series proposed by these scholars look to be largely in agreement.[10] On closer inspection, however, we notice that for the seventeenth century there are significant discrepancies: according to Biraben, between 1600 and 1700 the European population continued to grow, but at a considerably slower pace compared to the previous century, whereas McEvedy and Jones reckon that the first half of the seventeenth century, with a modest increase of just two million, was a period of crisis, or at least stagnation, followed by faster growth from 1650 to 1700, and much faster growth in the eighteenth century. Their figures clearly tally more with Livi-Bacci's scenario than with Cunningham and Grell's assertion that population growth leveled out around 1650.

Things are more complex than that, though, as these admittedly crude totals and general trends mask—again, especially for the seventeenth century— large differences among the various parts of Europe. McEvedy and Jones' work (see table 3.2) reveals that growth was stronger in north-western and Eastern Europe than in France (which was, in 1500, the most populous country in Europe), and in the central countries, not to mention southern Europe, whose population actually declined in the first half of the

Table 3.1: The European population from 1300 to 1800 (in millions):
two estimates

|  | McEvedy and Jones (1978) | | Biraben (1979) | |
| --- | --- | --- | --- | --- |
|  | Population | Index | Population | Index |
| 1300 | 79 | 97.5 | 82 | 102.5 |
| 1400 | 60 | 74.1 | 62 | 77.5 |
| 1500 | 81 | 100 | 80 | 100 |
| 1600 | 100 | 123.5 | 106 | 132.5 |
| 1650 | 105 | 129.6 | – | – |
| 1700 | 120 | 148.1 | 118 | 147.5 |
| 1750 | 140 | 172.8 | 138 | 172.5 |
| 1800 | 180 | 222.2 | 183 | 228.8 |

*Sources:* McEvedy and Jones 1978, 42–113; Biraben 1979, 16.

seventeenth century, and just managed by 1700 to reach the level it had
already attained one hundred years before.

It should be noted, however, that new estimates have now been produced for some European countries. In some cases (France and England,
for example[11]) the differences between old and new estimates are modest;
in others, they are quite considerable. The case of Germany is perhaps the
most striking. If Christian Pfister's calculations are correct,[12] in the course
of the sixteenth century the population of Germany nearly doubled, instead of just increasing by one-third, as estimated by McEvedy and Jones
(see table 3.3). Pfister actually believes that in 1618 it totaled 17.1 million, which means that in the following three decades Germany lost nearly
one-half of its inhabitants, at a massively negative annual rate of 18.2 per
thousand, and that it took another century for this country to go back to
the levels reached before the outbreak of the Thirty Years' War.

The case of Italy is also interesting and instructive. If we compare
McEvedy and Jones' estimates for Germany and Italy in tables 3.3 and 3.4,
we see that they suggest a slower growth for Italy during the sixteenth century, whereas the trends from 1600 to 1750 look exactly the same. More
accurate estimates show instead that Italy's population growth in the sixteenth century, while definitely slower when compared to the one estimated
by Pfister for Germany in the same period, was nevertheless considerably
greater than hinted at by McEvedy and Jones' figures.[13] The decline in the

Table 3.2: The European population from 1300–1800 (in millions): macro-regional differences

| Year | France | | "Northwest"[a] | | "South"[b] | | "Center"[c] | | "East"[d] | | Europe | |
|---|---|---|---|---|---|---|---|---|---|---|---|---|
| | Pop. | Index | Pop. | Index | Pop. | Index | Pop. | Index | Pop. | Index | Pop. | Index |
| 1300 | 16 | 107 | 9 | 99 | 23.8 | 107 | 17.6 | 94 | 12.5 | 78 | 79 | 98 |
| 1400 | 11 | 73 | 7 | 77 | 17.4 | 78 | 12.8 | 68 | 11.8 | 74 | 60 | 74 |
| 1500 | 15 | 100 | 9.1 | 100 | 22.2 | 100 | 18.7 | 100 | 16 | 100 | 81 | 100 |
| 1600 | 18.5 | 123 | 11.6 | 127 | 28.5 | 128 | 21.4 | 114 | 20 | 125 | 100 | 123 |
| 1650 | 21 | 140 | 13.5 | 148 | 26.2 | 118 | 21.8 | 117 | 22.5 | 141 | 105 | 130 |
| 1700 | 22 | 147 | 16.2 | 178 | 29.2 | 132 | 26.6 | 142 | 26 | 162 | 120 | 148 |
| 1750 | 24 | 160 | 18.5 | 203 | 34.8 | 157 | 29.7 | 159 | 33 | 206 | 140 | 173 |
| 1800 | 29 | 193 | 26.5 | 291 | 43.2 | 195 | 36.3 | 194 | 45 | 281 | 180 | 222 |

*Source*: McEvedy and Jones 1978, 42–113.
a "Northwest": British Isles, Scandinavia, Belgium, Luxembourg, the Netherlands.
b "South": Italy, Iberian Peninsula, the Balkans.
c "Centre": Germany, Switzerland, Austria, Czechoslovakia, Hungary, Romania.
d "East": Russia, Poland.

Table 3.3: The population of Germany between 1500 and 1750 (in millions): two estimates

| Year | McEvedy and Jones (1978) | | Pfister (1997) | |
|------|------------|-------|------------|---------|
|      | Population | Index | Population | Index   |
| 1500 | 9          | 100   | 9          | 100     |
| 1550 | –          | –     | 12.6       | 140     |
| 1600 | 12         | 133   | 16.2       | 180     |
| 1618 | –          | –     | 17.1       | 190     |
| 1650 | 11         | 122   | 9–10       | 100–111 |
| 1700 | 13         | 144   | 14.1       | 157     |
| 1750 | 15         | 167   | 17.5       | 194     |

*Sources:* McEvedy and Jones 1978, 69; Pfister 1997, 519.

first half of the seventeenth century—due more to the effects of plague than to the disruption of war—was also less severe than in Germany.

Other cases could be mentioned. Drawing on Wilhelm Bickel's pioneering work,[14] for example, McEvedy and Jones had proposed a total population of approximately 800,000 for Switzerland at the beginning of the sixteenth century,[15] a much higher figure than the 562,000 individuals subsequently estimated by Markus Mattmüller.[16] More importantly, even these new and more reliable national estimates may conceal vast regional differences. Thus, Pfister has found that between 1618 and 1648 some German regions were completely or largely spared by war and depopulation, whereas others experienced a veritable demographic collapse, with the number of their inhabitants falling by over 80 percent.[17] In Italy, the impression of a constant and generalized increase between 1650 and 1800 conveyed by table 3.4 disappears when data are disaggregated at a regional level.[18] Equally marked differences can be detected in Spain: between 1530 and 1787 the population of the Crown of Castile exactly doubled, from 3,919,000 to 7,833,000 people, but in Asturias and Galicia the number of inhabitants more than quadrupled, whereas in Castilla la Vieja, the most populous region in 1530, it increased by less than 20 percent.[19]

These numbers demonstrate that there were quite different demographic patterns across Europe and that population growth did not level out around 1650. Nevertheless, it can scarcely be denied that the sixteenth century

Table 3.4: The population of Italy between 1500 and 1750 (in millions):
two estimates

|  | McEvedy and Jones (1978) | | Del Panta et al. (1996) | |
| --- | --- | --- | --- | --- |
| Year | Population | Index | Population | Index |
| 1500 | 10 | 100 | 9 | 100 |
| 1550 | – | – | 11.5 | 128 |
| 1600 | 12 | 120 | 13.5 | 150 |
| 1650 | 11 | 110 | 11.7 | 130 |
| 1700 | 13 | 130 | 13.6 | 151 |
| 1750 | 15 | 150 | 15.8 | 176 |
| 1800 | 19 | 190 | 18.3 | 203 |

*Sources:* McEvedy and Jones 1978, 69; Del Panta, Livi-Bacci, Pinto and Sonnino 1996, 275.

was, in general, a time of demographic growth, and it seems hardly an ac-
cident that it corresponds to what historical climatologists have identified
as a warming phase lasting approximately from the 1470s to the 1580s or
1590s, when a long cooling period suddenly began, as in middle-latitude
areas such warming periods favor an increase in grain yields, which, in
turn, favor an upswing in the population growth rate.[20] However, the
Malthusian tendency of a population to increase geometrically, compared
to the tendency of resources to increase only arithmetically, may cause a
progressive unbalance between population and resources. Indeed, both
population figures and fragmentary evidence on declining yield rates from
various parts of Europe suggest that land was more and more intensively
cultivated, and that the soil was probably exhausted. Symptoms of over-
cropping can be noticed in southern Italy by the mid-sixteenth century,[21]
and in 1578 the Spanish agronomist, Juan de Arrieta, was giving voice "to
the fears of the Castilian peasantry that 'the land is becoming exhausted
and the fields are not as productive as they once were.'"[22] This was making
European rural economies increasingly vulnerable not only to occasional
bad weather, but also to a long-term worsening of climatic conditions,
whose main effect is to lower the elevation where crops can be cultivated,
thereby "decreasing the amount of land available for cultivation and leading in turn to either a decline in total output or more intense cultivation
and lower yields."[23] Since the end of the sixteenth century was marked by

the advent of a Little Ice Age, most spectacularly heralded by the threat-
ening advances of Alpine glaciers in the 1580s, it is reasonable to expect
"an increase in the frequency or intensity of famines from the end of the
sixteenth century, bringing a general decline in nutrition."[24] As a matter of
fact, the last decade was marked by the worst famine period of the whole
century: the Great Famine of the 1590s.

## THE GREAT FAMINE OF THE 1590s AND ITS LEGACY

All over Europe, the last decade of the sixteenth century "was a time when
the outriders of the Apocalypse were on the loose in much of Western
Europe: years of terrible famine, plague, war and disorder. There were repeated prophecies of the end of the world in 1600."[25] The most fearful of
the four horsemen was, however, famine: "Behold! What a famine God has
brought upon the land," an English preacher cried in a sermon at York in
the mid-1590s. "One year there has been hunger. The second there was a
dearth. And the third there was great cleanness of teeth."[26]

Signaled directly by disappointing production figures or indirectly by
lowering yield rates, increases in food prices, or heightened mortality,
dearth and famine hit the southern countries in the early part of the decade, the unfortunate outcome of a sequence of wet winters alternating
with drought in the summer months, and a few years later the northern
countries, where rye and wheat were at the mercy of severely cold winters and exceptionally rainy springs and summers, which rotted the crops
in the fields. Although the primary cause was the general deterioration in
the weather, Cunningham and Grell have suggested that the situation was
made worse by the almost total dependence of all European populations on
bread grains (mainly wheat in the Mediterranean countries and rye in the
north, supplemented by barley and oats) and by the demographic pressure
that had forced peasants to exhaust the available arable land, or to expand
it either by draining marshes or, more frequently, by putting grazing land
under the plough.[27] They have also argued that, while the Great Famine
struck all across Europe, its incidence in some places was more severe than
in others. In particular, they maintain that even though the countryside was
where the food was produced, towns were generally better places to live
during dearth or famine because "grain always moved—more correctly,

was moved—from areas of low purchasing power to areas of high purchasing power, irrespective of the relative degree of hunger and need."[28] It
would also seem to stand to reason that people forced to cultivate marginal
land were those most vulnerable to a poor harvest, and hence to dearth and
famine, for a cold period will predictably have "its greatest effects in marginal areas, particularly those at higher elevations."[29] Recent research on
the impact of the famines of the 1590s in northern Italy provides, however,
a more complex and somewhat surprising picture.

It is widely assumed that the effects of climatic change were most
acutely felt in the mountains and especially in the Alps, where a few glaciers expanded between 2,600 and 3,300 feet from 1580 to 1600, and de-
voured not only meadows and fields, but also hamlets that "must have been
put up in the belief, founded on experience of some length, that they would
be safe from such incursions."[30] In his analysis of the diary of Eustache
Piémond, notary and secretary to the small town of Saint-Antoine in the
Dauphiné, Mark Greengrass, remarks that although famine, plague, and
war occur very frequently in the diary, which runs from 1572 to 1608, "the
climatic conditions were far more important. He was a keen meteorologist
and his observations were quite precise... With advancing glaciers in the
Alps round Chamonix destroying villages at this period, it is difficult not
to take Piémond's meteorological evidence as an illustration from a village
only 80 miles from Chamonix of the effects of what has been termed the
'mini-ice age' of the latter half of the sixteenth century."[31] In fact, we know
for certain that many high-altitude hamlets were abandoned (if not altogether destroyed by the glaciers) and it is likely that the ecological processes
started by the worsening climatic conditions of the 1590s led to a sizeable
increase in the volume of Alpine seasonal emigration.[32] Yet, we should not
accept as self-evident that in the Alps the consequences of climatic change
were always and necessarily catastrophic. Based on an unusually broad
examination of parish records from a variety of northern Italian communities, a recent study has brought to light significant differences between
geo-ecological zones that cast serious doubts on the common view that in
northern Italy the impact of climatic worsening was essentially the same
"from the Alps to the Tiber."[33] In particular, it shows that the demographic
crisis of the early 1590s affected the plains much more seriously than the
Alpine uplands. This appears to have been mainly due to the different crop

regimes: since the crisis was essentially due to a grain shortage, mountain populations (whose diet was more varied, as they largely relied for their nutrition on animal husbandry) suffered less. In addition, it would seem that in most parts of the Italian Alps a low-pressure demographic regime, characterized by relatively low birth, marriage, and death rates, already prevailed in the sixteenth century, and allowed Alpine populations to keep their numbers largely in balance with local resources.[34]

While questioning the validity of some generalizations about the greater vulnerability of mountain populations, these findings confirm that the shortage of bread grains was the decisive problem faced by Europe during the famines of the 1590s. To cope with this shortage, grain could be bought and imported, sometimes creating paradoxical situations: in Sicily, which at that time was still the great granary of the Mediterranean, the wide-spread misery caused by frequent harvest failure was made worse by the fact that wheat continued to be exported.[35] However, the huge problems of the Mediterranean food supply could no longer be solved by Sicilian grain. The bad harvests which befell Italy in the late sixteenth century paved the way, as famously remarked by Fernand Braudel, "for the massive importa-tion of grain from the north, carried in Dutch, Hanseatic, and English sail-ing ships from the Baltic to the Mediterranean after the 1590s."[36] Indeed, grain from the north was imported not only by Mediterranean cities: "in this time of natural disaster, the Baltic grain trade appeared as an angel of mercy to many European consumers."[37]

Such an invasion of Mediterranean, French, English, and Dutch ports by grain ships from north-eastern Europe was a novelty of great impor-tance not only from an economic, but also from a political point of view. As several scholars have suggested, the significance of the "crisis of the 1590s" may ultimately reside in the impetus it gave to an enhanced view of government responsibilities: famines had often been the spur for communal action, but in the 1590s European governments were more brutally forced to play an active role, since they had to take urgent measures to provide relief for the poor, to protect industry, and above all to secure the food sup-ply. Especially in southern Europe, this demanded a transfer of responsibil-ity from the sphere of private charity to the domain of public action, which entailed an increase in taxation, and an extension of the control by state authorities over administration and justice.[38] It is therefore not unjustified to claim that out of the problems created by growing population pressure and of the resulting food shortages, "there came the basic structures of early modern European social welfare."[39]

This political, administrative, and social change is probably the main and most enduring legacy of the great famines of the 1590s. Rather surprisingly, it is less certain that the last years of the sixteenth century marked a turning point in European population history. As we have seen, in some parts of Europe demographic growth did not stop during the first half of the following century. In others it did, but this was apparently not the aftermath of the Great Famine, but the effect of either war or plague. What is more, although there is evidence that in the 1590s mortality surged in many places, one should not hasten to conclude that food shortage, resulting from acute population pressure upon increasingly scarce resources, was a common and obvious cause of widespread deaths.[40] Of course, both contemporary observers and modern historians have usually posited a link between population pressure, high food prices, and dearth-related mortality crises. But are they right?

## FAMINE, DISEASE, AND MORTALITY

The scholar who most seriously tried to tackle Laslett's question and to investigate if "peasants really starved" was the American historian Andrew Appleby, in a now classic book focused on the north-western English counties of Cumberland and Westmoreland, where in 1587–1588, 1597, and 1623 "thousands of people starved in what appears to have been a series of 'positive' Malthusian checks."[41] His argument was that in the late sixteenth century the population of the region had outstripped the food supply, thereby generating a disequilibrium that was brought to a crisis point by harvest failure. Exacerbated by a depression in the clothing industry, which made it difficult to pay for food from outside, this unbalance resulted in a series of famines which "skimmed off the surplus population through starvation aided by disease and emigration."[42] While recognizing the concurrence and close interdependence of several factors, Appleby was giving clear priority to hunger, and taking sides with a number of distinguished historians and historical demographers who had emphasized, especially in France, the importance of subsistence crises.

In an article published shortly after the end of World War II, the French historian, Jean Meuvret, reported that exceptional rises in the number of deaths in many areas of France invariably coincided with equally exceptional rises in the price of wheat—the best barometer of food crisis (*crise de subsistances*).[43] Subsequent studies[44] seemed to corroborate the theory, according to which the peaks in mortality that affected the whole of Europe from the Middle Ages to the eighteenth century could almost always be traced to subsistence crises: as intimated by the French peasant proverb according to which "first comes famine, then comes plague," Meuvret claimed, in a later work, that illness flourished against a background of famine.[45] This thesis was supported with great ingenuity by Appleby, who developed a method for differentiating between disease and famine in order to assess "the role of famine as a killer in its own right," and contended that mortality previously attributed to such diseases as plague or typhus was instead the result of starvation, if only *starvation* was defined broadly enough to include fatal intestinal disorders brought on by eating unsuitable food, such as rotting flesh or tree bark.[46] His verdict was unequivocally that the peasants really starved.

In recent years, however, the theory of subsistence crises has not received the empirical support that its proponents were expecting. To be sure, new evidence and new analyses have confirmed that mortality often responded to variation in the price of grain and other staple foods, although the intensity of the response differed from country to country.[47] However, on the whole, the correlation between famine, disease, and mortality seems to have been less close than was previously supposed. For one thing, although malnutrition certainly favors the spread of a certain number of illnesses such as cholera or measles, experts now maintain that its relationships with other infectious diseases is variable, or even (in the case of plague and smallpox) almost non-existent.[48] Moreover, clinical and experimental research has ascertained that there are special mechanisms within the body that allow it to adapt to conditions of extreme undernourishment and to survive. Many scholars are therefore reluctant to view food shortage as the primary cause of mortality crises in pre-industrial populations, and prefer to link them to epidemiological cycles largely unrelated to the state of nutrition of the population. According to Livi-Bacci, "there can be no doubt" that periods of high mortality were "almost always the result of an epidemic attack … triggered more by social dislocation than by malnutrition."[49]

This reversal of the previously dominant position has an interesting corollary when we wonder whether there was inequality in the face of famine. If mortality was closely related to nutrition, Livi-Bacci has reasoned, then "social groups who fed on a rich and varied diet should have enjoyed a lower mortality and greater life expectancy than the masses who lived in poverty and were, from time to time, the victims of serious shortages."[50] His finding that rich and poor were surprisingly equal in the face of death—and, in particular, equally unable to escape the attack of epidemic disease—is taken by him as another refutation of the theory linking mortality to nutrition. Yet this does not really mean that they were equal in the face of famine. Much depends, of course, on definitions. Cunningham and Grell, allegedly following "the characterization of the people of the sixteenth century" in distinguishing famine from dearth, have stated "that in time of dearth food stuffs are in short supply and thus become extremely expensive, but in times of famine, food stuffs cannot be bought at all, however rich one is."[51] This, however, contradicts what an Italian clergyman wrote in the early sixteenth century in a much-quoted *Treatise on Famine and Hunger*, namely that

> God sends three scourges to punish men for their sins: Famine, War and Pestilence. But of them all Famine, so severe as it is, is less terrible. For while War and Pestilence strike all men without distinction, Famine spares the priests, one can thus confess before one dies; it spares the notaries, so it is still possible to make a will; it spares finally the princes who oversee the safety of the state.[52]

## OVERCOMING DEARTH? THE NEW CROPS AND EIGHTEENTH-CENTURY POPULATION GROWTH

As we have seen, Livi-Bacci has argued that demographic crisis or stagnation characterized the population history of Europe until the beginning of the eighteenth century, when "the forces of modern expansion began to gather momentum." Table 3.1 confirms that between 1700 and 1800 the European population as a whole increased by approximately 50 percent, and in some regions (as shown by table 3.2) growth was considerably greater. Once again, the causes of such demographic growth are a matter of debate. According to some scholars, this increase was mainly an effect of what has been termed the *stabilization of mortality*. They point out that after 1660, most probably because of the preventive measures taken by European governments, plague epidemics grew suddenly fewer and further between, and that the end of the violent, short-term mortality fluctuations that had marked the so-called age of the plague brought about a substantial decline in death rates.[53] A different theory has been put forward by Thomas McKeown in his controversial book *The Modern Rise of Population*, where he contends that the single most important causal explanation of falling mortality (and, consequently, of population growth) in Europe was improvement in nutrition due to greater food supplies.[54] Both theses are open to objections. The general validity of the first thesis is contradicted by the discovery that in some parts of Europe population growth is attributable more to increasing nuptiality and fertility than to a decline in mortality.[55] On the other hand, McKeown's thesis sits uneasily with evidence from countries ranging from France and England, to Sweden and northern Italy, where population growth was apparently not accompanied by any improvement in nutrition.[56] Nevertheless, the introduction and spectacular diffusion in the eighteenth century of new food crops such as maize, potato, and buckwheat can hardly be overlooked, and even the main proponent of the theory of the stabilization of mortality recognized that these crops greatly assisted demographic growth.[57] Yet, once we concede that the increasing yields allowed by the new crops permitted a growth of population beyond what would otherwise have been possible, we may still wonder whether increased productivity also led to nutritional improvement: we might actually expect demographic expansion to have had an adverse effect on the quality of nutrition.[58] These are the questions we will try to explore in the concluding section of this chapter, starting from European society's growing ability to escape peacetime famines.

One of the merits of Appleby's mapping of the geography and chronology of subsistence crises in England was to raise novel and important questions about why some areas were more vulnerable to famine than others. Besides suggesting that in the late sixteenth and early seventeenth centuries there seemed to be "two Englands," with the north more clearly vulnerable than the south-east, his work brought into sharper relief the contrast between England and other European countries.[59] It is worth noting that Meuvret's subsistence-crisis theory rested on his analysis of mortality crises between 1677 and 1734, the classic period of great famines in France. By that time, however, or indeed by the mid-seventeenth century, both England and Holland had apparently ceased to be seriously and regularly affected by dearth. How did these two countries manage to develop such a resistance to famine? For England, one possible explanation resides in the rural population's increasing reliance on a mix of winter and spring cereals, whereas in France "the continuing stranglehold of winter cereals perpetuated the threat of dearth."[60] Following the iconoclastic theory proposed by the economic historian Ronald Seavoy,[61] a bolder and more ambitious argument has been advanced by Cunningham and Grell, who maintain that the ability of England and the United Provinces to withstand famine is due to the fact that they were the first European countries to get out of the Malthusian loop by moving from a peasant subsistence economy to a commercialized agriculture. This transition, they claim, took place between the end of the fifteenth century and the early decades of the sixteenth century as a response to the challenge posed by population growth: in England this challenge was met through the enclosures process, whereas in the Netherlands grains were replaced by industrial crops such as flax, hemp, hops, and rape-seed, bread grains now being imported cheaply from the Baltic.[62] Through different routes, England and the Netherlands were thus able to *refute* Malthus and to become free of the cycle of population growth occasioning peacetime dearth and famine.[63] In those countries where a peasant economic orientation continued to prevail, on the other hand, prospects seemed destined to become progressively gloomy.

The whole nutritional scenario was, however, deeply changed by the introduction of the new crops imported as part of the *Columbian exchange*.[64] Their success was not immediate, as witnessed by the slow and difficult diffusion of the potato, and the history of their progress is intertwined with that of famines. For a long time, the potato was the object of dislike and suspicion: both learned men and common folk regarded it as fit only for swine, and there were fears that it could give rise to scrofula, rickets, and many other evils.[65] Thus, although potatoes were cultivated in some European districts as early as the first years of the eighteenth century, diffusion on a large scale began only in the last decades of the eighteenth century, when serious famine in 1770–1772 and subsequent spells of bad weather and harvest failure affected Central and northern Europe.[66] The spread of maize was earlier and easier, but a powerful stimulus to put more land under maize cultivation was again provided, in 1816–1817, by a severe subsistence crisis.[67]

This simple chronology must warn us against hastily attributing the eighteenth-century population growth to the introduction of the new crops. Nevertheless, once adopted these crops played a crucial twofold role: on the one hand, particularly the potato in Central and northern Europe, and maize in southern Europe, increased considerably the foodstuff yield per unit of land; on the other hand, they made harvests less vulnerable to climatic fluctuations. A good example comes from the Alps. Prior to the introduction of the potato, the main weakness of Alpine agrarian ecosystems had been their lack of flexibility, as a high frequency of cold and wet spells ineluctably led to a simultaneous slump in grain, fruit, hay, and cheese production. Since the potato was a sturdier crop than summer grains, harvest failures, even in adverse meteorological conditions, became less likely. Thus, its incorporation into Alpine ecosystems, besides increasing productivity, made them more flexible, and therefore more resistant to climatic stress.[68]

Yet increased productivity did not necessarily entail an increase in the availability per head. Instead, many scholars believe that the introduction of the new crops restarted "a running battle between population and resources" by encouraging a multiplication of households and the relaxation of the old Malthusian preventive checks on marriage.[69] "As potatoes were substituted for the traditional foodstuffs", K. H. Connell wrote about Ireland, "a family's subsistence could be found from a diminished section of its holding": hence his famous argument linking Irish population growth to a dramatic increase in nuptiality made possible by the introduction of the potato.[70] This vicious circle was not ineluctable: in the Alps the introduction of the potato caused no abrupt decrease in the age of marriage or proportion of celibates, and in the course of the nineteenth century, as it had already happened in the late sixteenth century, social and cultural mechanisms conducive to a relatively low-pressure demographic regime helped preserve this area from famine.[71] The Irish famine of the 1840s is, however, a powerful reminder that demographic expansion could undermine the positive effects of higher productivity and greater harvest stability. Moreover, for many Europeans the adoption of maize and potato was an impoverishment of their diet, not an advance, and led to a deterioration in the overall nutritional level.[72] As David Grigg suggested thirty years ago in his influential book on population growth and agrarian change, after 1750 Europe had escaped from the Malthusian dilemma, but certainly not from many of the adverse consequences of rapid demographic rise: "many of the symptoms of population growth reappeared in the 1820s and 1830s, so that both contemporary observers and modern historians believed rural Europe to be overpopulated by mid-century."[73]

## CHAPTER FOUR

# Food and Politics: The Power of Bread in European Culture

VICTOR MAGAGNA

Food is a singularly cultural phenomenon. Although it is possible to adduce any number of material forces and factors that influence the food of any particular civilization, there is an obvious connection between a society's basic cultural values, and basic issues such as who is entitled to what kinds of food, on what occasions, and even what counts as a meal. Self-evident to those familiar with South Asia or East Asia, this testable proposition also holds for early modern Europe, where culture interacted with the political economy of food, just as was true for other dimensions of material life such as housing, and kinship. The central thesis of this essay is that culture—understood as core values or normative ideals—had an independent effect on food in multiple ways, ranging from issues of justice and entitlement, to sacred and secular modes of commensality. Although food can obviously be understood in a purely material fashion, the past cannot be adequately recovered if we rip it out of its cultural mix. Accordingly, what follows is divided into three broad thematic areas that analyze the link between culture and food from the vantage point of production, distribution, and consumption. The author freely admits that some of the casual connections may be speculative, but they are at least falsifiable and grounded in empirical evidence. The point is to draw the reader's attention to the way cultural values shaped the logic of food in early modern Europe, a society that was still largely feudal in character.[1]

## PRODUCTION: THE STAKEHOLDER HOUSEHOLD AND THE POLITICAL ECONOMY OF AGRICULTURE IN EUROPE 1500–1789

Let us begin with a loaf of bread. Anyone who has read the history and historiography of early modern Europe will be struck by the central role of bread in the European diet all the way from the Ural Mountains to Ireland. This humble but vital fact had solid material foundations in climate and soil, technological constraints, and the ever-present impact of social structure and its attendant distribution of wealth, status, and power. Just as important, however, was that the very ambiguity of bread gave it great culture salience as a sign of sufficiency or even prosperity, an issue of fair dealing and just prices, and a maker of both secular and sacred commensality. For example, whether rich or poor, or more or less powerful and privileged, Europeans expected bread to be part of a good diet, or even as an entitlement; and when those held responsible for the bread supply failed to deliver it or only at unreasonable prices, the result could be trouble, including, at the extreme, classic food riots. Similarly, bread was a source of sacred power in the ritual of transubstantiation in the Latin Mass, something even its Protestant critics acknowledged in their own complex attempt to construct a substitute for the ancient Catholic rite. Indeed, the cultural valence of bread can be seen by comparison with the history of the humble potato. The potato did become a basic component of the food of the poor by the end of the eighteenth century, particularly in Ireland and parts of Eastern and Central Europe. However, the progress of the potato was not a linear march based on single calculations of the economics of production and the advantages of its natural elements; instead, the potato often generated fierce resistance, precisely because of the culturally generated preference for bread, and the links between bread and status, security, and the definition of a full and satisfying meal. Given the importance of bread as a point of intersection between food and culture, we will focus on bread from its origins as grain to the event of final consumption.

Baked bread unremarkably requires milled or processed grain as a necessary condition of its existence, and flour or flour substitutes necessitate unprocessed grain, whether harvested in a wild form, or more commonly as a human-engineered domesticate. It is therefore essential to start any discussion of food and European culture with the process of its production, and specifically with the producers whose labor, land, or capital made possible the creation of a cereal-based food culture throughout the European region. This initial focus is important for two reasons. First, it will show the connection between the lives of the working population and the culture of food. Second, and more important, it illuminates the ways kinship and community help to shape the political economy of food through its connection to what will be called the *stakeholder household*.[2] Such a household was both a claimant to the food supply, and a holder of often substantial rights to property and entitlement that gave it real power in the chain of food production and distribution. With respect to the stakeholder household, a useful starting point is to imagine a cognitive map of early modern Europe that begins not with class or the state, but with the institutions of kinship and community at the core of European agriculture, and through which food was generated.

It is an unremarkable but vital fact that early modern Europe was as much a world of households as it was a world of markets, states, or individuals. Households made up of parents and children were often endowed with legal rights and obligations ranging from taxation to militia service and, most importantly, property rights. To be a member of a household was to have at least some minimal claim to security and subsistence, while being outside a household was to be literally alone, a stranger, wanderer, and potential outcast and criminal. In cultural terms, the sanctity of the household, like the sanctity of property, was rooted in Christian ethics, and sacred and secular law, and transgressions against the household were morally repulsive and legally subject to deep, culturally generated sanctions.

We can label this household the stakeholder household because members of this institution could make culturally accepted and often legally enforceable claims on human and material resources essential to food production. Such households therefore held a potent stake in a variety of economic and political organizations, ranging from the village or parish

community, to the emerging state. It was this stake that allowed its holders to control, to some extent, the flow of food-generating resources from
seeds and soil, to the grinding of grain, and the distribution of food stuffs
of all kinds. Bread begins with grain, and the stakeholder household always
had some margin of power over the whole chain of labor and marketing
that led to the functioning, or malfunctioning, of the food economy.

It is necessary to underscore the significance of the stakeholder household
because it is too easy to overlook it by focusing on markets and consumers. However, it was the decisions of households, ranging from compliance
with the rules to outright resistance, that controlled the aggregate level of
agricultural production and the quantity of food, including, ultimately, the
price and availability of bread for urban and rural consumers.

Moreover, culture was a source of empowerment as well as constraint
for the stakeholder household, because culture gave householders an almost unanswerable argument about why they were important, and why
their survival should be respected even by kings and aristocrats. Kinship in
early modern Europe was sacred, and sacred institutions could not simply
be over-ridden, or uprooted by the powerful for arbitrary or purely self-
interested reasons. The ability of ordinary people to mount a long struggle
against processes such as enclosure, public improvements, and general
changes in property law can be cited as evidence of the way stakeholder
households used both material and cultural power to enforce their claim to
a viable stake in the productive resources of their societies.

Culture, however, also restricted the ability of householders themselves
to adopt practices or styles of life that seemed to undermine the integrity
of the household institution. This is shown by the numerous legal and customary restrictions on such modern phenomena as divorce, romantic marriage, and the choice of occupation. As always, culture both enhanced and
limited the ability of individuals to choose or imagine a mode of existence
outside of established values.

The most significant point is that the cultural fortification of the stakeholder household contributed to the persistence of a political economy of
food in which the potential rapaciousness of strong hierarchies of wealth,
status, or power were constrained by the ability of those households with
a claim to a stake to affect the production and distribution of food. Such a
world was much less individualized and market-driven than is often thought,

and the net result is to make us appreciate how much early modern Europe was *early modern* and not simply a prototype or harbinger of modernity.

One final way that culture may have affected food production in Europe was through its consequences for the allocation of resources during a crisis such as crop failure or a war-induced famine. During such episodes, the enforceable claim to increasingly scarce resources was probably highly skewed in favor of both elites and productive rural and urban households with a stake in society. The destitute and the property-less without stable households could make a claim to relief based on Christian charity and the rules of sometimes effectual paternalism, but there was no real claim to equal entitlements, or social welfare based on still-forming notions of equal citizenship. This was still, and would long remain a hierarchy civilization and a civilization where a stake in, rather than outside hierarchy mattered more than abstract conceptions of the claims of individuals. To produce in stable household units was to simultaneously have the right to a recognized claim to neighborly and state support in times of dearth.[3]

## DISTRIBUTION: THE MORAL MARKET AND THE CULTURALLY SANCTIONED REGULATION OF FOOD

At this point we have crossed the always interlinked boundary between production and distribution—the production of food grain and the distribution of the means of making bread. Even though more a story of urban than of rural societies, it should be kept in mind that the distribution of food through institutions such as the market and the state also affected rural communities, and links the stakeholder household to networks of exchange and consumption. As is true of production, the distribution of food was a cultural matter as well as a matter of material fact, and it is here that we necessarily encounter the work of Karl Polanyi, E. P. Thompson, and others who have made an eloquent, if debatable case for the idea of a moral economy.[4]

According to this perspective, the existence of an extra- or anti-commercial moral economy tied to deep ideals of justice and reciprocity meant that the distribution of vital goods such as food could not be simply reduced to the movement of supply and demand, or the logic of profit. Instead, the moral economy put limits on what groups such as merchants could do with the food supply, because popular notions of rights and fairness meant that human need, and not market logic, had the first claim on the distribution of food, thus enabling even the very powerless to make a claim for social subsistence. Ultimately, the moral economy is conceptual shorthand for a world where the market for vital subsistence goods was restricted, pre-commercially organized, and even opposed to the calculus of profit and loss.

Although it is easy to show the many ways in which the moral-economy tradition can be qualified or even disproved in some cases, there is no doubt that early modern Europe did treat food very differently than other goods, and a high level of commercialization of the food supply did not preclude the regulation of food markets through culturally sanctioned institutions and values with a strong moral component. Specifically, food grain and cooked foods such as (and above all) bread were understood by elites and commoners to have a kind of moral power and sanctity that could not be completely reduced to economic logic. Simply put, in a confrontation between the needs of people, and the dictates of profit and the market, the latter often lost the contest both at the level of cultural values, and at the level of decisions, made by governments, communities, or households.

However, as already indicated in the discussion of production, this was not a moral economy of equality in the sense of empowering individuals as equal citizens or consumers to make claims on society's stock of subsistence. If there was a robust moral economy, it was a hierarchical economy, where criteria such as status and kinship made some substantially more equal and empow-ered than others when market principles were superseded by extra-market distribution. For example, we know that food riots carried out in the name of just or fair prices and subsistence needs did occur when merchants and others were considered to have engaged in immoral practices such as hoarding, or price gouging during a period of dearth. What seems less clear is that such an act was an assertion of a universal right tied to a specifically moral economy, or a particular demand regarding the rights and privileges of those with a larger stake in local communities. More important is that there is no evidence to suggest that ordinary people were extra- or anti-commercial and therefore opposed in principle to the commercialization of food distribution.

Indeed, the moral-economy argument draws an extreme and probably false dichotomy between a pre-commercial economy, called the moral economy, and its supposed opposite, called the market economy. The net result is to undercut the moral economy's salutary reminder that cultural

values, including moral principles of entitlement, served to particularly
regulate food markets by delimiting what could be sold when, and where,
and at what prices in specific circumstances, such as normal harvest years
as opposed to episodes of dearth. The people of early modern Europe were
evidently capable of balancing a sense of the legitimacy of market exchange
with a belief in the limits of the market imposed by fundamental, if hierarchical, moral values. The just price for a loaf of bread is perhaps the classic
case of this mix of the commercial and the moral, because the justice of a
price entails a market-derived price regulated by morality.

What can be proposed as an alternative to the starkest versions of moral
economy that still link markets and cultural values is the idea of the moral
market. Just as with all civilizations in all times, early modern Europe
hedged the scope of the market with moral ideas and formal and informal
rules, prescribing when the market should be allowed to work, and when
it should be constrained by cultural values concerning rights and privileges
that were not necessarily incompatible with commerce. A moral market
is simultaneously a market and a moral construction, where real human
beings operate with a complex calculus of prices and equity. Cultures will
necessarily vary in terms of the particulars of this calculus, but this simply
shows how culture matters in concrete ways.[5]

In early modern Europe, the logic of moral markets was perhaps most
visible and deeply entrenched in the distribution of bread, and the means
by which to market particular kinds of un-milled and milled grain and
flour. The history of this is well known and quite rich, and it is therefore useful to emphasize only two critical examples having to do with the
rule of government in formal market regulation and the role of merchants
in the distribution of food.

At the level of an emerging territorial and monopolistic state, there is no
doubt that territorial rulers and officials saw part of their rights and duties
as including the regulation of food markets in order to guarantee the security of the food supply against the failure of the market in the face of natural
and human disasters. This took the concrete form of everything from the
creation of fair and useful standards of exchange such as weights, measures,
and sovereign coinage, to the creation of food reserves consisting of public
granaries and long-term contracts with merchants who could facilitate government sales and purchases of grain. The consequence was the more and

often less explicit construction of a subsistence infrastructure, which could be transparently understood by elites and commoners as a tangible manifestation of the princes' grace and good works. Although France is often seen as the standard in this regard, the examples include Russia, England (both before and after 1630), and the Iberian Kingdoms of Spain, and Portugal.[6]

Even though the prince's attempt to create a subsistence infrastructure through territorial regulation can be seen as a pragmatic tool to maintain order and pre-empt popular violence, it can also be seen as the result of a culture that understood the role of a Christian ruler as involving a householder's or familial obligation to secure the rule over subjects in spiritual and material terms. In the absence of such cultural underpinnings, it is difficult to see why war-driven rulers would invest scarce governmental capital in policing the price of bread and the flow of high-quality food to rural and particularly urban households. Similarly, it is hard to believe that embattled monarchs such as Charles I of England (r. 1625–1649) would risk the wrath of powerful mercantile interests if they themselves did not believe in the morality they professed and the culture behind it.[7]

The role of princely paternalism in the distribution of food can be seen very clearly in the French Crown's intervention in food markets throughout the Ancien Régime. Royal officials repeatedly regulated the sale of grain, the milling of flour, the prices of bread and bread products, and the quality of food in general. Whether this was efficient or inefficient is beside the point, because what is relevant is how these forms of regulation corresponded to the logic of a culture where markets were normal and valued, but always subject to moral constraints, including those enforced by the prince. Not every loaf of bread was stamped with a princely seal; yet, all bread was in one or another way tied to a territorial ruler whose state or estate included a culturally validated claim to inspect, value, or, if necessary, command the means of making and baking bread. To this extent, the moral markets of early modern Europe established the state as a key player in the political economy of food, a position it would never relinquish despite the various European experiments with free trade and market liberalism (itself being one rendering of a moral market).[8]

If territorial rulers regulated the distribution of food, including bread, through a centralized, statist version of moral market logic, merchants who traded in grain or flour, and baked it into a final product were themselves subject to the self-enforcing constraints of cultural logic and its attendant moral values. Merchants and millers are often pictured as nascent capitalists who operated by a strict, wealth-maximizing logic and who therefore opposed traditional moral principles as applied to the market. This makes for a linear story of over-regulated merchants who pressed for the abolition of constraints such as guilds, and who regulated prices in the interests of expanded commerce and commercial liberalization. However, does this view represent the whole of commercial reality or is it a partial vision that needs serious qualification?

Simply on the basis of logic, it can be doubted if most merchants dealing in food saw themselves as outside the cultural order or in opposition to moral market practices. As with other social groups, merchants were members of households, rural and urban communities, churches, and ultimately, an expending state. It is unreasonable to suppose that merchants' values were not shaped by these institutions, nor is it really possible to imagine how merchants could have operated differently in early modern Europe, where fair-trading and just prices crated a standard by which good and bad could be evaluated. In this context, merchants probably gained more than they lost from working with, and not against customary values. Indeed, merchants who processed or traded in food would have needed the support of consumer households if they wanted stable prices and sufficient consumer demand, and these would not have been easily forthcoming for merchants who could be branded as malefactors who starved the people. In addition, merchants of all kinds depended on credit, and credit, in turn, depended on reputation. Reputation could be damaged or destroyed for a merchant who was seen as unfair or immoral in trading food—something that needs more investigation from economic historians.[9]

The moral constraints on merchant behavior can also be brought into clear focus through the example of the role of guilds in the early modern economy. Guilds and other similar merchant associations played a variety of roles in Europe well into the 1800s. In addition to providing price and quality control along with an opportunity for monopoly ventures in some cases, guilds had charitable and convivial functions, ultimately rooted in Christian notions of confraternity. Given their multiple material and moral purposes, it can be hypothesized that the guilds' policing of their members served to imbue in many merchants a sense of what was, and what was not ethical behavior in the market place. This would have been strongly reinforced by the religious underpinnings of guild institutions, particularly in Catholic countries. But whether Catholic or Protestant, guilds were conservative groups that must have taught and enforced a conventional code of trading—practices that would have reinforced rather than undercut the larger structure of moral markets.

The distributional role of merchants can thus be visualized as a spatial hierarchy of artisans and merchants ranging from local distributors, millers, and bakers to wholesale merchants operating on a regional, national, or international level. There is no reason to presume that any of these groups were unaffected by, or hostile to, prevalent cultural values concerning issues such as fair trading and just prices on the sale of the most important of all commodities: food.

In sum, the concept of moral markets helps to resolve an apparent paradox in the history of early modern Europe. The paradox is the apparent coexistence of a highly commercial civilization, especially in the north-west, and an economic morality that was deeply concerned about limits to the scope of market behavior. However, there is no paradox, because Europeans accepted the logic of a market economy regulated formally and informally through moral principles emphasizing justice and the subsistence needs of households, graded according to a hierarchy of status, property, and power. What held markets and morality together was a culture that apparently saw no inherent contradiction between profit, wealth, and ethical behaviour.[10]

## CONSUMPTION: SECULAR AND SACRED COMMENSALITY

We now enter the realm of consumption, the final destination of foods such as bread that were used as the substance and symbols of the European meal. It is critical not to reduce this to a simplistic story of dietary health, calories consumed, or the individuating effects of consumer choice. Early modernity can naturally be understood from all of these perspectives, but what is most significant are the many ways in which early modern European food consumption differed from its twentieth- and twenty-first-century descendants. The most striking and important variation was the stratification of foods and cooking styles by social status, and the location of most consumption within households.[11]

In order to render this rich complexity more analytically manageable, this section will focus on commensality in its secular and sacred modalities. Commensality refers to the rules that defined who could, and who could not eat together at what times, and in what places. Although it is misleading to describe early modern Europe as hermetically divided into secular and sacred, the distinction is useful as a way of capturing the point that some occasions were more, and others were less invested with religious meaning. Secular, therefore, describes minimally religious events such as daily household meals, while sacred indicates maximally sacred events with a primarily religious purpose. A reasonable case can be made that patterns of commensality, or shared eating, reveal more cogently than any other activity the links between European culture and European food.

With respect to the more secular forms of commensality, the imprint of culture is strongest in the tendency of European societies to stratify consumption according to informal and formal rules of exclusion and inclusion. In the limiting case, certain foods such as wild game were reserved for aristocrats, but in all areas of life the quality and types of food as well as the quantity, and of who could eat with whom was hierarchically determined to the extent that superiors and inferiors would rarely have shared a loaf of bread. Even within households, parents and elders ate as a group apart from children and servants, and to some degree, to be invited to eat with others was a bonding mechanism that signified acceptance and possible membership in the commensal group; to eat the king's bread was therefore to be acceded a role in the ranks of royal power, just as eating with a particular family signified at least a quasi-kinship tie. All of this hierarchical commensality was underwritten by sumptuary laws and, more importantly, social custom. In this world, the idea of an individual consumer exercising market sovereignty according to personal preferences simply had no place.

More than an index of wealth and income inequality, the hierarchical stratification of commensality was a product of a culture that at least, to some extent, valued hierarchy and status as both means and ends, and believed inequality should be transparent and socially ratified in daily practice. This may be the reason why status-segregated commensality was not a major source of protestor resistance—something that would likely occur in a self-consciously egalitarian culture.[12]

The consumption of something as basic as bread, therefore, had a part to play in the customs of commensality that acted both as bonding mechanisms for group members, and boundary markers separating insiders from outsiders. To violate such a cultural code was to risk social sanctions that could escalate into a confrontation with the basic identity of a whole way of life.

However, if commensality was highly stratified, it was also characterized at all levels of society by the salience of the household as the actual physical location of commensality in its more secular mode. Early modern Europe seems to have been a civilization with few restaurants, and apart from ceremonial meals in extra-familial institutions such as guilds and civic corporations, the economic role of the household was reinforced by its centrality in the preparation and consumption of food. When foodstuffs were turned into finished products such as bread, they were typically baked at home or, at least, were purchased and then complimented by home-made products. While practically impossible in many poor, urban households, it still served as a cultural norm that reinforced the sense of a society as one divided and united by the bands of kinship. To engage in commensality outside the household was a rare, ritualized event that corresponded to a truly special occasion, more or less secular, or sacred in nature.

When we move from the more mundane and everyday, to the more sacred occasions of European life, food and culture once more interact in illuminating ways. At the core of every European society was one or another typically state-protected churches, a fact persistent and durable enough to largely withstand the exciting saga of the Reformation. What was distinctive about any natural or trans-natural church was not only its doctrine or liturgy, but the way in which it understood the sacred ritual of the Eucharist, and within the Mass, the nature of liturgical food, particularly bread. For many centuries, what would become the Catholic Church defined the Mass as a literal reconstitution of the last supper, and the last, or Eucharistic bread as a literal embodiment of Christ's body. This highly concretized, sacred reality was disputed by some Protestant churches, whose theologians chose to see the divine service as a remembrance, and the bread and wine as symbolic reminders, but Catholics and Protestants alike agreed on attributing to bread the role of a sacred instrument of divine purposes. Moreover, the consumption of divine bread served as a form of religious commensality that drew a religious circle around the members of a congregation or large church, even for those among the laity who only ate bread as vicarious spectators.[13]

This brief sketch of sacred and secular commensality illuminates two important points about culture and food in early modern Europe. First, food culture was obviously still shaped in large part by long-established religious values concerning issues such as purity and salvation. Second, and more importantly for food culture, early modern Europeans attributed great cultural power to food, and food could not be separated from its meaningful contexts of ceremony, status, or kinship. The idea of treating food as culturally neutral and purely an issue of income, taste, or nutrition could have no purchase when so much of what was culturally vital such as religious practice was expressed, in part, through the group consumption of culturally valued and, therefore, valuable foods, including bread.

## A BRIEF CASE STUDY: BRANDENBURG-PRUSSIA 1500–1800

Aptly termed the *Iron Kingdom,* the complex territory of Brandenburg-Prussia (or simply *Prussia*) in North-Eastern Europe can be used as an illuminating and well-documented brief case study of some of the major themes of this essay. Specifically, Prussia can be drawn upon for a more detailed analysis of the vitally important issue of the relationship between culture, food, and the state. Of the many forces driving change in early modern Europe, the state was one of the most significant, and the consolidation of territorial state around princes, bureaucrats, and (occasionally) representative assemblies moved much of Europe from the more to the less feudal—at least in institutional terms.[14]

Crucially, however, the early modern state was itself a carrier and organizer of culture as well as a structure of domination—a set of political institutions. The rich symbolism of early modern European states is a testament to the cultural investment of rulers in communicating to their subjects and their place in a larger European civilization, where alternative networks of power such as churches, and corporate towns and cities could still provide rival foci of loyalty and mobilization. Given the emphasis on states and war over the past three decades, it is necessary to re-emphasize the role of states in the more mundane aspects of their subjects' lives, including the production, distribution, and consumption of food.

Prussia is uniquely useful as a window into states, culture, and food, because more so than with the more organically constituted states such as England, France, and Russia, Prussia was, from its origins, a conscious project of its ruling dynasty. It thus allows us to see how monarchs consciously, and as a matter of strategy, interacted with their subjects' food supply, particularly in terms of their interaction with the stakeholder's household and with the problem of moral markets. In addition, the Prussian state nicely illustrates the complex cultural and institutional ties between religious belief and practice in early modern Europe.

The first point to make about Prussia is how much its history defies a linear model of political change that focuses exclusively on structures of material power and attempts to calculate state-building outcomes on the basis of fiscal and economic resources. To be sure, Prussia fits the model of a state organized for war and taxation, but its history is much more the history of institutions and culture than a story of large predatory states taking advantage of weaker neighbors.

At the risk of teleology, we can say that Prussia began its existence as a loosely integrated network of villagers, nobles, feudal jurisdictions, towns and cities, and representative estates that might have disappeared, or been absorbed by powerful neighbors in the 1500s. In a Holy Roman Imperial Germany that in 1618 (on the eve of 30 years of war) consisted of 150,000 villages, 2,200 towns and cities, and dozens of well-established princely and dual territories, what was originally called Brandenburg-Prussia differed from the well-integrated, bureaucratized monarchy of Frederick the Great in 1756 (the eve of the Seven Years' War).

What held this network of political and social institutions together as a structuring matrix was its ruling Hohenzollern dynasty, a very clear instance of the stakeholder's household writ large. Although not recognized as true and formal kings until the eighteenth century, the Hohenzollerns were already amassing the property rights, legal jurisdictions, and territorial patrimonies and privileges in the 1600s that would give them a more solidly bounded so-called state in the 1700s, alongside a claim of importance in the European balance of power. Nearly extinguished by Sweden's unexpected expansion into the Germanys in the Thirty Years' War (1618–1648), Brandenburg-Prussia would perhaps, not ironically, emerge strong.[15] Following the ordeal (by the 1660s and by the 1690s), what was rapidly becoming Prussia proper would start to project military power out of proportion to its few million inhabitants.

Even though it used to be conventional to see this surge of power as a linear function of its bureaucrat army, it is better to see it as the result of the wide scope of power resources that the Hohenzollern household could draw on to both consolidate, and then further expand its dominion over people and territory.[16] As the largest feudal landholder in its realm, the Hohenzollerns are robust examples of the domain state whose rulers could, to some extent, bypass obstreperous representative estates, and rule on the basis of familiar resources that did not yet require permanent monetary taxation of the entire non-noble population. True, the domain state began to wane in the 1600s, but in combination with its many courts and related legal jurisdictions, rights over coinage and commerce, and general police powers over the material and moral lives of its subjects, the ruling dynasty, in close alliance with its nobility, exercised more of an institutional presence than can be measured by simple economic and demographic data.[17]

Moreover, the Hohenzollerns could tap the cultural power of widespread models of good princely rule that emphasized the paternal justice and good order provided by the ruling house over its sometimes resistant subjects. As long as the dynasty at least appeared to be protective of its subjects' interests in peace as well as during war, it could claim a cultural legitimacy that had roots in the ancient west, and was echoed by the other princes of the Empire, including the Imperial House of Hapsburg. This cultural capital was reinforced by the right of the Hohenzollerns as rulers of Brandenburg to act as one of the select few electors of a new Emperor whenever a vacancy occurred.

In addition to these more secular power resources, the Hohenzollerns could claim to plausibly represent the best interests of the Christian faith as protectors of the territorial church, particularly because the Reformation had made Prussia more or less permanently Lutheran, and thus in need of a secular prince who could regulate the faith in the absence of the Papacy.

In sum, the Hohenzollerns could arguably pose as the supreme war leaders, law-finders, feudal overloads, and religious protectors in their many territories, both in domain and non-domain territories. It is necessary to emphasize this, because it is essential in understanding how culture and food intersected in the emerging territorial states of early modern Europe. It was this set of power resources that allowed early modern European rulers to intervene more expansively into the food supply of their populations, and to do so by plausibly claiming an enhanced economic role both as duty and right.

With respect to food production, the story of the Hohenzollerns should begin with what can be viewed as their role as the premier stakeholder household of the realm. As large landholders (who also governed consumer towns and eventually promoted commerce as a means of taxation), the dynasty had a vested incentive to guarantee at least some tolerable level of food production and distribution for its subjects, if only to pre-empt rebellion, and generate the grains needed for hungry armies. Should Prussia fail, after all, the house of Hohenzollern would sink in the wreckage, and this sort of patrimonial interest should not be underestimated anywhere in Europe where monarchs still perceived their rule as partly a property right. (It is easy to ignore the potency of kinship and the survival of the ruling house as motivators of state building at a distance of several centuries of political developments.)

With respect to the production of food and the role of the dynasty, the vital starting point is the recognition that the entire Hohenzollern enterprise rested on an ultimately negotiated, if strained alliance between landed nobility, the Junkers, and the ruling house and its administration. Given the largely rural character of Prussia's economy and social structure until the 1800s, the Hohenzollerns' necessity for stable elite support could only be met through close political, economic, and military cooperation with local nobilities who had the resources and human power to serve as bureaucrats and army officers of a sometimes shaky state. In exchange for their human and material support, the dynasty, in part, created and, in part, ratified the Junkers' political and economic power at the local level, even though the autonomous standing of noble-dominated estate assemblies was gradually reduced by power-building rulers.

Central to the dynastic underpinning of Junker power was the central government's partly tacit and partly legal recognition of the Junkers' right to control the bonded agricultural population; and it is in the mix of noble-controlled serfdom, dynastic politics, and culture that we can begin to see how territorial states affected the production of food. A majority of Prussians may not have been serfs by 1600, but there is no doubt that so-called serf villages provided the necessary labor for the vital grain production of Prussian Junkers' landed estates.[18] Without that labor, much of the basic rye supply would not have been available for human consumption, despite the existence of a stratum of free smallholders and middle farmers. Moreover, without the organizational overlay of the Junker estate, the dynasty could not have mobilized the conscript soldiers who were vital to the native core of the Prussian war machine. Serfdom, or more properly *unfree labor*, was consequently more important than any other economic institution in keeping the dynasty solvent and resilient enough to expand against the opposition of much larger neighbors such as Austria.

Yet it is a caricature to see unfree labor as only a structure of economic production, or of power and domination. Serfdom also had a cultural logic that made sense in an early modern Europe that valued hierarchy and stability rather than legal equality and change. At the same time, Prussia's unfree rural population had a recognized cultural and legal status that cannot be described as simply base, degraded, or rightless. Serfs were not slaves, and they had enforceable rights and privileges that could be (and were) invoked against their Junker lords in the local courts of the ruler. Humble status did not mean negative status, and Prussian serfdom can be seen as a customary, culturally validated exchange of unfree, mandatory labor for permanent use rights to land, stable households, and a minimum set of protections against arbitrary power.

More importantly, it may be suggested, without torturing the evidence, that what made this system workable was its respect for the stakeholder household as a cultural ideal that included, rather that excluded the unfree rural population. That population formed more or less self-reproducing households that held a stake in the land, the viability of village institutions, and ultimately, the survival of the protective role of the Hohenzollern house. Without the dynasty, the unfree, as well as the free, or even the privileged could be exposed to the ravages of war and invasion, as had happened in the 1630s and 1640s.

Indeed, we can speculate that it was the indirect but real connection between the Hohenzollerns and the rural population that made possible the gradual extension of the rulers' power into the production of Prussia's food supply. By the 1700s this intervention took the two primary forms of military conscription and the judicial ordering of the lord–serf relationship. The dynasty regularly conscripted a proportion of able-bodied males into its military forces, but—and this is the important qualifier—with great care for its possible negative effects on the household-based regime of agricultural production. Conscripts typically returned home to help in agriculture labor, and this cannot but have helped to support both the dynasty and the survival of ordinary stakeholder households. If only dimly, this can be explained as at least a minimal effort by the dynasty to validate the cultural value of the household at all levels of society, not just at the level of the Junker elite.

However, law as well as war offered the dynasty a point of access to food production, because the ruler's courts, legal codes, and legal officials came to play a significant role in daily rural life for free and unfree alike. The rights and obligations of unfree labor came to be increasingly the subject matter of state law and jurisdiction, and this may have substantially modified the inherent harshness of unfree labor. More specifically, law and dynasty jurisdiction created an institutional bond between the rural population and the dynasty that underscored their mutual dependence in a great chain of rights, duties, and privileges. Ultimately, this kind of intervention created the framework of property rights determining the institution of agricultural production.

What all of this seems to mean is that the early modern state and its ruler used a common cultural vocabulary of values such as kinship, property, and hierarchy to expand the ties of power and compliance in a still-dangerous and resistant world. Prussia was fairly unique in this regard, but the very unlikeliness of its relative success shows how power could be built in early modern Europe on more than military and purely material foundations.

As with its counterparts elsewhere, the house of Hohenzollern also acted to regulate the distribution and consumption of food, partly through its own institutions, and partly through the mediation of extra-bureaucratic groups and institutions such as voluntary societies and the church (despite its control by the state administration). Since these are not as distinctive in Prussia as the regulation of unfree labor, they can be considered briefly as further illustration of general European patterns of culture, politics, and food.

Similar to its sometime enemy and ally, France, the Prussian dynasty also attempted to regulate the flow of food through what was a rudimentary, if increasingly complex distribution network. By the 1700s this form of state-owned grain magazine helped to mitigate the effects of dearth on the general population, and shows once again the importance of a paternal and hierarchical cultural model that looked back to Christian charity, and forward to Enlightened notions of state regulation. In regulating food production, the dynasty could additionally call on a broad Central European tradition of police and land ordinances that looked to territorial rule and the territorial ruler as a potentially well-ordered household along the lines of the 1500s.

When we enter the sphere of consumption, what is striking is not the dynastic effort to pass sumptuary laws and rules applicable to society at large, but its apparent willingness to regulate its own consumption to meet the culturally shaped expectations of Prussian society, at least at the elite level. In the 1600s, the house of Hohenzollern ostentatiously consumed in the Baroque style, perhaps in order to show that people's weariness with war and forced austerity could be overcome through magnificent commensality and good taste. But in the 1700s this changed decisively, as Prussian rulers voluntarily reduced their daily consumption of luxuries, donned plain (even military) dress, and conformed themselves to a revived, yet traditional model of kingship as frugal and pious—something even the skeptical Frederick the Great could not abandon. This indicates just how potent culture was, because it was a response to deeply rooted sentiments about how a monarch's consumption of anything and everything, including food, should conform to a hierarchical, but just, ideal of power and consumption symbolized by the quantity and quality of diet.

Obviously, Prussia was in some ways unique, as these remarks have shown; but what is much clearer is how the remarkable experience of Prussian state building can be used as an index of the interaction of food, culture, and politics in early modern Europe. The production, distribution, and consumption of food in Europe rested on a matrix of cultural values and expectations that affected what both ordinary people and the mightiest rulers could do in shaping their world to meet their interests. Even in Prussian markets, food had a moral dimension larger than war.

## CONCLUSION: CULTURE AND FOOD IN EARLY MODERN EUROPE

We have now reached the end of an extended speculation about food culture in early modern European civilization. It is legitimate to use the term *food culture* rather than simply culture and food, because Europeans understood food in terms of deeply rooted, cultural core values that had a bearing on issues as complex and diverse as justice, hierarchy, and sacred salvation. To underestimate the power of culture in this context is to ignore that its history matters so much, and as vitally as a study of both similarity and of salient difference.

Moreover, what is most evident about early modern Europe is that food and food culture contributed to European distinctiveness, and helped to provide a basis for linking people together, as well as dividing them through common practices and values.

In part, the cultural significance of food shows up in the way Europeans understood food as what can be called a public commodity; as with all commodities, food and food grain could be legitimately bought and sold, but in the case of food, this vital commodity was also invested with the key public purpose of providing the stable basis for the survival of households, the hierarchy, or the sacred order. The public, in the form of the populace or the prince, could therefore intervene in the market for food in legitimate ways that ranged from crowd action to price regulation. As a commodity with a public purpose, food is a striking indicator of the distinctive ability of early modern Europeans to balance a robust commercial economy with larger moral values in a synthesis Europeans would only begin to change fundamentally in the 1800s and 1900s.

However, much research needs to be done on the links between culture and food, both in Europe and beyond. For example, we know that Imperial China and other Confucian societies had an ancient theory and practice of government-funded granaries that were explicitly designed to provide price stability and famine pre-emption through sales and grants. It would be useful to know how much, and in what ways this differed from the Christian paternalism of early modern European states, and what specific cultural values informed the relationship between morality and the market in East Asia. Similarly, despite its apparent individualism, comparative work might show how much Europe, as was the case with other civilizations, valued kin groups and households, and how European kinship did and did not vary in comparative terms.

Finally, throughout this text we have followed bread from its production and distribution, to the moment of its consumption. Although bread no longer has the cultural, material, or literal weight it once possessed, it is still central to the European diet and way of life. It is worth remembering that bread is also a culturally generated fact. It points back to the legacy of a European food culture that expressed the core values of a dynamic, but still conservative civilization, where moral values contributed to the ordering of everyday material existence.

## POST-SCRIPT: KINSHIP, CLASS, AND COMMUNITY IN THE CULTURE OF FOOD

Readers who come to the study of history with a more class- or community-based, analytic focus may be disappointed by this essay's emphasis on the stakeholder household as the unit of description and explanation. However, the author believes this emphasis is methodologically justified by the following three points concerning the writing of historical social science.

First, the focus on kinship does not in any way invalidate class-based models of explanation. However, these macro-structures are typically used in causal terms to explain large-scale and long-term change. As a result, they are less useful in dealing with culture, because culture logically implies continuity rather than disjunctive change; and culture appears most clearly and at its most empirically relevant when we focus on smaller-scale units of organization such as the household, where cultural values are most in evidence as micro-level incentives. The stakeholder household is useful for this as an early modern institution accommodating cultural values such as religion in daily life, even if they were not always visible.

The second point is that although kinship is important in all civilizations, the ideal of a stable, conjugal household, defined in part by its proprietary claim of a stake in property and status, seems distinctly (although not uniquely) European, and particularly early modern and European. There were few parts of Europe where households with stakeholder claims were unimportant to non-existent between 1500 and 1800; and it is precisely the combination of kinship with a proprietary stake in society that makes European households different from ritually defined lineages, castles, or simple extended groups of kin.

Finally, the essay has emphasized the household owing to its obvious empirical importance in all aspects of life. Early modern Europe did not apparently have that many large-scale extra-kinship institutions apart from, or in opposition to, the household; and institution-like states and churches were themselves organized, in part, along household lines and patterns. What made an institution such as the village or the town work was the labor of many linked, but bounded and distinct households with varying levels of stakeholder claims, rights, and duties. Indeed, the importance of the household was ultimately recognized by that large-scale institution of the state, because states kept records and monitored people statistically, largely through the use of household units.

## CHAPTER FIVE

# Eating Out in Early Modern Europe

BEAT KÜMIN

When no lesser figure than Heinrich Julius, Prince of Brunswick-Wolfenbüttel (r. 1589–1613), staked his literary claims with a tragicomedy on the themes of fraud, greed, and other human failings, he chose to associate them with a publican. *Von einem Wirthe oder Gastgeber,* published in 1594, tells the story of the keeper of the Golden Lion who, having earned a fortune by over-charging, resolved to repent following his abduction by the devil. At one point, a Bavarian character named Lendle recalls a particularly terrible dining experience, featuring an:

> awful, smelly, moody and dirty…cook,…a table cloth as filthy, as if someone…had cleaned his bottom with it,…hard, mouldy bread, gnawed at by mice,…plates not properly washed for eight days,…a dish of intestines, which…looked as terrible as if they had only just been pulled from the ox,…a piece of beef one could smell rather than see,…sauerkraut…as unappealingly served as to be impossible to eat, [and] wine as sour as vinegar.[1]

While such tales may have struck a chord with contemporaries (and indeed some modern food scholars), we do well to remember that public houses served many early modern authors as vehicles to convey symbolic rather than realistic messages.[2] Furthermore, even in such a blatantly moralistic tale, some passing references—for example, when the keeper asks his servant to go "to the market and look whether you can find something good, with which I may serve my guests the better"—suggest that commercial food provision may have been a little more differentiated than testimonies such as Lendle's imply.[3]

This chapter aims to survey various forms of eating out—simply defined as meals taken outside a person's home[4]—between the late sixteenth and eighteenth centuries in their own right rather than as rudimentary prehistories of the modern restaurant; that is, the gastronomic culture of the bourgeoisie in the age of industrialization and urbanization, which has tended to monopolize discussions in the field.[5] The argument, focusing primarily on evidence from German- and English-speaking Europe, is structured in three parts: catering infrastructure, dining contexts, and variables affecting the quality of provision.

## CATERING INFRASTRUCTURE

Early modern Europeans had considerable choice in terms of catering services. The single most important institution was the inn, a fully privileged public house entitled to serve hot meals and banquets as well as alcoholic drinks. From the late Middle Ages, travellers could count on an extensive network, with one (or more) establishments in nearly every major settlement, particularly along transit routes. Local and territorial authorities regulated provision in manorial customs, town statutes, and an increasing body of state legislation, invariably insisting on general access, reasonable prices, and the monitoring of moral behavior. Some—such as the ordinance of the Bavarian Elector Maximilian of 1631—added detailed instructions on the number of courses as well as the common combination of meat and fish dishes in the so-called ordinary (the *table d'hôte* served at a set time to regular diners), alongside the obligation to provide a cheaper menu for visitors of lesser means and to allow social elites to compose meals according to their personal preferences. Most inns also offered take-away provision, giving locals and strangers the chance to purchase hot and cold meals for consumption in their homes (especially when large groups had to be catered for) or temporary accommodation.[6]

Drinking houses served cold snacks such as bread, cheese, fruit, salad, ham, and sausages to accompany their wine, ale/beer, or mead/cider. Numbers could be very high, especially in areas with extensive home-brewing (such as England) or viticulture (such as France and Italy), and growth proved notoriously difficult to prevent, as operators needed little more than a large-sized lounge and a few barrels of alcohol to get going. A special case among European drinking houses was the London tavern, surely the most direct ancestor of the modern restaurant, where patrons found a dazzling spectrum of delicacies by the seventeenth century. Keepers of these extremely commercialized institutions catered for every whim of their well-heeled clientele, serving practically round the clock, developing reputations for gastronomic sophistication, and fulfilling any peculiar wishes by sending servants to fetch the desired products from the nearest provider.[7]

Another type of establishment targeted the fast-food and convenience market. From the high Middle Ages, cook shops (*traiteurs, Gar-/Wurstküchen*) operated in all major cities, fair towns, and pilgrimage centers. Usually lacking the right to sell alcoholic beverages (although many allowed customers to bring their own), they offered quick access to hot food, typically various spit-roasted meats, soups, and oven-baked meals.[8] Locations like pre-Revolutionary Paris devised intricate distinctions between different specialists (*traiteurs, rôtisseurs, patisseurs,* and so on); some with permission to host large parties, some without; thus creating a system which prompted owners to jealously watch out for any encroachments by their rivals. Most towns, however, allowed a greater degree of flexibility, often under the supervision of a dedicated guild. London's Cooks' Company, for example, traced its origins to 1170 and received a formal charter in 1482.[9] Several *Garküchen* flourished in Hannover from the fourteenth century. According to a council ordinance from 1360, they had to "roast and cook, clean and salt dishes, to the best of the cooks' abilities." Town officials monitored compliance and after a merger with a private operator in 1642, the city-owned establishment contained a basement with a small lounge, kitchen, and meat pantry plus a ground-floor lounge, three chambers on the first-floor, an attic with smoking facilities, and a pig-sty outside. By the eighteenth century, here and elsewhere, cook shops faced stiff competition from newly-emerged dining tables (*Speisetische*), which offered regulars a subscription scheme for discounted lunches.[10]

Sometimes there were further options. Many guilds operated hostelries for apprentices and journeymen. The richer companies also owned halls, where they staged feasts and banquets for members as well as guests.[11] In Catholic areas, monasteries continued their time-honored hospitality tradition, especially by running guest houses for travellers and pilgrims.[12] Furthermore, from the mid-seventeenth century, the coffee house made its appearance in major cities, first in Mediterranean ports such as Constantinople and Venice (1647), then in London, Vienna, and Paris. An extensive literature discusses their important role in the sociability of higher social groups, but with a view to the spread of new colonial beverages and the emergence of the political public sphere rather than in terms of food provision. Here, the emphasis lay on hot, non-alcoholic drinks and an atmosphere conducive to the exchange and discussion of information among a selective set of patrons.[13] Food, in contrast, moves center stage in the history of the modern restaurant, which started in 1760s Paris. Expanding from an original concentration on restorative bouillons for a medically aware clientele toward a differentiated menu catering for the culinary tastes of the ascending bourgeoisie, restaurants became focal points for urban representation and an institutionalized gastronomic discourse in specialized periodicals.[14] Their innovatory achievements may lie less in areas such as quality awareness and choice (both of which prosperous early modern consumers were accustomed to) than in the exclusive concentration on leisure dining and fashionable "slow food." Last but not least, quick bites were available from countless market stalls and itinerant sellers. Depending on budget, taste, and situation, customers could find anything from cheap pies right up to fresh oysters; in a Mediterranean city such as Naples toward the end of the Ancien Régime even delicacies such as chocolate, ice cream, sorbets, nuts, and melons were available.[15]

## CONTEXTS FOR EATING OUT

Meals outside the home could be taken both locally and at a greater distance from the regular place of residence (with the latter defined here as situations involving at least one overnight stay). A closer examination of the sources produces a wide range of settings in both categories, pointing to the considerable degree of economic differentiation and spatial mobility in this period. Factors such as urbanization, near-constant warfare, mass pilgrimages, stagecoach networks, and overseas expansion—highlighted in this volume's "Introduction"—all boosted the frequency of eating out in early modern Europe. Specialized advice literature was also available: in his guide to travellers' fare published in 1561, Guglielmo Grataroli recommended light morning meals (to avoid stomach problems en route) and to keep away from fish (which was rarely served fresh).[16]

At the most basic level, easily transportable victuals such as bread, fruit, and cheese could be taken from home for consumption at mealtimes elsewhere (Grataroli suggested snacks such as marzipan and pastries), but such informal arrangements leave few traces in the records. For historians, the reconstruction of regular, everyday life is often more challenging than research on extraordinary events.

In contrast to the present day, where eating out constitutes a popular leisure activity for substantial sections of society, most dining away from home in preindustrial times involved laborers, unmarried workers, and other lower members of society. One key reason was the lack of suitable kitchen facilities. In large cities such as London, in particular, many people lacked both designated areas for cooking and the resources (firewood, kitchen utensils) to prepare fresh meals at home every day.[17] The situation was even worse for vagrants and the homeless, groups which increased in size due to worsening socio-economic conditions from the sixteenth century onward. Such "masterless (wo)men" roaming the land in search for food, work, and money caused great anxiety among contemporaries.[18] Their sustenance options ranged from the use of cook shops and street sellers (if in possession of disposable income), via searching for free food (in nature or rubbish dumps), to begging, and—particularly in periods of dearth and harvest failure, when early modern law courts could show a degree of understanding for necessity-based crime—theft.[19]

Business dining took two basic forms: meals provided by employers as part of their remuneration package and the use of catering services by workers and officials having to make individual arrangements. Employers' fare did not always have to be basic, although bread, cereal-based dishes, and ale/watered-down wine were common. A glimpse into the accounts of the St Mary Magdalene hospital in Münster (Germany) around 1600 shows agricultural day laborers (just like normal inmates) receiving meat on three days of the week (resulting in an astonishing per capita level of 230 pounds/year in 1570), various kinds of preserved fish on Fridays and during fasting periods (37 pounds/year), and a beer ratio of between 3.5 and 5 pints a day. This was much more, of course, than for independent, lower-level households, but (both in terms of quality and quantity) less than for local elites.[20] Commercial catering for workers, too, could be fairly decent. In eighteenth-century Vienna, the basic menu (costing eight Kreuzers) involved shared bread and goblets, but the ten-Kreuzer option provided customers with their own roll, serviette, and glass.[21]

Higher up the social scale, the borderlines between a business lunch and a pleasure meal could be blurred. Apprentices who lived in the households of craftsmen sometimes chose to eat in specialized hostelries rather than at the table of their mistress. There was no necessity to dine out, but the decision gave live-in adolescents a chance to temporarily escape the masters' supervision, socialize with their peers, and thus combine a physiological need with a leisure pursuit.[22] Somebody else who knew how to combine business and pleasure was the London navy official Samuel Pepys in the 1660s. His uniquely detailed diary reveals him as an almost obsessive frequenter of public houses, be it for a quick drink with colleagues, amorous adventures in suburban alehouses, or a full meal at a reputable eatery. On April 18, 1666, for example, he had a "bit of meat and dined alone" at the Swan in Westminster, on further occasions he ate at the King's Head, Charing Cross, or at a dining club in another London tavern.[23] In contrast to other parts of Europe, where visits to fast-food outlets carried a social stigma, higher-ranking Londoners—according to an early eighteenth-century observer—seem to have had no hesitation in using their services:

There are Cooks Shops [now] in all Parts of the Town, where it is very common to go and chuse upon the Spit the Part you like, and to eat it there.... Generally four Spits, one over another, carry round each five or six Pieces of Butcher's Meat, Beef, Mutton, Veal, Pork, and Lamb; you have what Quantity you please cut off, fat, lean, much or little done; with this, a little Salt and Mustard upon the Side of a Plate, a Bottle of Beer, and a Roll; and there is your whole Feast.... A *Frenchman* of any Distinction would think it a great Scandal in *France* to be seen to eat in such a Place; and indeed, Custom will not allow it there; but in *England* they laugh at such Niceties.... a Gentleman of 1500 Livres a Year enters a Cook's Shop without fear of being at all despis'd for it, and there dines for his Shilling to his Heart's Content. I have often eat [*sic*] in that manner with a Gentleman of my Acquaintance that is very rich, and was a Member of the House of Commons.[24]

Further occasions for dining out locally included receptions for various dignitaries and celebrations marking rites of passage. Both had representative dimensions and thus often above-average provision, sometimes bordering on excess. Early modern authorities tried to impose limitations on weddings in particular. The relevant ordinance of the Imperial City of Strasbourg issued in 1664 outlawed banquets held on private premises. All families had to use guild halls or inns, where their behavior—and the observance of strict cost ceilings for each category of citizen—could be controlled. Furthermore, in contrast to the widespread addition of lavish breakfasts and suppers, one main reception starting at eleven o'clock had to suffice.[25] At the annual auditing of accounts of the Münster hospital encountered above, city officials were treated to numerous large glasses of wine and beer each and 6 to 12 different meat dishes (mutton, beef, veal, chicken, and pork, as well as shellfish and venison). In the same city during the mid-seventeenth century, the dean and chaplains of the church of St Mary Überwasser regularly dined in a nunnery dominated by the local nobility. Lunches featured six dishes (with four different kinds of meat) and dinners three dishes, but on feast days such as kermis, midday provision increased to two courses of six dishes each (including ham, smoked fish, sausages, tongue, fresh meat, and six different desserts) washed down with "as much wine, as they desire."[26] Lower down the ranks, villagers such as the Sussex churchwarden and overseer of the poor, Thomas Turner, participated in similar, if less extravagant, events. As a member of the parish vestry, he regularly went to meetings in the local victualing house, where he dined—on April 19, 1756—"on a buttock of beef and ham, and plum pudding and greens" and—some three months later—"on a piece of pork and peas with a baked beggar's pudding."[27]

Turner can also serve as an initial example of meals taken further away. He earned his living as a shopkeeper, which brought him into contact with customers and suppliers from the wider region. Every so often, he visited nearby market towns, although he hardly ever stayed away for more than one night. His diary records numerous inn meals during such trips: on October 11, 1757, at the Bull's Head in Battle Market, it consisted of "a rump of beef boiled, a loin of veal roasted, a roast goose and a currant suet pudding and an apple-pie"; on May 1, 1764, at the White Hart in Lewes, of "a fillet of veal roasted, a ham boiled, a fore-quarter of lamb roasted, 2 hot pigeon pasties, 2 raisin and currant puddings, greens, potatoes and green salad" (the reason for such "elegant a dinner," taken in the company of twenty others, being negotiations with the heirs of a gentleman); and a few months later, at the George in Hailsham, of a "forequarter of lamb roasted, a piece of beef roasted, a giblet and pigeon pasty, boiled and roasted chicken, ham, plum pudding, carrots, cabbage, French beans etc" (this time, enhanced provision reflected the simultaneous session of magistrates granting beer licenses).[28]

A more regular kind of work mobility characterized itinerant professions such as soldiers, merchants, diplomats, friars, and scholars. Many frequented inns as Turner did (Erasmus famously contrasted French establishments—distinguished by personalized and sophisticated service—with German hostelries—restricted to set meals of porridges, warmed-up meat, and moldy cheese—in a satirical colloquy often taken at face value[29]), while others found places at private tables. Perhaps the most prominent hosts were Martin Luther and his wife Katharina, who entertained numerous pupils, friends, and theologians at their Wittenberg home.[30]

Early modern Europeans also travelled for cultural reasons. Catholics embarked on mass pilgrimages to regional and (inter)national shrines—a phenomenon which depended on both a dense network of catering facilities en route and a highly developed infrastructure near the holy places themselves (where the ratio of public houses to inhabitants could be as low as 1:20).[31] At the same time, members of social elites from all confessions rounded off their education by means of extended *Grand Tours* around the sights and princely courts of Europe. In terms of dining, the latter offered highly elaborate meals prepared in the French fashion, with all eyes and rituals centered on the person of the monarch. From the late seventeenth century, such long-distance journeys became much easier due to the emergence of a regular and reliable stagecoach service.[32] The latter's staging posts coincided with postal inns, where provision had to keep pace with an increasingly cosmopolitan clientele, making comparisons and complaining about things they did not like. On his wanderings through late-eighteenth-century England, for example, German clergyman Carl Philip Moritz commented unfavorably on the cold meat, salad, and eggs that constituted his normal lunch fare in the Midlands.[33]

Towards the end of the Ancien Régime, ever-more foreign guests explored beauty spots such as Italy or the Alps purely for personal edification. Through the combination of several factors—enhanced transport and accommodation facilities, the rise of the middle-class consumer, exponential growth in travel literature—the early modern period laid important foundations for the take off of mass tourism in the nineteenth century. On some routes, particularly in the Alps, visitors resorted to picnics,[34] but the bulk of catering was provided by innkeepers. According to a guide to Switzerland written in the late 1700s, they typically served a soup, three courses, a dessert, and half a measure [28 fluid oz] of table wine for the price of 1 fl. Unsurprisingly, quality levels varied (at an isolated mountain hostelry in 1771, startled diners faced a "stinking marmot spiked with white maggots" and "rancid" salad), but top-level, urban establishments, as well as rural inns benefitting from fresh produce and skilled chefs, could satisfy even the most demanding palates (one traveller praised the "terrific" red Neuchâtel wine alongside the "delicious mountain butter" and knew "nothing tastier than young potatoes and chestnuts *à la crème,* and carps out of Lake Geneva, prepared by the innkeeper [of Bex in the 1780s] after his peculiar fashion").[35]

As a result of a dispute over excessive charges (vehemently denied by the hosts), we have a detailed record of all main meals served to the Count of Lippe and his extensive entourage during a stay at the Roman Emperor inn at Wesel (Westphalia) in July 1802. For breakfast, the source notes coffee, white bread and butter for all (plus, for the highest guests eating a little later, roast veal, pastries, and liqueur). At lunchtime, the noble party enjoyed a beef consommé, 2 meats and 2 vegetables, roast and salad; cherry compote; fruit, butter, and cheese for 2/3 of a Reichstaler (while the servants received a beef soup, beans with bacon, and salad, charged at just over 1/3 of a Taler). For the Count's dinner, taken privately on a table with a "clean" cloth and serviettes, the menu comprised oat soup; bowls with cauliflower, peas, carps, roast chicken, roast pork rib; two dishes with cutlets, two with cherry compote, and two with salad; plus—for dessert—confectionary, fruit, almonds, and sultanas with bread and cheese, all accompanied by red Rhine wine, for 1 Taler (while the servants, catered for in another room, had to settle for ragout, roast veal, salad, beer, and cumin liqueur priced at less than half a Taler).[36] The initial soup or light course, the combination of several meats, and the inclusion of salads/fruit and sweets—as well as different beverage choices depending on social status—all seem typical for inn catering at this time.[37]

## REGIONAL AND CHRONOLOGICAL VARIABLES

Generalizations for an entire continent are always hazardous. An interrelated set of religious, political, and cultural transformations, as well as geographical diversity require historians of early modern Europe to consider (at least) regional and chronological variables. Both have already been touched upon, but deserve to be addressed in some more depth.

Detailed assessments of regional differences are complicated by the uneven state of research. Some areas, such as England, France, and the Holy Roman Empire, have been studied in much more detail than the European periphery. This pattern may reflect uneven density and quality of provision, as spotlights on Scottish and Mediterranean landscapes reveal a less developed—and less satisfactory—network of catering establishments than in more central parts of the continent.[38] Aragonese law prevented hostelries from providing food for their visitors as late as the seventeenth century (in the village of Mukalavòs on January 18, 1654, the English Levant merchant, Robert Bargrave, "suffered the Inconvenience of that troublesom Law, of buying our own Provisions out of the Ostella; for which, Hunger and Cold made me very angry with the Viceroy"), and while no such restrictions applied in the Ottoman-controlled Balkans (at Burgoss [Lüleburgaz near Constantinople] on September 12, 1652, Bargrave found, "a stately Cane [khan or caravanserai] for Travellers, [to which] the Charitable Founder has bequeathd Provision for a dayly Supper to all Travellers Gratis: viz: for every Company where Armes are hung up, and a Carpet Spread, a Sufficiency of Bread, & admirable Pottage made of Mutton & wheat"), kitchen and dining facilities were clearly less elaborate than in Central European towns.[39]

Another fundamental dividing line separated beer- and wine-drinking regions, with northern and eastern parts of Europe belonging to the former and southern/western areas to the latter. There was a degree of fluctuation (Bavaria abandoned viticulture only during the Little Ice Age from the sixteenth century) and greater choice for social elites (with imported wine available, at a premium, for those who could afford it). A related culinary equator separated butter-preferring northern cuisines from oil-based southern European cooking.[40] In addition, of course, each area had specialities linked to its climate (for example, in terms of fruit or drinks such as cider), location (fresh fish in places near rivers, lakes, and coasts), and agricultural regimes (mutton and dairy products in pastoral regions). Early modern Bavarian tables, for example, were noted for the prominence of *Sauerkraut* and cereal-based noodles or porridges.[41] Further factors such as confession (for example, the existence of fasting periods in Catholic territories) should also be taken into account.

Turning to chronological change, a first major development was the widening of food and drink choices in the course of European expansion. While maize quickly became a staple in northern Italy, the rise of potatoes only occurred from the late eighteenth century onward. Alongside this, chocolate, tea, and, above all, coffee established themselves in catering establishments from the late seventeenth century.[42] The latter contributed to a process of typological differentiation, which added brandy shops, gin palaces, and coffee houses to the traditional range. The rapid spread of strong spirits and liqueurs—boosted in the case of brandy by demand from soldiers and in the case of gin by comparatively low taxation—worried authorities greatly; by the early 1700s, in fact, the perceived dangers of large-scale alcohol abuse caused a moral panic in England.[43]

Inn historians agree that comfort, service, and provisions improved over the course of the early modern period—certainly in the best houses. Hosts had to keep pace with the emerging urban civil society, new forms of sociability (salons, coffee houses) associated with the bourgeois public sphere, changing culinary tastes (moving toward lighter, less heavily spiced dishes), and a refinement of manners inspired by princely courts.[44] This manifested itself in table arrangements (serviettes, introduction of forks), Baroque elaborations (of room decorations as well as table displays), more private dining facilities (including room service), and professionalization trends among catering staff. In the Swiss city of Bern, for example, complaints by visitors about small and cold rooms at the Golden Falcon prompted an extensive renovation project costing over 10,000 crowns in the 1730s. The result was a representative building with an elegant frontage and Palazzo-style galleries. At the same inn (now effectively an early hotel), a 1726 inventory documents a fully equipped kitchen with 3 spits, 5 frying pans, 3 fish kettles, 2 big casseroles, 2 pastry forms, several pots, a coffee mill, and a host of other utensils.[45]

Numerous similar cases could be added from other towns. On a trading card of 1769, the keeper of the Roman Emperor in Frankfurt/Main proudly displayed a prospect of his imposing mansion and assured prospective guests of "the most civil Treatment and most commodious Apartments, with the best of every sort of Provisions & Wine." At another inn in the same city, Jean Fréderic Lippert recommended himself "en qualité de cuisinier expert," who "fournira lets mets les plus exquis" and "les meilleurs Vins soit du pays soit étrangers."[46] The *table d'hôte* system remained common, but evidence for à la carte can also be found. By 1785, it seems to have become the standard in Vienna. One newspaper advert for a new establishment announced that each of its tables would carry a bill with a list of dishes and prices, and the city's address book of 1792 explained that Viennese innkeepers catered for all guests separately, allowing choice over dining times, quantity, and quality of provision—in other words, something approaching modern restaurant dining. One stranger, used to eating in larger groups, promptly complained about the "apportionment" of meals and the decline of sociability during his stay at the White Swan in 1800.[47]

By the eighteenth century, public-house catering could be really quite sophisticated. In England, there are instances of highly skilled cooks transferring their knowledge from the kitchens of social elites to the running of their own businesses, as when William Verral, previously employed by the Duke of Newcastle as an assistant to the famous French cook Pierre Clouet, took over the White Hart inn at Lewes in 1738. He is now best-remembered for publishing a cookery book—one of the few to provide a reliable impression of French cookery in England in the middle of the eighteenth century. London tavern chefs, too, could acquire sufficiently high reputations to create demand for the dissemination of their recipes. Francis Collingwood, principal cook at the Crown and Anchor in the Strand, co-authored *The Universal Cook* (1792)—a comprehensive hands-on collection covering meat, gravy, vegetable, pudding, and liquor preparation, as well as "Little elegant Dishes for Suppers"—with his tavern colleague, John Woollams.[48] Even in provincial Bavaria, there is evidence for innkeepers carefully monitoring culinary fashions. When called upon to host a banquet for local church officials on Corpus Christi day 1740, Franz Jakob Weiß—host of the Post inn at the town of Bruck between Augsburg and Munich—included a dessert called *Mandelschmarrn,* described in a contemporary cook book as follows:

**Sweet almond dish...**

For this one takes two pounds of almonds / two pounds of sugar / the juice of three lemons / and thinly-cut slices / also of two oranges / lemon preserve / a little lemon and orange spirit / so that it has a strong flavour / the almonds have to be cut in long slices / all this has to be stirred together / and when the tart plate is heated / smeared with white wax / and wiped clean again / arrange large or small piles on it, according to preference / and to prevent the piles from dispersing / one can dip a knife in cold water / and use it to re-form the large or small piles / and sprinkle well-scraped pistachios over it / and bake it nicely light yellow.[49]

Among many further changes, a final trend deserves special mention: the synergetic relationship between catering institutions and the emergence of a commercialized leisure industry in the Age of Enlightenment. From the seventeenth and especially eighteenth centuries, major towns such as Paris, London, Dresden, and Vienna (often, in fact, those with a princely court) catered for an expanding proportion of residents with spare resources, disposable time, and a growing appetite for entertainment. New types of infrastructure included theatres, assembly rooms, pleasure gardens, and large amusement parks, sometimes with artificial lighting enabling a gradual conquest of the night. In a related process, townspeople discovered the surrounding countryside as an attractive destination for leisurely walks and visits to beer gardens or—as in the suburbs of Paris—leafy *guinguettes* (outdoor wine taverns). Here visitors encountered a colorful mix of men,

FIGURE 5.1: Trading card of the keeper of the Black Eagle inn at Nuremberg in the Holy Roman Empire, for his newly purchased Dutzendteich public house located half an hour outside the city. The text advertises the addition of an "English Garden" with many amusements and high-quality catering, illustrated by grapes, wine bottles, elegant glasses and a meat dish (engraving by J. L. Stahl). 3686.4.37.62; Trade Card of Georg Uhl, Inn-keeper, *Zum Schwartzen Adler* and *Zum Dutzendteich*; 1770–1790 {nd}. Waddesdon, The Rothschild Collection (The National Trust). Image; University of Central England Digital Services. © The National Trust, Waddesdon Manor.

women, and children from different social groups, attracted by music, dancing, and other entertainments organized by entrepreneurial publicans (see figure 5.1). Vienna offered a particularly impressive range of facilities. One popular destination was the Sommerpalais in the Baroque Augarten, where a wide cross-section of society met to enjoy attractive views and the culinary creations of renowned chefs. On the most popular occasions, such as the opening of a new season, visitors (including dressed-up members of the middling and lower sort) had to queue to get a table. Over in the Prater

park, literally hundreds of specialized catering establishments—ranging
from simple taverns to outdoor eating lounges set in fanciful decors—vied
for custom with leisure attractions such as fireworks and open-air concerts.
Prosperous groups also wined and dined at the countless spas catering for
the fashionable interest in medical services (already encountered as a factor
in the genesis of the restaurant).[50]

## CONCLUSION

There were plenty of dining establishments catering for a wide range of
groups, needs, and budgets in the early modern period. Inns providing
extensive set meals were by far the most common types used by travellers
(whose numbers grew dramatically after the introduction of regular stagecoach services from the late 1600s), but many people decided to eat out
closer to home, be it for reasons of work, conviviality, or because they
lacked the facilities to prepare food themselves. Cook shops, hostelries,
employers, charitable institutions, and street sellers catered for this section of the market. Dining out was thus neither a phenomenon restricted
to members of the elite, nor always the result of necessity. Recent research
in related fields detects elements of a commercialized leisure culture well
before the industrial age,[51] an impression supported here by the discerning
eating habits of prosperous London consumers (using taverns much like
modern restaurants), the emergence of proto-tourism in areas such as the
Central Alps (which attracted visitors for reasons unrelated to work or religion), and the institutionalization of a pleasure industry (linked, in turn,
to the rise of civil society and its associational culture) in many towns.
Sitting down at their tables, Europeans encountered regional peculiarities,
varieties in the quality of provision, an expanding range of food and beverage choices (now including spirits and colonial goods), and—in the leading
houses—services reflecting the latest culinary tastes and courtly fashions.

## CHAPTER SIX

# Professional Cooking, Kitchens, and Service Work: *Accomplisht* Cookery

SARA PENNELL

The subtitle of this chapter is adapted from that of a cookery book, published in England in 1660: Robert May's *The Accomplisht Cook*. Relatively little is known about May (?1588–?1664), other than what he (or his publisher, Nathaniel Brooke) presented in the book's prefatorial, biographical material. However, what is there provided the contemporary reader with the requisite confirmation of May's authority to write such a book with such a title: he was a professional cook with an occupational track record of forty years and more standing.[1] For the modern historian, such texts supply an entry point, albeit rather indirect, into the structures and operations of the "art and mystery of cookery" (the book's own subtitle): that is, the provision of food preparation and service in large-scale domestic, institutional, and commercial environments, in exchange for payment, perquisites, and/or position.

This chapter will draw on published cookery books (from Germany, France, and Italy, as well as England), as well as the biographies of the cooks to whom printed cookery texts were attributed, and elite and middling household accounts, to consider the occupational hierarchies involved in professional food production, as well as the degree of professionalization in the provision of cookery. What cooks such as May understood as cookery were the techniques and, above all, skill involved in the preparation and presentation of complex made dishes such as the olios and ragoûts fashionable in the mid-seventeenth century, and pastryworks.[2] It was distinguishable from mere food provisioning, by immersion in the "art and mystery" underpinning it, a knowledge traditionally provided through training and apprenticeship within urban guilds, noble households, and large-scale institutions (for example, monasteries, universities, and hospitals). Yet, as this chapter will show, while the strictly organized guild structures of medieval towns and cities, and the service wings of great houses provided a framework for both the development and diversification of food preparation professions, the weakening and reordering of such systems across the period 1600–1800 reframed not only who could be a wage-earning cook (especially in regard to the sex of the practitioner), and how, but what indeed cookery was—an increasingly commercial endeavor, rather than simply a medieval mystery.

## THE ARTS OF COOKERY: OCCUPATIONAL ORGANIZATION AND DIVERSIFICATION

What constitutes professional cookery in the early modern period? One answer would be that membership of a guild concerned with food preparation denoted someone as occupationally a cook. Yet amongst the large number of guilds concerned with food provision and preparation, there were only a small number of professional, specifically cooks' guilds across Europe in late medieval Europe; and even fewer by the end of our period.[3] They were understandably concentrated in larger centers—for example Paris, London, Venice—where a market for the catering and coordination skills of the cook could be sustained.[4]

Such specialist cooks' guilds reflect a distinction that we need to understand in order to grasp what happens to these same guilds across our period; cookery was constituted as a distinct art, involving the preparation of elaborate dishes as well as the orchestration of complex meals. The May 1616 Charter granted to the Cooks' Company of London by James I makes this explicit, commending the membership for their services "as well at the Royal Feaste of our Coronacon at the intertayninge of our deere brother the Kinge of Denmarke, the Marriadge of my well beloved daughter the Ladie Elizabeth, our annual Feastes of Sainte George, as at the intertayninge of Forraine Princes and upon other occasions."[5] The same company's Minute Books from 1663 regularly record what was perceived as normal activity of city cooks, through the misconduct of members: fines were frequently levied for insufficient staffing of large-scale feasts held at other livery companies, for employment of non-Company cooks at such events, and complaints against other companies, notably the Bakers', for making and selling "baked pyes, puddens, and other bakemeates properly belonging to the Cookes trade."[6]

This London conflict reveals, of course, that the territory of the cook, in this city at least, was encroached upon by other trades with the equipment (and knowledge) to cook certain foods. In the English capital, the provision of prepared food in taverns, inns, and ordinaries (which we can group under the heading *victualing*) proliferated, despite the claims of the Cooks' Company that such provision might encroach upon its occupational territory.[7] In November 1713, an entry in the Company's Court Book records this problem, in seeking "to obtain an Act of Common Council to oblige all persons exercising the trade of Cooks within the City to bind apprentices to this Company and that no person useing the trade of a Cooke may for the future be admitted of any other Company."[8] The origins of the restaurant in pre-Revolutionary France are not only to be found in the output of the *traiteurs* (cook-caterers') guild, but also in flourishing sites beyond the control of such groups—notably the more marginal locus of the *cabaret à assiette.*[9]

In Georgian London and late-eighteenth-century Paris, then, cooks appear to have been subject to dilution of professional status (in contrast to other service-oriented occupations, such as the apothecaries). Yet this is by no means a universal story, for in other European cities and urban centers, distinctive occupational groupings were increasingly recognized. Even very niche food-production/preparation trades were, in French cities, subject to extending formal organization and distinction from the late seventeenth century onward. By 1702, the *pâtissiers* (incorporating the *cuisiniers*), butchers, *épiciers,* grain merchants, bakers, poultry and meat dressers (*poulailleurs et rôtisseurs*), vinegar and mustard producers, and distillers of Lyon in France had all either sought, or been granted, powers of regulation and policing.[10] This move toward, rather than away from formal recognition of occupational boundaries, is characterized by historians as a particular consequence of Louis XIV's absolutism, but does not mean that professionalization was advancing and accepted. Rather, such developments reflect contemporary concerns to battle the problem of occupational cross-fertilization with regulation rather than liberalization. Indeed, even so-called free or unregulated Lyonnais trades, such as that of the *cabaretiers,* or eating-house keepers, were expected to meet certain standards and be self-policing.[11]

The variable character of guild organization of, and between food-preparation trades across early modern Europe reflects not only the mutability, but also the growing necessity of a diversified occupational spectrum. Certainly, a wide range of food-producing trades, moving well beyond just cooks, flourished in centers without a guild tradition. The first, later eighteenth-century trade directories for the expanding industrial cities of the English Midlands and north-west, such as Liverpool, reveal this: John Gore's 1766 *The Liverpool Directory* lists pork-dealers (manufacturing sausages and pork-pies) and confectioners, as well as myriad victualers, but no cooks per se.[12]

What promotes this occupational diversification? Certainly, occupational protectionism plays its part up to 1800, but demographic change is also significant. The growth of sixteenth-century London, as F. J. Fisher explained in a seminal 1954 account, required a substantive shift in the patterns of feeding the city. Moreover, the inadequacy of the metropolis' building stock in providing all inhabitants with the means to cook on their own hearths, as well as the round-the-clock labor of many, left them without the time to cook for themselves, stimulated the provision of both leisure-oriented and necessary commercial cookery without the control of guilds.[13] Changing patterns of dining, with a move (if not a complete shift) toward more privatized collective eating, and away from highly orchestrated, visible feasting also contributed to the migration of expertise from the territory of the guild cook, to that of the tavern or domestically employed cook.

Beyond large urban centers, cookery professionals were predominantly employed in elite domestic settings (notably royal and aristocratic households), and in large-scale institutional settings such as religious institutions, colleges, and hospitals. Yet while the largest medieval households sustained a roll-call of specialists from cooks to waferers, and small armies of table servants, from butlers to panters (in charge of a household's bread supply and serving), the spatial and cultural reorganization of domestic eating impacted seventeenth- and eighteenth-century culinary service, and created new modes of domestic service within more modest households.[14] The cook nevertheless remained as a key figure, occupying an elevated position in the noble household, albeit, for the most part, answerable (and inferior) to the house steward (the French *maître d'hôtel,* the Italian *scalco*). This hierarchy says something about the secondary role of the food itself in the logistics of the banquet spectacle in early modern Europe. Indeed, at the end of the infamous and disastrous festivities staged by the Prince de Condé for Louis XIV in April 1671, it is the *maître d'hôtel,* François Vatel, who commits suicide, not the head cook.[15]

However, increasingly there were households where a cook's expertise and renown placed him in a more direct and less permanent relationship with his master. French chefs were politically sensitive, satirical targets for Georgian English commentators, precisely because they were highly sought after by, and influential within, the households of prominent political players such as the Whig statesman, Thomas Pelham-Holles (1693–1768), Duke of Newcastle. Pierre Clouet, ducal head chef during the 1730s, gained notoriety not only for his French origins, but for the extravagance which was proverbially associated with them, a famous example being his alleged use of "the gravy of twenty-two partridges for sauce for a brace," to quote the chef's chief apologist, William Verral (1715–1761).[16]

The increasing (and international) mobility of high-status cooks such as Clouet meant that service for life in one household became the exception rather than the rule. Robert May moved between the households of several noble and gentry Catholic families in his fifty-year career; at a more modest level, Verral himself started out in the Sussex kitchens of Pelham-Holles, and then set up as an inn-cook and -keeper.[17] Some degree of recognition of changing professional trajectories is also in evidence in seventeenth-century France, where cooks trained at the royal court were given special leave to enter the commercial sector by the Parisian cooks' guild, without needing to retrain.[18]

But cooks and the multiple divisions of culinary labor familiar in late medieval Europe were no longer employed in only royal, papal, and the largest noble households. By the end of the seventeenth century even provincial gentry households might support some specialized culinary personnel, and a 1690 "Plan of a Person of Quality's Family" suggested at least four cooks as a minimum: one for French-style cooking, one for English, one for pastrywork, and one for roasting.[19] Sir Justinian Isham (1611–1675) of Langport Hall (Northamptonshire) did indeed employ a (male) pastry chef, who taught his motherless daughters one of the key domestic skills expected of genteel young women—the art of pastrywork. By the close of the following century, cooks were commonplace in middling British households.[20]

At the same time however, in England at least, the diffusion of commercially available specialists meant that in-house pastry chefs were hardly needed; in April 1763, Charles Fairfax (d. 1772), Viscount Fairfax of Gilling Castle (Yorkshire), could source a dessert of wet and dry sweetmeats from a French confectioner working in York, at the cost of fifteen guineas (about £1,100 sterling in today's money; figure 6.1).[21] As with cooks, confectioners and pastrymen were highly mobile, relocating internationally in

FIGURE 6.1: An idealized mid-eighteenth-century French pâtissier's shop, as depicted by Robert Bénard for the entry "Pâtissier," in the *Encyclopédie ou Dictionnaire raisonné des sciences, des arts et des métiers, par une Société de Gens de lettres* (Paris, 1751–1777). Wellcome Library, London © Wellcome Images.

search of better employment opportunities, and thereby creating a reputation for their homeland as the best source for such skills. Italian confectioners were especially *en vogue* in early modern Paris and London;
Francesco Procopio (1650/1?–1727) came originally from Palermo, to
found the legendary eponymous Parisian café (Procope), while "the king-
pin of London confectioners," the Italian-born Domenico Negri, advertised himself as maker of "all sorts of ices, fruits and creams in the best
Italian manner" at the sign of the Pineapple in Berkeley Square, London
from 1757.[22]

The skills of table service were also being re-assigned across the seventeenth and eighteenth centuries. While specialized Renaissance service techniques, such as carving and napery folding were printed for the delectation
of early modern readers in texts such as Matthias Giegher's *Li tre trat-
tati* (Padua, 1639) and May's *Accomplisht Cook,* the personnel expert in
them—the *trinciante* of the Renaissance Italian household, the ewerers
of the English table—were disappearing from view, to be substituted by
multi-tasking servants. Carving was itself increasingly conceived as something a well-educated gentleman should undertake himself at table, rather
than a servant's duty, while the adoption of the fork diminished the need
for formal, pre-meal handwashing, aided by a towel-wielding servant.[23]
The chamber-maids and footmen superseding these specialized positions
were depicted as less skilled and thus less respected in the very servants'
manuals that sought to teach their many attributes to the uninitiated. This
is especially the case where these roles were taken on by women, as they
increasingly were in middling and urban artisanal households. The section
on "directions for such who desire to be chamber-maids" in the popular English publication, *The Compleat Servant-Maid, or Young Maidens
Tutor* (first published in London, 1670) makes it clear that to occupy such
a position for a gentlewoman would necessitate knowledge (if not actual
mastery) of a broad array of domestic skills:

> You must not only learn how to dress, wash and starch very well...
> but you must learn to work all sorts of needlework...to make all
> manner of spoonmeats, to raise paste, to dress meat well...to make
> sauces both for fish and flesh, to garnish dishes...to see that every-
> thing be served in well and handsomely to the table.[24]

In addition to these culinary requirements, there was also the hope that the chamber-maid would know how to purchase goods at market: in effect, to be proficient in the range of activities previously assigned to distinct servants. As a court case from Nantes in 1639, concerning the status of a step-daughter in her step-mother's household, reveals, food purchasing and preparation were considered servile and among the "low chores which servants do"; by not undertaking these tasks, the step-mother defended, her step-daughter could not claim she was being treated as little more than a servant.[25]

## PROFESSIONAL KNOWLEDGE: CIRCULATIONS AND LIMITATIONS

Both in what they cooked, and as importantly, how they disseminated their knowledge of dishes prepared and equipment used, culinary professionals clearly had an impact on gastronomic experience in early modern Europe. The impact of what has sometimes been called the first wave of French nouvelle cuisine in the mid-seventeenth century was experienced across the continent, well into the eighteenth century. Although François Pierre la Varenne's modern reputation as *the* architect of this shift to the more modern is over-emphasized in detriment to Italians such as Bartolomeo Scappi, who came before, it is undeniable that elite gastronomy changed substantially between 1600 and 1700. The medieval spicings involving saffron, ginger, and mace were supplanted by pepper, salt, and common herbs (parsley, thyme) in what we now know as a bouquet garni. Sugar and dried fruits, so long a feature of elite savory dishes, were mostly dethroned, in favor of more piquant, acidic flavorings, such as citrus juices, capers, and vinegar. Butter-enriched coulis, or thick, intense sauces, using the concentrated essences of flesh and fowl, dressed concoctions of boiled meat cuts, to produce the fricassées, ragouts, and olios (something of a "soup-stew hybrid," to use Lehmann's description) that characterize late-seventeenth-century, French-influenced cuisine. By 1700, these *made* dishes, along with potages or soups that feature so heavily in Massialot's *Cuisinier roial et bourgeois* (Paris, 1691), and dressed vegetables as distinct dishes, were pushing primarily sweet dishes to the latter stages of a meal, alongside the recasting of the late medieval-banquet course as dessert.[26]

We know about these developments primarily through the cookery books in which they are detailed. Nevertheless, it is important that we do not overstate the significance of events such as the banquets held for the Gonzaga Dukes of Mantua, detailed in Bartolomeo Stefani's *L'arte di ben cucinare* (Mantua, 1662), or the Francophile dishes served forth in the royally sanctioned menus in Patrick Lamb's *The Royal Cook* (London, 1710).[27] We simply do not know how many people read or owned these texts; and only a select, usually courtier and aristocratic audience would actually eat the dishes exemplified in such texts. This proviso established, it is through the publications of known professionals, be they stewards such as Antonio Latini (1642–1696), author of *Lo scalco all moderna* (Naples, 1692–1694), or master cooks, such as May and Lamb, that historians have gauged what constituted professional as opposed to non-professional knowledge. Yet such texts are also evidence of the development of cookery as a commercial, as much as a professional activity for culinary practition-ers. Indeed, the books themselves clearly mark a departure: from culinary knowledge as part of a culture of secrets to protect, to being separable, immensely saleable knowledge.

Texts concerned with food were notably among the first to leave the newly invented presses in Europe in the late fifteenth century, but this is no simple demonstration of a lay demand for, or interest in recipe texts. These early texts were primarily intended to showcase and celebrate the art of professional cookery, rather than make experts of the lay audience. Bartolomeo Scappi's *Opera* (Rome, 1570) and Marx Rumpolt's *Ein New Kochbuch* (Frankfurt, 1581) paraded professional cookery as it should be practiced, illustrating optimal spatial arrangements and equipment (in over 150 woodcuts by Just Amman, in the case of Rumpolt). Active profes-sional engagement needed to be demonstrated in these texts, to confirm the authority of the contents. Thus in "the cookbook that changed the world" (as Sarah Peterson calls it), *Le Cuisinier François* (Paris, 1651; English translation London, 1653), its author, the titular *cuisinier*, François Pierre la Varenne, makes it clear in his dedication to his master, Louis Chalon du Blé, Marquis d'Uxelles (d. 1658), that he is a practicing professional.[28] Indeed, La Varenne and his English counterpart (and so-called borrower) May, primarily addressed their texts to fellow trained masters of cookery; going even further, William Rabisha, in his *The Whole Body of Cookery*

*Dissected* (London, 1661), declared that the book could be of no use to any "kitchen-wench and such as never served their times" (that is, one who has not undertaken the proper apprenticeship).[29]

This professional strand of cookery writing did not quickly wither away in the eighteenth century, contrary to some accounts. Vincent La Chapelle's *Cuisinier moderne* (first published in England in 1733 as *The Modern Cook;* then published in an expanded French edition in the Hague in 1735) was clearly addressed to the male professional practitioner such as Chapelle himself.[30] In France, such professional texts indeed prevailed over more domestically directed publications, with the notable exception of the bestseller attributed to one Menon, *La Cuisinière bourgeoise* (Paris, 1746 and subsequent editions).[31] The first appearance in print of Dutch baking and pastry recipes, in 1753 in the text *Volmaakte Onderrichtinge ten Dienste de Koek-bakkers of hunne Leerlingen* (*Perfect Instructions to Serve the Pastry-bakers or Their Students*), was still titularly framed as a professional, rather than domestic text, indicating the dominance of guild-regulated baking and pastry-making in the Low Countries up until the middle of the eighteenth century.[32]

Yet alongside this courtly and specialist text genre in England (and arguably in its stead in Germany and the Netherlands), there quickly developed a market for manuals which spoke to non-specialist *gentle readers,* embodied in titles such as *de Verstandige kok of Sorghvuldige Huyshoudster* (*The Sensible Cook or Careful Householder*), first published in Amsterdam in 1667.[33] These texts identified certain culinary preparations as being distinctively feminized, undertaken by the gentlewoman in her (genteel) household: sweetmeats, pastrywork, and distilling. Such texts effectively represent the passage of cookery from a protected art to a set of actions to be undertaken by anybody able to read and follow clear instruction. So, whereas Rabisha railed against the upstart "kitchen wench," just over a century later, Richard Briggs, a noted tavern-keeper in his plagiarizing *The English Art of Cookery, According to the Present Practice* (London, 1788), acknowledged both the lay "learner" and the vast body of domestic servants with no specific training expected to undertake cookery as part of their employment, as being amongst his potential readers, taking pains to avoid overly stylized "language and high Terms" which might render "the Art of Cookery embarrassing."[34] Briggs' book comes close to being the late-eighteenth-century equivalent of a modern celebrity chef's print output, in that it represents another strand of commercial engagement, as much as being a testament to his professional expertise.

The wider cultural and economic influences that shaped and often limited the horizons of culinary professionals in early modern Europe lie beyond the covers of a cookbook, however. In aristocratic and royal households, expertise and knowledge were often subordinated to political and diplomatic concerns, custom, and (of course) the tastes of the chief consumers. For guild feasts, and annual events such as the City of London's Lord Mayor's day feasts held every October 29 at the accession of the new incumbent, the cooks employed would have had to take into account available budget and produce, local custom, and other specific restrictions. The 1673 feast, which fell on a Wednesday, appears to have been dominated by fish dishes, in an echo of pre-Reformation practices and possibly also a nod towards the increasingly pro-Catholic regime of Charles II.[35] In the following century, George III's modest palate and desire to moderate expenditure on court cuisine was the subject of contemporary satire, in the infamous circa 1762 print "The Kitchen Metamorphoz'd"; the royal cook is depicted smoking a pipe, "to close up the Orifices in my Belly," for want of food, while an extremely thin cat, "Grimalkin," stalks in the background.[36] In later seventeenth-century and eighteenth-century Italy and Spain, political upheaval and accompanying economic turbulence signaled a closing-down of culinary horizons, or at least a focus on earlier culinary traditions. In cookery publications of this period, there is either a demonstrable turn to the local, or a repetition of established dishes, rather than wholesale alignment with the nouvelle techniques and tastes inaugurated by La Varenne and others.[37] The high flown art of the professional cook in the pre-restaurant era was thus often brought down to earth by his working environment, political and economic necessity, and other constraints.

## TECHNOLOGIES AND RATIONALIZATION

Professional cookery and its delivery in early modern Europe demanded not only high levels of specialist staffing, but also technological and material changes in the kitchen itself. The gold standard of Renaissance kitchens is anatomized in Scappi's *Opera*, where his exhaustive visual presentation of equipment—from spits, to pastrycutters, to mandolins (depicted with few, if any differences to the modern forms of these utensils)—and specialized rooms, emphasized in concert with the printed recipes what a cook (and his many staff) could achieve within a state-of-the-art environment.[38] The built-in stove, with circular recesses for purpose-made vessels, provided a way to cook with more temperature control than afforded over an open flame. Scappi depicts a stove in the *Opera* (plate depicting *Cucina principale*) and by the middle of the following century, French culinary authors assumed their readers would have one at their disposal; La Varenne even gives a definition of the verb *to stove* in his prefatorial material.[39]

The saucepan, illustrated in Scappi (plate *Diversi instrumenti*) and employed in mid-seventeenth-century French cookery texts, was the ideal stove-top vessel with its heat-distributing flat bottom; its diffusion is, in part, explained by the contemporary innovation of sauces thickened with butter and flour, rather than breadcrumbs and almonds. Artefactual survivals suggest that saucepans and perhaps stewpans often came in graduated sets, with individual pans numbered; more modest versions of the massive nineteenth-century *batteries de cuisine*.[40] It is possible therefore, that the six saucepans (two of copper and four of brass) owned by Jonathan Carter, a St Sepulchre (London) innkeeper, whose estate was inventoried in March 1736, constituted part of, or a complete graduated set.[41]

Another technology that we can identify in the professional kitchen at the beginning of our period, but also available in much more modest domestic kitchens (indeed, widely present by 1700 in middling households in London), is the mechanized jack for roasting meat. Although Scappi does illustrate two in the *Opera* (plates *Molinello con tre spedi* and *Cucina fatta a Campana* featuring a smoke-jack), its spread beyond these imagined settings may have been due to deployment in more modest commercial kitchens, where man- (or dog-)power dedicated solely to such monotonous tasks was not in endless supply.[42] The 1688 inventory of Roger Parks, a cook living in the parish of St Martin's in the Fields, London, listed in his "shopp" both "a jack, weight and chain" and "a range in the chimney," as well as "2 saucepans" and other tools of the trade (colander, chopping block, brass ladle, and skimmer); Parks' domestic chattels amounted to no more than £12 11s 6d (no more than a quarter or half the annual wage of a live-in male cook in an early modern elite household), reiterating that this was no Scappi-scale operation.[43]

The locus of operations for the cook and other food professionals was also shifting. Certainly, many of the designated preparation spaces and associated equipment of the professional domestic kitchen, as delineated in a late Renaissance text such as Rumpolt or Scappi were still incorporated in Baroque palaces and aristocratic houses. However, the horizontal expansion of such houses, and indeed the explicit architectural separation made between service and living/entertainment quarters, meant that the cook/chef and his kitchen staff were becoming even further removed from the service and display of the food they had prepared. Jean-François Blondel's 1737–1738 plan and elevation of a separate "*bâtiment des Cuisines*" suitable for a *Trianon* (pleasure palace), and to be placed "*au côté gauche de la cour du château*" ("on the left-hand side in the palace courtyard") exemplifies this, in being all on one ground-floor level and containing within it all the conceivable offices associated with food preparation, and key servant accommodation.[44] In urban centers such as Paris, newly built aristocratic *hôtels* and townhouses increasingly located the food preparation areas below ground-floor level from the early seventeenth century—a location adopted in England at much the same time in the so-called villa houses of greater London, at Ham (Surrey: built 1610), and Eagle Manor (Wimbledon: 1613).[45] The creation of equipment to keep food hot (dish-warmers, tin covers) was a response not only to diners' wishes to eat their food at a palatable temperature, but also to the extensive geographies of service in such houses, and neo-Palladian buildings such as Uppark (East Sussex), where by the early nineteenth century, food prepared in the separated kitchen wing had to travel along underground passages on heated trolleys for it to arrive in the dining room in the main body of the house.[46]

The order and number of dishes sent to the table was also shifting within professional prescription. Although *service á la française* was the dominant mode of table arrangement, it was evolving, from the medieval mode of overlapping courses of intermingled flavors, toward settings of several dishes, increasingly differentiated and ordered by their savory or sweet taste.[47] The number of dishes served forth was also subject to reduction (and, by implication, refinement). Changing dining practices, notably moving from the rectangular to the oval or round table, required fewer dishes, now within easier reach of all diners; Pinkard notes in her analysis of Nicolas de Bonnefons' menu for twelve people, published in *Les Delices de la Campagne* (second edition, Paris, 1656) that only eight dishes per course were specified, in contrast to the more traditional twelve.[48] This reduction in the number of dishes also reflected growing sensibilities of the physiological impact of, as well as the moral weakness inherent in gluttony.[49]

The triumph of the dessert as a distinct (and very sweet) course, and the role of professional confectioners in its execution is evident from the end of the seventeenth century in France, and catalogued in specialist texts such as François Massialot's *Nouvelle instruction pour les confitures, les liqueurs et les fruits* (Paris, 1692).[50] By the middle of the eighteenth century, in the largest urban centers of Europe, confectioners offered up not only the sweetmeats to furnish the dessert, but also the accoutrements to set off these dishes on the table, such as centerpieces, parterres, glasswares, and porcelain dessert services. Domenico Negri's tradecard declared he could furnish "Entertainments in the new[est] fashions" and that he sold "all sorts of Desarts [i.e. dessert settings], Flowers, frames & glass-work at the lowest price." This last claim is of course relative: in 1765, Negri supplied the Duke of Gordon with a dessert laid out in the deeply fashionable garden style, for the princely sum of £25 7s 6d (nearly £1,900 sterling in today's money).[51] In the advertising of such comprehensive services, it is clear that by the end of the eighteenth century the culinary professional, be he cook, *traiteur,* or confectioner, could be much more than simply an artist; such men and women offered their skills as a highly valued commodity.

## GENDER AND PROFESSIONAL COOKERY

The presence of women within professional, or rather, commercial culinary provision across this period is an important feature in this changing landscape of cookery. Where women were able to enter those areas of the food-service economy, such as tavern-keeping, that were not regulated by guilds or limited only to male citizens, they did so in large numbers; for example, in south-west Germany and the Low Countries. Elsewhere, as in eighteenth-century Lyon, women selling their culinary skills skirted round the restrictions placed on them doing so as best they could.[52] Moreover, while city and other regulations might formally restrict women working as cooks and specialist food providers in the early modern market, such legal barriers were more often in evidence in their breach than in their observance. This is certainly the case in seventeenth-century London; the Cooks' Company observed the commonplace exclusion of women from their ranks in principle, but the apprenticeship and other records (although very patchy), suggest young girls were allowed to enter the company membership.[53]

As Gilly Lehmann has also stressed, there was, in practice, no clear dominance of either French or male cooks in elite English households across the eighteenth century, and by the end of the century, female cooks cum housekeepers dominated the middling service market (being paid notably much less than their male counterparts, as Field's research shows). Indeed, in later eighteenth-century satirical prints, while French cooks were always depicted as male (and skinny), English household cooks were often female (and fat).[54] In England, women could also operate in the less regulated area of confectionery without attracting legal redress. Mary Eales, whose book *Mrs Mary Eales's Receipts* was published in 1718, was noted on the title-page as a confectioner to the "late Queen Anne."[55] While this may have been a publisher's puff, as a thorough search of the royal household records for Anne's reign does not show an Eales doing service, it is clear Eales was engaged in confectionery commercially; a manuscript collection of the recipes later published is to be found in the Bodleian Library, having been sold by Eales herself for the then-vast sum of five guineas.[56] Elsewhere in Europe there is evidence of slower integration; in the partially surviving documentation for the 1796 Bologna census, no female cooks are mentioned.[57]

Even in England, the emergence of the woman cook across our period is not straightforwardly a story of professional acceptance, however. Names that have become familiar to British food historians—Hannah Wolley and Hannah Glasse, to name but two—as authors of popular cookery books in this period, have life stories which bear witness to the difficult circumstances in which women sought to make money from their domestic skills. Wolley (?1622–c. 1674) was twice widowed, and all her publications date to her periods of widowhood; in this sense, her culinary writing was not a chosen path, but a necessary one. Glasse was illegitimate, and although she married an estate steward, her life following his death in 1747 (the year her most famous book, *The Art of Cookery Made Plain and Easy*, was first published) saw her declared bankrupt twice, and committed to a London debtors' prison.[58] It is also clear that British women cookery authors were in a distinct continental minority until the nineteenth century; by way of example, the first Italian cookery book attributed to a woman (but possibly not written by one) was not published until 1771.[59]

Beyond cookery, food provisioning more broadly supplied women with occupational opportunities, both within mainstream urban and rural economies. Married women were active, if not exactly visible partners in the taverns, cookshops, and other victualing trades of both the early modern Dutch Republic and London.[60] Within the more marginal "economy of makeshifts" that impoverished men and women survived within throughout early modern Europe, the likes of Mary Rabson, a single woman of St Sepulchre's parish, London, could scrape a living from food, too. Rabson died in lodgings in May 1739 in possession of a pie peel (a slice for moving items in and out of ovens), cake board, rolling pin, and a brass *nossell* (nozzle; for icing); she may have earned her living baking cakes and pies to sell on the streets, just as the (male) "Colly Molly Puff" seller depicted by Marcellus Laroon II did.[61]

Learning housewifery, or more specifically cookery, was indeed a popular destination for pauper girls from English parishes, since the ability to cook could engage women in seasonal or temporary trade beyond their own hearths.[62] Special occasions and transient populations in administrative centers and burgeoning resort towns provided employment useful to women who sought to integrate monied labor with domestic tasks, too. Suzanne Fumette, wife of a Lyonnais master textile maker, was presented before the city authorities in May 1680 for making and selling biscuits to supplement her household's income.[63] More successfully, the sizeable sum of £1 3s. 3d was paid to one Mrs Webb, who catered for the household of Captain Thomas Bowrey, a merchant from Stepney (London), during his family's stay in Bath in June 1699. Although Bowrey's group lodged with a Major and Madam Long, separate payments in Bowrey's accounts are made to Webb for the purchase and preparation of itemized foods. Dressing victuals on a temporary footing such as this gave Webb a monthly income that compared very well with contemporary wages paid to live-in cooks.[64]

## INTERFACES BETWEEN PROFESSIONAL COOKERY AND DOMESTIC COOKERY

To conclude this overview of professional cookery and its commercialization across the period covered by this volume, it is worth highlighting an area of food preparation which straddles the professional/domestic boundary, in early modern England at least, in such a way as to emphasize the problems of clearly demarcating a boundary between the domestic, and the professional or commercial. Pastrywork was never separated from cookery as a distinctive occupational practice with its own guild in London or the rest of England. At the same time, pastrymaking and pastrywork were already identified at the beginning of our period as key genteel female aptitudes. Yet how was one to learn pastrywork if one did not grow up in a household equipped with a pastryman like Sir Justinian Isham's (see above)?

A small number of published cookery texts from the late seventeenth century and early eighteenth century suggest an answer. *The Young Cook's Monitor; or Directions for Cookery and Distilling Being a Choice Compendium of Excellent Receipts. Made Public for the Use and Benefit of My Schollars* by M. H. (London, 1683; second enlarged edition, 1690), and Mary Tillinghast's *Rare and Excellent Receipts, Experienc'd and Taught by Mrs Mary Tillinghast and now Printed for the Use of her Scholars Only* (London, 1678) appear to be intended as handbooks to accompany face-to-face instruction (as opposed to simply ventriloquizing such instruction). Very little is known about Mary Tillinghast and nothing is known in any of the existing specialist bibliographies of cookery literature about M. H., who may well have been the printer, William Downing's, invention.[65] There also survives a trade card, masquerading as an invitation, dating to c. 1680, which invites women (it is addressed explicitly to "Madam"), to attend a dinner put on by the "Ladies & Gentlewomen Practitioners in the Art of Pastery and Cookery" taught by one Nathaniel Meystnor.[66] Perhaps the best known teacher-cook is Edward Kidder (c. 1665/6–1739), whose published *Receipts of Pastry and Cookery* exists in variant published forms (engraved and latterly printed), datable to circa 1720–1740.[67] Kidder was quite the pastry entrepreneur, running schools in several different London locations from at least the early 1700s, switching between locations on different days of the week.[68]

There was then, as these varied texts suggest, an acknowledged market for didactic materials which actively linked to actual teaching of these pastrymaking and cookery skills, in existence before and beyond 1700. In Edinburgh, Lady Grisell Baillie (1665–1746) attended cookery lessons with a Mr Addison in April 1696, for which £1 6s was laid out.[69]

The beautifully calligraphed folio manuscript signed by Hannah Bisaker/ Hannah Buchanan in several places, and inscribed July/August/September 1692, suggests that Bisaker may well have been a student at a London pastry school.[70] The manuscript contains mainly recipes for pastrywork alongside some recipes for other baked goods and general cookery. All the pastry recipes are accompanied by a drawing of the form that the pie or tart case could take. Most telling, however, are the directions for the recipe for "cold butter paist" (enriched shortcrust/flaky pastry) which suggest a face-to-face lesson lay behind the text, which closed "...then lay yor Bottom in First Fill Close and Garnish *as I have taught you always* Putting Liquor into your Pye Before you bake it."[71]

But it is unlikely Bisaker was training to become a professional pastry-woman; her lessons, if she had them, were to enhance her domestic skills in advance of her marriage (which is also recorded in the pages of her manuscript) and perhaps indeed specifically followed to enhance her marital prospects. Yet the possibility remains that, in late seventeenth-century London, there was nothing to stop Bisaker, like Hannah Wolley before her, and other women after her, deploying those skills commercially. It is this freedom and the transferability of cookery skills between domestic and commercial environs, increasingly without the threat of legal sanction or guild opposition, which transformed the profession of cookery in Europe by 1800.

## CONCLUSION

The role of professional cooks in shaping what was eaten by society at large is captured, to some extent, in the pages of the books attributed to them. This is a period of pronounced culinary and technical innovation, yet the relationship between professional cookery and such developments is complex, and complicated by the circulations of both print and manuscript recipe texts, the varied geography of commercial cookery, and the possibly unknowable role played by forces such as custom, itself framed by religious and moral beliefs, medico-therapeutic values, and localized economic and social constraints.[72]

The distinction made in this chapter and the next—between professional or commercial cookery, and domestic cookery—is, of course, entirely artificial, for in all but the poorest households throughout much of Europe by 1800 domestic preparation and presentation of food was not being undertaken by family members, but by paid or indentured servants to that household. At the same time, a distinctive but highly diverse commercial culture of food provision operated, not just in large cities such as London and Paris, but also in smaller provincial leisure towns, such as spas or those servicing travelers on the Grand Tour, en route to Rome and Naples, and the inns and taverns of early modern Europe's highways and byways.[73] The paid provision of prepared foodstuffs entailed, in effect, a kaleidoscopic variety of authorized and informal practitioners, as in other service sectors. As a potential consumer, the degree to which one's cook was a professional depended very much on where one was, what one could afford, and what one wanted. Likewise, amongst practitioners, one might be a cook by virtue of guild membership, but one might also be an innkeeper, or an author, or none of the above.[74] While the end of the eighteenth century saw the coronation of what we might recognize as the celebrity chef, in France and in England such novelties did not replace the useful services of the likes of Mrs Webb, preparing dressed soles for visitors in Georgian Bath.[75]

## CHAPTER SEVEN

# Family and Domesticity: Cooking, Eating, and Making Homes

SARA PENNELL

While the previous chapter has concerned itself with the outward face of food preparation and service, through exploration of the "art and mystery" of cookery (to quote the subtitle of May 1660), this chapter turns us toward its conventional counterpart, housewifery; that is, the preparation and presentation of food within the household, for the household. However, as I have argued in chapter 6, the relationship between professional or commercial cookery and domestic cookery is by no means oppositional. As research has demonstrated, housewives were rarely *just* that across the seventeenth and eighteenth centuries. At the lower (and indeed lowest) end of the economic scale, early modern women fitted food preparation for the household within a broad and fluid range of productive and commercial activities, as well as working alongside domestic servants in their own households; while at the upper end, although examples of aristocratic domestic paragons live on in fulsome funerary monuments, the realities of domestic service and changing ideologies of femininity meant that fewer such women actually participated in cooking, preserving, and distilling, but rather supervised these activities.[1] It would indeed be wrong to see domestic food production as solely the preserve of the hearth-tied housewife, just as it is too simplistic to see the hearth as a site of routinized, low-skilled female labor. We should also not be nostalgic about early modern domestic food production; this was not some golden age of domestic goddess-hood, but rather an era in which food processing and preparation consumed a sizeable and wearying proportion of available domestic labor time.[2]

Any survey of the place of food preparation and consumption within the early modern domestic environment must take into account not only the textual registers of such practices (in prescriptive literature as well as domestic papers), but also the archaeological and artefactual record—from the layout of surviving hearths to cesspit remains. Food preparation and presentation in all its dimensions was a technical activity and mastery (or rather, mistressing?) of it required multiple knowledge registers.[3] The dissemination of this knowledge to one's own family members—most specifically from mothers to daughters, but also from masters and mistresses to servants—was gendered, to be sure, but against the "compleat housewife" (Smith 1727) we need to set the *incomplete* or disinclined housewife. This chapter, while concentrating on English sources, with some material from France and northern Europe, will therefore debate what constituted, for contemporaries, a well-ordered hearth in terms of its equipment and management, and how changing technologies, social practices, and moral expectations affected domestic preparation and provision of food.

## DOMESTIC IDEALS: HOUSEWIFERY AND DOMESTICITY

It is difficult to avoid the persona of the good housewife in seventeenth- and eighteenth-century Europe, so interwoven was it in Christian domestic ideology. In England she is invoked not merely in conduct books and household manuals, but in sermons, ballads, and funerary inscriptions: Lady Mary Digges (c. 1590–1631), wife to Sir Dudley Digges (1582/3–1639), is memorialized in Chilham (Kent) parish church as "such a House Wife, Such a constant Housekeeper, as for Example for ye best of Wives."[4] In the contemporary English-language literature promoting the "commendable art of Housewifery," the call to be a good housewife framed a particularly feminized set of domestic responsibilities—frugality, charity, familial loyalty—which were particularly crystallized within domestic food preparation.[5]

However, this is not to say that the early modern housewife, even in her idealized forms, was a submissive tool of patriarchy; culturally constructed notions of aptitude and propriety embodied in virtuous housewives such as Mary Digges validated the centrality of domestic order, and its communal visibility was crucial.[6] Œconomy (*mesnagement* in early modern France), or right household government, was not solely the preserve of the male household head, but also of his female partner. The quotidian actions of the hearth and its utensils fed into, and sustained œconomic management, and so positioned housewives, as well as their husbands, at the heart of household ordering, both practical and moral.[7] This moral responsibility can be glimpsed not just in the language of cookery texts and conduct books specifically aimed at the female reader, but in images such as William Hogarth's *Gin Lane* (1751), where the ragged mother heads for the pawn-broker's with her hanging pot to secure money for her next draught of gin. In real-life counterpoint, when the overseers of the poor of Dorchester-on-Thames (Oxfordshire) in 1727 paid 1s. 8d to Mary Bassell so she could redeem her skillet from pawn, they sought to support her return not only to the hearth, but to society.[8]

The good housewife is nevertheless far from being an unchanging or untroubled prescriptive persona across the seventeenth and eighteenth centuries. Readers of such texts were exposed to increasing friction on the written page between differing conceptions of femininity and feminine knowledge. Self-sufficiency and sound domestic practices are moral precepts that cookery texts continued to enshrine across the seventeenth and eighteenth centuries; Gervase Markham's Jacobean *The English Housewife* (first published as Book II of the 1615 compendium *Country Contentments*) is echoed in the advertisement of the contents of *The Compleat Housewife* (London, 1727) as "directions for the dressing after the best most natural and wholesome manner, such provisions as are the product of our own country and in such a manner that is agreeable to English palates."[9] Yet while Markham nominally addressed his text to "the English House-wife," it was actually directed at audiences undifferentiated explicitly by gender; by 1750 English-language culinary authors spoke in distinctly feminized tones of an explicitly domestic conception of the household, to an audience prefigured as female.[10]

Furthermore, whereas Markham's housewife was imagined as a competent all-rounder in the domestic production of foodstuffs, medicines, beer, and other domestic necessities, Smith's readers were more likely to be *habituées* of commercial shops as much as the open market, mistresses of at least one servant, clients of laundresses, apothecaries, physicians, and other services, and most significantly, urban, rather than rural inhabitants. The same audience could also access more critical and condemnatory accounts of women's domestic skills as the only attributes worth developing: Eliza Haywood declared that the modern mid-eighteenth-century "lady of Condition, should learn just as much of Cookery and of Work, as to know when she is imposed upon by those she employs in both those necessary Occasions, but no more."[11] This may run counter to the prevailing idea that it is across the long eighteenth century that the roots were laid down of what was to become clearly defined as domesticity by the nineteenth century. Yet while production and reproduction, in forms such as needlework and child-rearing, were central to this emerging ideology of domesticity, practices which were of necessity more engaged with the body, for example "kitchen physick" and the more corporeal aspects of food preparation (butchering and meat curing, for example) were relocated to the margins of the ideal household, if not beyond it.[12]

## COOKING THE BOOKS: THE KNOWLEDGE ECONOMY OF THE DOMESTIC COOK

How then should we locate food preparation and cookery, and knowledge of them in the early modern household? Many histories of food consumption start with available texts,[13] but printed cookery books and associated literature (household manuals, servants' guides) of course only supply a partial, prescriptive, and usually reactive account of what might be termed the knowledge economy of domestic food production and consumption. By contrast, the active knowledge of the food preparer/cook was neither simply domestic nor static. Awareness of foodstuffs, especially those novelties coming from the east and west, needed to be constantly renewed and updated to take account of different qualities and strengths, just as their use needed adjustment according to the requirements of specific consumers. Likewise, kitchen and other food-preparation equipment demanded not only expertise in use and maintenance but also a keen sense of value: buying a new cooking pot was a sizeable investment, so evaluating wear and tear, and when to replace it were crucial skills.

Cookery books can nevertheless serve as a (if not the only) widely disseminated index of what were contemporarily deemed acceptable culinary practices amongst the audiences who could access them. The following brief survey of this knowledge may be Anglocentric, but reflects a widely acknowledged trend: that culinary texts explicitly embodying non-professional knowledge were relatively rare outside of English-, German-, and Dutch-speaking territories until the mid-eighteenth century.[14] What this says about the English market for such knowledge has been debated by Lehmann, Mennell, and others, but it is accepted that the domestic compendia which begin to make their appearance in late-seventeenth-century England, with their breadth of content (from how to manage servants to how to gild wood to make it appear as leather), were chiefly responding to the diversification—socially, geographically, and in terms of gender—of the audiences for print.[15]

The success of some of these books signals a voracious appetite for them, although canny publishing strategies deploying plagiarism and piracy have to be taken into account, too.[16] After 1727, E. Smith's *Compleat Housewife* re-appeared regularly until its eighteenth edition of 1773, while Elizabeth Moxon's *English Housewifery* (Leeds, c. 1741) and Hannah Glasse's still-celebrated *Art of Cookery* (London, 1747) were comparably popular, with re-printings carrying both titles into the following century.[17] At 5s 6d, Smith's text was not cheap, but its titular compendiousness may have lured purchasers. Less is known about actual print runs of cookery books, but in 1733 the printer Charles Ackers undertook to print 2,000 copies of *Miss Mary Eales's Receipts,* to be sold at 2s. 6d each.[18] Eales' book was a relatively specialist work, so arguably the print run was gauged accordingly and a more general work, such as Smith's or Moxon's, might be expected to sell in much greater numbers.

Books like Smith's and Glasse's might have been intended only for consumption by "independent, property-holding households," but they were not the only texts in the field.[19] Books such as *The Compleat Servant-Maid,* or *Young Maidens Tutor* (London, 1677) addressed their titular audiences directly, and were advertised specifically for them, while the cookery books amongst Samuel Pepys' "Penny Merriments" collection of ephemeral cheap print were well within the reach of a maid (or her beau) with six-pence to spare. Selling for just that, *The Compleat Cook, or Accomplished Servant-Maids Necessary Companion* (London, 1685), evoked in brief the sentiments of the larger *Compleat Servant Maid,* and in its twenty-two pages collected together an array of basic dishes, preserves, and medicinal cures, "as the most Useful and best Approved Curiosity is that of Cookery" (Preface).

The conservatism or innovatory nature of these housewife-addressed cookery books has been discussed elsewhere;[20] but the print presence of recipes is only the tip of the culinary knowledge economy in early modern England and its colonies, Germany and the Netherlands, and probably elsewhere too. Manuscript recipe compilations, often begun and maintained by aristocratic individuals in the sixteenth and seventeenth centuries, but increasingly also by genteel, so-called middling compilers in the eighteenth, survive in many British, American, and continental archives, as well as in untold numbers in private hands.[21] These compilations suggest that culinary innovation, diffusion, and adaptation were expected in the early modern domestic kitchen (if not always acted upon). The fricassées, ragoûts, and other made, or complex meat- and fish-based dishes, and the new-style sauces (made with roux bases or via emulsion, rather than using breadcrumbs or almonds as a thickener) populating noble tables in mid-seventeenth-century France and England, find their way into manuscript compilations surprisingly quickly later in the century, suggesting a shared interest in, if not actual taste for this century's nouvelle cuisine.[22] Recipe exchange and modification within familial and social networks ensured further dissemination of information (if not actual preparation) of dishes whose origins are residually hinted at in headings such as "a French kick-shawe" (Anglicizing the French *quelquechose,* a complicated made dish) and "beef Allamode."[23] Less swift in their diffusion were the recipes for dishes which required truly specialist equipment. Ice creams and sorbets, dependent on proximity to an icehouse and also ideally to be served forth in specialist vessels, do not surface quite so frequently, and when they do, it is usually explicable by very particular circumstances of compilation.

The manuscript recipe collection of Lady Ann Fanshawe (1625–1680) is believed to contain the earliest English-language recipes for both ice cream and drinking chocolate committed to text; but Fanshawe was unusual in being exposed to these preparations during her husband's embassy in Madrid in the 1660s.[24]

## FROM PRESCRIPTION TO PRACTICE

Given the problems of associating cookery book/recipe compilation ownership with actual usage, it is difficult to argue for such texts representing reliable registers of domestic tastes and preferences, not least when the texts move from being instructional literature, to being heirlooms and family artefacts.[25] Yet annotations and additions do on occasion mark that a dish was not merely recreated from the recipe, but compared with others, and judged good. Anne Lisle's otherwise list-like recipe compilation, dating to c. 1748, is mostly silent on the qualities of the culinary and medicinal recipes collected, which makes her annotation of the recipe for "Cheese cakes Mrs Phillipps" as "the best I ever eat [sic]" all the more notable. By contrast, those recipes crossed through and marked "good for nothing" (as in a recipe for pickled cucumbers in the compilation attributed to Lettice Pudsey in the Folger Shakespeare Library) denote those which have been tried, tested, and found wanting.[26]

What was actually prepared and eaten domestically is nevertheless difficult to substantiate without ancillary evidence. The late-eighteenth-century/early-nineteenth-century manuscript recipe collection attributed to the Lomas family of Bollington (Cheshire), suggests that the recipes were collected for use, as much as for reasons of education or entertainment, since details of menus and drawings of table layouts for actual meals, dated between 1805–1806, are sketched into the volume; in at least two of these layouts, dishes mentioned are also present in the text as recipes.[27] The coming together of a recipe collection with a set of household accounts, diaries, or correspondence outside of aristocratic settings is frustratingly rare. Benjamin Browne (1664–1748), a Lake District farmer whose wife Elizabeth compiled a recipe book which survives alongside a run of domestic accounts, allows us to consider what might have been eaten in the Browne household. Thus, the regular purchases of cockles could have been destined for pickling, as outlined in one recipe, while the Venice treacle and salad oil detailed as ingredients in the recipe for "Lugatellus [sic: usually Lucatello's] balsam" (a multi-ingredient cure-all), were frequently purchased in sizeable quantities. This also reminds us that the early modern household produced many of its own medications in the same spaces, using the same equipment, and from the same sources as its food.[28]

Although no recipe collection survives for the household of Thomas Turner (1729–1793), the shopkeeper-cum-schoolmaster in the village of East Hoathly (East Sussex), his diary covering the years 1756–1765 provides one of the few surviving records of what one household ate, on a nearly daily basis, for its main daily meal across a decade. This records the seasonality of Turner's eating, his regular consumption of leftovers, and the frequency with which food "gifts" from neighbors, customers (perhaps as payments in kind), and friends, featured on his table.[29] While not necessarily archetypal, mid-Georgian English cuisine, his dietary record nevertheless supplies a sense of the rhythms of food consumption, with unspectacular daily eating—sometimes not even meriting description beyond "[T]he remains of yesterday's dinner"—punctuated by more memorable, sociable eating.

In Turner's daily consumption, savory and sweet boiled puddings and roasted meats predominate, rather than complicated made dishes; but he and his household regularly consumed fresh vegetables as accompaniments. This, along with evidence from other non-elite household accounts of the purchase of seeds and plants for kitchen gardens, as well as archaeobotanical findings, suggests that the increased presence of recipes for distinct side dishes beyond the salads and pickled vegetables of earlier texts in mid-eighteenth-century printed cookery books was a response to existing practice, rather than creating it.[30] Turner was also very much an opportunistic eater, in that the food gifts he was given were quickly consumed. The wife of the local estate steward dispatched a veal pasty to the recently bereaved Thomas in July 1761; and if the speed with which he consumed this present is any gauge of the esteem in which it was held, its appearance on the following day's dinner table was respectful in the extreme.[31] Turner's table does reflect, too, the localized nature of both food provision and food styles that still prevailed in mid-eighteenth-century England. While published cookery texts were moving toward a more homogenized, if not precisely *national* cuisine in England, Turner was eating dishes which have now entered the folkloric lexicon of *regional* dishes: what is now known as "Sussex pond pudding," turns up on several occasions as "raisin butter pond pudding" and "currant pond pudding."[32]

If we had access to Turner's domestic rubbish (assuming he had no pig or poultry to feed the last leftovers to), we might also be able to enlarge upon what he ate and did not record in his diary, since archaeological evidence extends our knowledge of what was likely to be eaten domestically. Although pork (as opposed to bacon and cured meat) was increasingly deemed, in English-language dietary and culinary texts alike, a meat best eaten by laborers, palaeo-archaeological analysis of disposed bones demonstrates it was widely consumed, certainly more than the occasional inventory reference to bacon and sausages in the chimney might indicate. The presence of a broad range of fruit seeds and pips in early modern domestic-waste pits such as those excavated in St Ebbe's parish, Oxford, reveals that just because cookery books do not mention the consumption of fruit other than in the form of pickles, conserves, and sweetmeats very often, it does not mean they were not consumed; a mid-to late-eighteenth-century cesspit on this site contained the seeds/pits of blackberry, grape, fig, gooseberry, black- and red-currant, strawberry, pear or apple, plum, and black mulberry.[33] This is indeed a growth area for academics across disciplines, with great potential for revolutionizing our understanding of food-preparation methods, and the interplay of diet and health in the past.[34]

## POTS, PANS, PLACE

Early modern visual images supply a confusing picture of what equipment and settings might have been available to the early modern domestic cook. On the one hand, we have scenes evoking the well-supplied kitchen, with plump scullery maids hard at work (or taking a rest from) scouring heaped brass and copper pans, or the material and moral excesses of a fat kitchen; at the other end of the spectrum, there are the peasant interiors, such as those by Adrien von Ostade (Haarlem/Holland, 1610–1685) and Louis le Nain (Laon/France, 1600/10–1648), where modesty and poverty are materialized in a single dish of food for the family, or a lonely pot hanging within the fireplace.[35] Such images are, however, freighted, and alone cannot be taken as windows into the equipping of the early modern kitchen, either wealthy or impoverished. Rather, the disposition of key objects within the images serve as visual shorthand: pots tell us we are in a kitchen, lots of pots tell us it is a wealthy kitchen, while overturned and cracked pots warn of a household undone.[36]

Pre- and post-mortem inventories, while undeniably problematic documents, have certainly enriched our knowledge of what, materially, lay between the superabundance and squalor of the artistic fat and lean kitchens. Pardailhé-Galabrun, in her analysis of 3,000 eighteenth-century Parisian inventories is struck by the "abundance" and "differentiated applications" of kitchen equipment, even in modest households: for her, the litany of different spoon types found, from soup to skimming, from jam to coffee, embodies this diversity.[37] This variety is not a unique feature of Parisian hearths either; the early modern cooking hearth in much of northern Europe, except in the poorest households, was a locus of technically sophisticated, sometimes highly decorated tools and multiple vessels in myriad materials.[38]

As we have seen in chapter 6, the impact of coal as a domestic fuel, as well as innovations in culinary technique, re-equipped the domestic, as well as the professional cooking hearth in much of early modern England. But coal was by no means all-conquering in the rest of Europe. In eighteenth-century Paris, coal did not supersede wood as a cooking fuel in as spectacular a fashion as it did in London in the preceding century, while in seventeenth-century Holland (and indeed, the north-west of England) the environmental conditions gave peat continued prominence (as seen in Pieter de Hooch's 1670–1675 canvas, "The Fireside," with its immaculately laid peat fire and laden peat bucket).[39]

Where coal was deployed, and where wood was a secure and plentiful fuel resource, hearths were equipped with more mechanized and specialized tools by 1800 (figure 7.1). By the middle of the eighteenth century, some form of mechanized jack appeared in 50 percent of Overton and Whittle's Kent inventory sample, while 33 percent owned a saucepan; in Paris too, such jacks were deployed in wealthier households.[40] Parisians were also equipped with a diverse and precisely named array of cooking pots and pans with specialist purposes: from fish kettles (*poissonnière*), to the *huguenote*, a tightly lidded pot apparently used by Protestants wishing to conceal their cooking of meat on fast days.[41] This degree of specialization in

FIGURE 7.1: The kitchen from the dolls' house known as "May Foster's House" (made c. 1800). Very few pre-1800 kitchens survive in historic contexts with contemporary layouts and contents; although within a dolls' house, because of the date of its construction, this kitchen does evoke how a late Georgian hearth may have been equipped in a genteel English household. Photo © Victoria and Albert Museum, London.

cooking pot names might have been lacking in comparable English households (although regional terminology can complicate identification), but by the middle of the eighteenth century, the presence of stewpans and skillets, porridge pots, tea kettles, boilers, and pots in copper, tin, bellmetal, and brass, suggests diversification and specialization by usage. This said, both Parisian and English inventories across the period display a common property; what differentiates wealthier households from poorer ones in their cooking equipment is not necessarily more specialized tools, but rather a greater quantity of a similar range of tools, and better quality materials.[42]

Even in those areas where fish kettles and saucepans did not make such an impact, and the reading of the inventory evidence "suggests the continuation of very simple methods of cooking," there were small but perceptible shifts in the form and variety of cooking equipment; for example, from the use of brass to the use of cheaper tinned cooking vessels, and the entry into households of a broad range of cheap tinwares, from basting spoons, to dredging boxes, and colanders.[43] The dredging box is a prime example of a novel utensil that quantitative inventory analyses miss (because they are usually not valued separately), and yet which other sources indicate as increasingly common in the English kitchen.[44] Containing seasoned flour or breadcrumbs, the dredging-box had a perforated lid, so that contents could be sifted over the roasting joint, in the manner of the modern flour dredger it resembles. Significantly, this process is not employed by English cookery writers much before 1700, although both Gervase Markham and Hannah Wolley do explicitly mention the technique. By the middle of the eighteenth century, dredging had become a common recipe direction in the roasting of all types of meat and dredging boxes appear as key kitchen equipment in visual evocations of the ideal kitchen, such as the frontispiece to Martha Bradley's 1760 *The British Housewife,* where one sits at the far left end of the mantel-shelf over the cooking hearth.[45]

The cooking hearth itself may not, of course, have been in a space denominated as a kitchen; in a sample of 600 non-elite inventories from London, Norwich, the Thames Valley, and Westmorland, between 1650 and 1750, concentrations of cooking equipment were found in spaces as variously named as "back parlour," "bodystead," "lodging chamber," "fire chamber," "buttery," "house," and "cellar." The notarial households of early modern Nantes, studied by Hardwick, rarely contained a room named as a kitchen, although the material culture around one of the (most commonly two) hearths clearly designated it as a cooking hearth. In eighteenth-century Paris, 45 percent of Pardailhé-Galabrun's sample inventories mention a kitchen, "or at least a room, bedroom, hall, closet, ante-chamber...serving as a kitchen."[46] Some designations reflect geographical distinctiveness (bodystead and firehouse were used in north-west England to denote the space in which the chief cooking hearth sat), while others simply recognize the spatial constraints on urban dwellers, where cooking, sleeping, and general living were confined to one or two rooms. Indeed a kitchen might not contain a hearth at all, instead being used for food processing and storage alone; this is certainly the case in early modern Kent.[47]

The location of kitchens below ground level is a distinctly urban phenomenon of our period. In England, although a small number of elite cellar kitchens were built prior to the Fire of London in 1666—such as at

Ham House (Surrey), built in 1610, with all its main service rooms below ground level—the basement kitchen developed further in the post-Fire period. In the new-style townhouses being built on horizontally restrictive plots, kitchen and other service rooms were situated below stairs to maximize spatial use, and isolate the main hearth from the living quarters on the floors above.[48] In eighteenth-century Paris, although kitchens were also listed in inventories on the first, second, and third floors of decedents' properties, they were increasingly noted to be on the ground floors and in the basements of housing stock.[49] Limitations on urban domestic space in both cities nevertheless designated the kitchen as the only space for food preparation and storage: much non-elite urban housing lacked ancillary preparation or storage rooms, other than multi-purpose yards, cellars, and passage-ways.

Even if we can see the kitchen slowly emerging as a distinctive space for specialized practices across the seventeenth century, this did not mean food could not be prepared elsewhere. Thus, the presence of chafing dishes and toasting forks in bed chambers allowed for late-night, or sick-room, cooking, while the lodger in a single room two floors up had no choice but to cook at the hearth with which her room was (hopefully) equipped. Nor were the spaces in which the main bulk of a household's cooking was undertaken solely limited to cooking. Just as the twenty-first-century kitchen might also be a study, a *rec* room, and dining space, so the early modern kitchen might be characterized as the household's forum. Alongside cooking and eating, business might be transacted, trades pursued, pet birds kept, instruments played, weaponry stored, Bibles read (aloud), and murders committed.[50]

The early modern kitchen was indeed, to use the modern term, a live–work space. Its manifestation as a natural philosophical workplace is borne out in high art, in renderings of the confusion of the alchemist's kitchen/laboratory by artists such as David Teniers (1610–1690). More prosaically, inventory and taxation data demonstrates the difficulties of separating out domestic and occupational usage within the kitchen. In eighteenth-century Paris, 4 *limonadiers* of a sample of 62 used their kitchens to prepare their goods, while a further 9 used spaces designated as *laboratoires* and shops as their cooking space, too.[51] The English Hearth Tax, which operated between 1662 and 1689, and taxed each household on the number of working hearths, did not easily distinguish between commercial or industrial hearths, and domestic ones; in 1665 a clarification of the exemptions from its payment was issued, which stated that ovens, forges, and furnaces which shared a hearth used for other purposes were not exempted from the tax.[52] The kitchen as a site of employment for the swelling ranks of domestic servants has been noted in the previous chapter; but as Carolyn Steedman has argued, this does not mean it was not also a site for poetics, philosophy, and subversion, alongside the drudgery amongst the dishcloths.[53]

Rural kitchens continued to be sites of food production for multiple ends: for the household, for the community, for the market.[54] Although the early modern period has been characterized as an era in which domestic production for domestic consumption of beer, bread, dairy stuffs, and cured/processed meats declined in favor of market purchasing and more specialized and large-scale commercial production of foodstuffs, some English regions, such as Kent, reveal a more complex picture: an intensification of domestically sited brewing and dairying that may have benefitted both the household, and local and metropolitan markets simultaneously, represented in increasing inventory registers of butteries and brewing equipment, milk houses, and dairying items. Moreover, much of this redirection of production for the household toward that for the market was due to women.[55] In agrarian regions, the seasonal flow of foodstuffs from field and pasture transformed households into processing plants, with cheese lofts, apple lofts, salting troughs, and mustard mills all attesting in inventories to the productive and processing capacities of early modern households.[56] Details of thefts of livestock and food from north-west English regional court depositions plot the extensive domestic geography of food storage, too: in August 1675, Annas Bele of Rash (Cumberland) was found to have "very fatt mutton in the pott, and severall peices [*sic*] of sueet [*sic*: suet, or rendered animal fat] in the arke, & a sueet loafe [suet loaf] in the Chimney and fower [four] skins in the dunghill," all from the sheep she was accused of stealing from the fellside.[57]

## EATING AND NOT EATING: HOME-MAKING/BREAKING

Challenges to culinary knowledge and practice highlight the centrality of food preparation and provisioning to the good order of the early modern household. Œconomy was diminished, and indeed destroyed when food was either not plentiful, or badly-prepared, or the systems (moral as well as practical) to sustain it malfunctioned. It was not simply the hearth that was at the heart of the well-ordered household, but specifically the kitchen hearth and its products.

There were many sanctioned occasions in which food preparation was limited within the household. Fasting may not have prevailed in its fullest Catholic form across the whole of Europe in the seventeenth and eighteenth centuries, but collective abstinence from food for the purposes of commemoration and public humiliation, even in Protestant territories such as England and its Anglican colonies, saw the state circumscribing domestic food preparation and consumption. In early-seventeenth-century London, it was still possible to be prosecuted by the church authorities for eating flesh on a designated fast day, while Samuel Pepys found to his horror that he had to fast more fully than he had planned on the public fast designated to commemorate the execution of King Charles I, on January 30, 1663: "a solemne fast for the King's murther. And we were forced to keep it more than we would have done, having forgot to take any victuals into the house." The presence of a whole chapter, "For a fast-dinner," in Glasse's 1747 *Art of Cookery Made Plain and Easy* also speaks to the continuing expectation of English observance on these days well into the eighteenth century.[58]

More disruptive to the moral balance of the household than such temporary abstinence, was the absence altogether of a kitchen, or a meaningful concentration of cooking equipment in a household. How indeed did the Parisian cook, his wife, and four daughters under the age of eight, inventoried in the Marais district in 1662, prepare food in their one-room lodgings? Such a lack did not mean the occupants did not eat there, but it does suggest the food they did consume was not of their own making (ironically, in this case). For the inhabitants of the largest urban centers in early modern Europe, eating out was not solely a leisure activity, but rather one frequently endured by necessity in the absence of sufficient facilities.[59]

Tensions over no food at home could boil over into domestic violence. Wendy Wall's evocative phrase, "blood in the kitchen," reminds us that, as a site of bodily slaughter (the throttled chicken, the caught hare) as well as bodily repair through kitchen physic, the early modern kitchen was not necessarily always a place of gleaming pots and well-ordered provisioning.[60] Although Wall's work has foregrounded the dramatic potential in the early modern kitchen and its corruption, the relationship of real kitchens to violence is not just contained within the evisceration of animal flesh. Female control of the hearth inspired copious imaginings of female wickedness, although the petty treason of husband-killing was in reality much rarer than the converse crime. Highly publicized and fictionalized accounts of "murderous wives" depicted women fatally striking spouses with spits and frying pans, while cases alleging malicious or fatal poisoning at table insinuated that wives could manipulate their culinary and medicinal skills for despicable ends.[61] Real though was the report in the *Gentleman's Magazine* in 1731 of the seemingly accidental poisoning of Messrs Whitehorn and Dokes, distillers of Kensington, who, "dining together, were poyson'd by a hard pudding, which Mr Whitehorn's wife had made for his dinner." The tragedy was explained as the "mistake of a girl whom she had sent for beaten ginger, which proved yellow arsenic." Yet this casualty report leaves several questions hanging, not least about the mistress's supervision of her kitchen servants, and the wisdom of storing arsenic in the same place as one's spices.[62]

This violence, and the hortatory tone of prescriptions about housewifery apart, there is nevertheless notably little evidence to suggest that poor culinary skills, or slovenly housekeeping alone constituted grounds for marital discord and violence. Margaret Hunt, in her work on domestic violence in eighteenth-century London, cites only one case in which poor cookery (the burning of dinner) provoked a husband's abuse of his wife, while in early modern Wildberg and Ebhausen (Germany) only 6 percent of church court marital-conflict cases concerned a wife's poor provision of food (compared to 24% recording a husband's drunkenness as cause).[63] More prosaically, domestic cooking and eating acted as catalysts for the articulation of mundane, though possibly plate-throwing levels of domestic disgruntlement. Alice, wife to John Richards, a Dorset yeoman farmer, was not averse to picking an argument with her husband at the dinner table. On February 14, 1701, Richards reported that "at table I had words with Alice about my son John, which became at last very high, and the next day after dinner she began to renew the quarrel violently," while Samuel and Elizabeth Pepys had regular disagreements at table, and about what he perceived as her slovenly housekeeping and management of servants.[64] Beyond the household, the use of saucepans and cooking pots as the instruments announcing the cuckolded husband in seventeenth-century "rough music" and skimmingtons transformed the cooking hearth, its equipment, and actions around it into the key locus where the ordered household should be rooted.[65]

## DOMESTIC HOSPITALITY AND SOCIABILITY

Household food preparation was undoubtedly a repetitive, often tedious activity that took up several hours per day, with even greater effort expended at crucial points in the agricultural cycle (the slaughter of livestock, harvestide).[66] However, non-quotidian eating and socializing around eating marked times when food preparation embodied key moral qualities of the ordered household: as a hospitable, charitable, and neighborly organism.

Rites of passage, holy days, and festivals were all marked with special foods and conduct around food, in Protestant areas as in Catholic; Jan Steen's 1662 "Twelfth Night" (Museum of Fine Arts, Boston), with its extended family celebrating Epiphany with waffles and merrymaking, illustrates the weakness of Protestant prohibitions of such popish holidays, as does Samuel Pepys' massive twenty-shilling expenditure on a Twelfth-Night cake in 1668.[67] Cookery texts can tell us something of these specialized dishes, especially through nomenclature, such as the "bride pie" in Robert May's 1660 *Accomplisht Cook* ("for a Wedding to pass away the time"), but so can material culture.[68] In the marital and post-mortem inventories of the seventeenth- and eighteenth-century southwestern German communities of Wildberg and Ebhausen, specialist cake-making equipment for the festive *Mutscheln* (mussel-cakes) was far from rare, even in the poorest households, supporting the idea that female expertise in production of complex pastries and cakes was by no means limited to gentlewomen, nor alienated to commercial producers.[69]

Other celebratory dishes are not so distinguishable. The many cream- and grain-based porridges and possets (warmed milk or cream, curdled with alcohol, and flavored with herbs and spices) in English culinary texts are not explicitly named as post-birth celebratory (and restorative) dishes, but many would have been prepared in such circumstances. The yearly accounts of the Lathams, an artisan family engaged in husbandry and textile production in north-west England, show that such dishes were not purely the preserve of the elite either, with purchases of sugar, alcohol, raisins, and spices following the births of several of their eight children recorded along-side payments to local midwives. The survival of decorative posset pots, in glass, decorated earthenwares, and porcelain, reiterates the rite-of-passage significance of these domestically produced foods.[70]

More often than not, however, we get little sense of the explicit culinary dimensions of domestic celebration/commemoration. A rare insight is given in the set of funeral accounts that survive for Benjamin Browne's family between the end of the seventeenth and mid-eighteenth centuries, in which we witness the bereaved family moving from providing home-made food for mourners to purchasing the bulk of the funeral meats. Thus in April 1700, at the burial of his baby daughter Jane, Browne supplied the mourners with "a good veal of our own and three good pieces of powdered beef which gave our relation and most of our neighbourhood a snack of cold meat before they went to the church." By contrast, at Browne's own funeral in 1748 his son George appears to have purchased all the chicken, fruit, cakes, wine, and ale served to family, and mourners.[71]

Domestic sociability enabled its participants to locate themselves within their local communities, "illuminate the success of the household," and experience new foods and material culture around food, such as the well-laundered napery which Nantaise notaries owned in such abundance in the seventeenth century.[72] Thomas Turner's mid-eighteenth-century diary, useful for its register of the quotidian repetitiveness of eating, also demonstrates how certain meals were infused with the offering of appropriate sociability. An elaborate meal was served forth for the visit of Mrs Jeremiah French (wife to the village's largest, non-noble landowner) and her daughter on Tuesday December 1, 1761: "a goose roasted, a piece of beef boiled, a raisin butter pond pudding, cabbage, turnips and apple sause [sic]." This was undoubtedly an exceptional weekday repast, served forth in acknowledgement of his guests' superior standing. But Turner's œconomy is not far from the surface, even in this formal meal: it not only utilized a gift from a grateful neighbor (the goose, from a Mrs Brown, received on November 28, 1761), it also provided Turner with enough leftovers to suffice for the following two days' dinners.[73]

Turner's diary also records his expectations of the sort of foods that registered appropriate sociability. Having served up "two roasted ducks (of our own breed), a piece of bacon, a leg of mutton, cauliflowers and carrots, with a currant pond pudding boiled" to Mr and Mrs George Beard in August 1756, Turner was less than gracious (but perhaps quite smug) about the meal to which he was treated at the Beards' home, on October 27 of the same year: "I dined at Mr Beard's on a part of a leg of mutton hashed (but spoiled in the doing), a pigeon pudding and cold plum pudding, but all in very bad order." Turner also felt that he deserved better than the "leg of very ordinary ewe half boiled...and sauce which looked like what is vomited up by sucking children," which was offered at his Uncle Hill's for Sunday dinner on October 17, 1756; there is sadly no entry recording what Turner offered his relative by way of culinary retaliation.[74]

For all Turner's disappointment in meals "in very bad order," what we witness in mid-eighteenth-century rural Sussex is a distinctively more informal mode of collective eating, in which the food quality, company, and material display as much as etiquette, and the "honours of the table" were of chief concern. "Of doing the Honours of a Table," a chapter in *The Art of Cookery, or the Compleat-Housewife* (London, 1758), showcases these more relaxed relationships around food sharing. The dominant active figure is "the lady at the head of the table," not her husband; and in both the old English and more modish French methods of service described, it is the mistress of the house, not the master, who directs the pattern and rate of eating. Furthermore, the imagined guests at this table are all construed as equals alongside their hosts:

> everyone helps himself as he likes, and where he likes...we suppose that every one who dines with us, dines as well every day at home, and therefore we make no pother about his eating, as if he was at a feast.[75]

Using the household as a site for leisure, and specifically food-related leisure, be it Turner's neighborly dinners or a gossipy tea-table gathering, is materially measurable in the growing ownership of not only cutlery, but sets of cutlery, and of not only isolated ceramic pieces, but full tea and coffee equipages and dessert sets, in England at least.[76] Whilst new Meissen and Chelsea porcelains may not have been within the reach of many consumers, by the end of the eighteenth century provincial potteries in Liverpool,

Lowestoft, and, of course, the Midlands, were producing attractive and affordable alternatives to deck the middling table.[77] And if new table goods
were still out of reach, the availability of similar goods secondhand was
growing, through the formalized guild-regulated disposal of such commodities in Italy, France, and the Low Countries, and the commercial auction
sales of Georgian Britain.[78]

## CONCLUSION

This material multiplication of food service goods, coupled with greater
access to different foodstuffs—at neighbors' households, as well as in the
course of travelling and extra-domestic food consumption[79]—reframed
early modern domestic eating beyond that needed simply to survive, as an
experience not simply captured in the term *feasting*, nor limited to elites, as
it had so often been during the sixteenth century. Greater attention to the
domestic table as a site for sociability, and demonstrations of status and
taste across the long eighteenth century meant that the kitchen supplying
what was served forth needed to attend to not only culinary changes in
taste, but also the œconomics underpinning such shifts. If many housewives,
in England at least, became more distanced from the heat of the kitchen fire
by virtue of the percolation of domestic service down the social spectrum,
prescriptive literatures continued to depict them as the linchpins of domestic order, and their cookery (even if it was only textually manifest, in their
compilation of manuscript recipe collections) as the pre-eminent badge of a
household working as it should.

## CHAPTER EIGHT

# Body and Soul, or Living Physically in the Kitchen

DAVID GENTILCORE

In 1556 the rector of the Jesuit college in Louvain wrote to the founder and general of the Society of Jesus, Ignatius of Loyola, with a query about the diet of the college's residents.[1] Although it was located in Flemish Brabant, the Louvain college was made up of Jesuits from different parts of Europe and the rector, Adrian Adriaenssens, was unsure what sorts of foods to serve the community, especially when individual members were unwell. Ignatius offered a balanced reply, on the one hand praising the rector's frugality when it came to nourishment, whilst on the other suggesting that this should not extend to the care of the sick. They should be allowed to follow the physician's medical and dietary advice, including whatever special foods and drink he might recommend. Forcing a "coarser" diet on those used to eating well, especially if they were in a weakened state, would do more harm than good. The advice did not apply to those who were in full health, however, who ought to consume those foods considered common and ordinary in the region. For example, residents should get used to drinking beer, cider, or water—whatever was usually drunk there—rather than wine, if that was an imported luxury. This general rule of thumb should also be flexible enough to cater to the different bodily constitutions and temperaments of individual residents, by varying diets in the name of maintaining health. But the rector would have to be vigilant that "superfluous things" did not enter the menu under the guise of medical "necessity." The college should provide "all that is needed for health," but not to the extent of consuming foods that catered only to the senses.

Just under two centuries later, two French followers of Ignatius equated the excellence in cookery of their own times with higher levels of delicacy and refinement. Pierre Brumoy and Guillaume-Hyacinthe Bougeant were both teachers at the Jesuits' prestigious Parisian college of Louis-le-Grand and had both published works on a variety of subjects, historical, literary, and devotional. Their forty-page scholarly essay prefacing François Marin's 1739 cookery treatise, *Les dons de Comus,* brought cookery into wider philosophic debates. Evidently, Brumoy and Bougeant were not afraid to be associated with a book that referred in its title to "the gifts of Comus," the Graeco-Roman deity of merrymaking and festive excess, who here "seasons" the foods brought by the other gods.

Whilst the two French Jesuits acknowledged the harmful effects of food that, from the time of Adam's fall, human beings were forced to ingest in order "to sustain a frail machine," they also believed human beings were of a higher level than the animals. Man's constant "progress" proved this.[2] Since the earliest human history, "habit gave birth to distaste, distaste led to curiosity, curiosity to experimentation, and experimentation to sensuality. [Man] tastes, he tries, he chooses; little by little he turns into an art the most simple action, the most natural. Here, we have the history of cookery, as well as most of the arts." Luxury and civilization were closely linked and ultimately had beneficial effects, furnishing "delicacy, magnificence and profusion." Not that Brumoy and Bougeant were advocating intemperance, of course; rather, that vice should not be equated with "the innocent art of cookery." Constant innovation in the kitchen, according to the two Jesuits, was a sign of culinary superiority and refinement. "Modern" cookery was an improvement over what had preceded it. Without sacrificing variety, it was "simpler, more hygienic [*plus propre*], more delicate and perhaps even more learned."

How much times had changed, from the Counter-Reformation of Ignatius to the Rococo-meats-Enlightenment of Brumoy and Bougeant. The contrast between Ignatius's dietary suggestions of 1556 and the ideas expressed by two Jesuits in 1739 reveals more than the extent to which the Society of Jesus had evolved over the course of 185 years, negotiating its way into elite and influential parts of society, throughout Catholic Europe and beyond. It reveals how much medical ideas about food and diet had changed; even the very idea of disease prevention through diet had altered significantly. This is the first theme of this chapter. And yet, even if their advice took different forms and was buttressed by changing medical theories, physicians still felt obliged to counsel moderation and restraint. Living a healthy life, which meant eating *properly,* remained a moral obligation, even while the advice on how to do this changed. And because this world was intimately connected with the next, what was good (or bad) for the body was good (or bad) for the soul. Our focus will be on the body, the natural province of both medicine and cookery; however, one of the seven deadly sins, gluttony (*gula*), and its paired virtue, abstinence, strongly influenced perceptions of diet and health. The ongoing tension between the two extremes of gluttony and abstinence, with moderation somewhere in the middle, will form our second theme—an undercurrent to the first. We shall take an almost circular journey from a religiously influenced moderation, through to Baroque elaboration, toward a different, more taste-related, refined simplicity. All of this during a period when heavily spiced food gave way to natural tastes, foodstuffs from the New World gradually made inroads, concoction was replaced by fermentation and insensible transpiration, and vegetables went from being dangerous to not only healthy, but downright fashionable.

## LIVING PHYSICALLY

Ignatius's particular vision of the relationship between diet and devotion, and the positive contribution that a correct diet could make, were partly conditioned by his own experiences and the frailty of his own body. His advice was firmly rooted in the Hippocratic–Galenic notions of his own time regarding the important role of diet in the prevention of disease through a regulation of the balance of the four humors (see below). At the same time, Ignatius's worry—that eating for our health, which was itself good and necessary, could easily lead to us becoming ensnared by our appetite, tempted by pleasure—was straight out of St Augustine's exploration of the sense of taste.[3] As St Augustine himself acknowledged, there were different ways of allaying the temptations of an "incontinent appetite"; the reins should be neither too slack nor too tight. Ignatius did so by initiating a new dietary model, markedly different from the rigors of the early Christian and medieval models, but still in keeping with the spirit of the Counter-Reformation: not austere and frugal, but one located between the courtly sumptuousness and refinement of some aristocratic religious orders, and the simplicity and sameness of the strict monastic diet on the other. It was the sort of diet considered necessary to fuel the social elites in leading the religiously active life the Jesuits valued so much.

During the time of Ignatius, ideas about how best to regulate the six so-called non-natural things—food and drink, air, motion and rest, sleep and waking, repletion and evacuation, strong emotions and passions—vis-à-vis the individual body, the humoral balance of which varied from person to person, made up the field of hygiene or regimen. The theoretical frame-work was provided by the advice of two ancient physicians: Hippocrates and his systematic interpreter, Galen. According to Galen, proper regimen balanced the temperament of the humors within the individual body and its parts, including the psychic functions.[4] Galen's works had been codified and published earlier in the sixteenth century as part of the Galenic revival of the Renaissance. It was responsible for a new genre of medical writing on healthy eating, mixing moral philosophy and medical advice. It proved not only very successful in publishing terms but long-lived in terms of the way it structured thinking about the relationship between food and drink, eating, and health. The readership of these works was literate, cultured, with the luxury of being able to worry about maintaining a healthy diet, and to be concerned about what others in society would think.

This was a time when *living physically* meant living according to the dictates of *physic*: the maintenance of health and treatment of disease in the individual body, according to its circumstances in the natural world, by the following of a tailored manner of living. Not everyone was in favor of the moderation and temperance imposed by regimen. The say-ing in full—"to live physically is to live miserably"—reminds us of that.[5] However, everyone who could choose what to eat and how to eat it would certainly have been influenced by these medical ideas. Ignatius's letter refers to some of the concepts. A healthy regimen was one that: (1) respected the needs of the individual body, with different people eating different things;

(2) varied according to one's social status and condition; and, (3) differed from region to region, in line with local custom. Gender would have been another factor, since women's bodies were generally regarded as being temperamentally cooler and wetter then men's; but of course it was not applicable to Ignatius's Jesuits. To appreciate why all of these factors could influence health and disease we need to understand something of contemporary notions of how food interacted with the body.

The texture or substance of different foods, and how their varying qualities determined their interactions with a person's own humoral balance and bodily complexion, was at the basis of dietary opinions expressed by the authors. Different foods had different properties. Cooking was believed to render foods more palatable and more digestible, whilst allowing the cook to counteract a food's perceived adverse qualities by balancing them with corrective condiments. Cold and moist lettuce needed to be tempered, quite literally *seasoned* (in its original sense of *to make ready*), with hot and drying ingredients such as salt and pepper, in order to make it suitable for the human body. Qualitative properties such as hot or cold, dry or moist came in different intensities or *degrees*. At the one end of the spectrum, a first-degree food such as white bread altered a balanced body only slightly, making it an ideal food. At the other end, fourth-degree foods forcibly altered the body: for example garlic, hot to the fourth degree, which supplied too much heat. Most foods were second-degree or more and had to be corrected in some way to make them humorally balanced. Simple dishes were to be preferred to rich ones, because the latter abounded in potentially contrasting ingredients that made digestion difficult. The most harmful dish of all, "a food fit to kill man," according to the Roman physician Scipione Mercurio, was the rich Spanish stew *olla podrida* (which Mercurio spelt *putrida*), also fashionable at Italian courts, whose putrefying perniciousness in the stomach was evident in its very name.[6]

All of this is important because according to the Galenic theory of digestion one became what one ate. The most important stage of digestion was when the foods entered the stomach, beginning a process called *concoction*. During concoction the stomach cooked the food with its heat, in a similar manner to an enclosed kettle on a fire. Since the stomach's heat could not be regulated, one had to be careful about what foods went into the kettle, not overburdening it, and in which order. When food had been thoroughly concocted the resulting liquid, *chyle,* went to the liver, to be turned into blood and thence distributed throughout the body.

Ignatius was also attentive to issues of habit and status. One should eat what one was accustomed to eating; change was considered unhealthy. This put people coming from outside, such as well-travelled Jesuits or European colonists in the New World, in a slight quandary: how far to adapt, without putting one's own, now-foreign *complexion* (humoral balance) in jeopardy? It was also awkward for northern European physicians, since the Galenic tradition was a Mediterranean one and dealt with foods of that region: veal, olive oil, wine, figs, and so on. The advice given was harder to apply in, say, the Low Countries or the Swiss Alps. It is not surprising, then, that dietary manuals written by northern Europeans vary widely from region to region, sometimes going to great lengths to defend established, native food customs in the face of ancient medical authority. In terms of status, there was no point in forcing heavy or crass foods, such as beans, on those used to eating lighter foods, such as game birds. In its assertion that only well-exercised people, such as laborers, could tolerate heavy foods, medical theory was reinforcing and reflecting contemporary social structure and status, which had themselves intensified during the sixteenth century. Many of these notions about foodstuffs would persist even when their Galenic underpinning had been replaced by other physiological theories.

When it came to Ignatius's recommendation to avoid "superfluity" in diet, saintly figures of the age went much further, opting to live in a perpetual fast. Archbishop Carlo Borromeo of Milan, despite being a cardinal of the Catholic Church, a Milanese patrician, and heir to vast estates, eschewed all creature comforts, according to contemporary hagiographers.[7] When Borromeo was not depicted amongst the poor and plague victims, he was represented alone at table, in solitary devotion, bread and water his only nourishment (figure 8.1). Other Counter-Reformation saints went even further than this. Not content merely to eat the very minimum, they actually sought to punish their appetites. The Franciscan, Giuseppe da Copertino, abstained from even bread and wine, and sprinkled his plate of simple herbs or beans with "a bitter powder"—a sort of anti-condiment. This became his regimen: when he had to eat meat because ordered to do so by his superior, "his overcharged stomach immediately rebelled and rejected the meat."[8]

FIGURE 8.1: The abstemious eater. "St Carlo Borromeo at Supper," painting by Daniele Crispi (1628). Church of Santa Maria della Passione, Milan. Photograph by Giovanni Dall'Orto.

Just how far should one go? Medical writers acknowledged that the occasional fast might be good for one's health, concocting excess humors that had collected in the stomach, in addition to the undeniable spiritual benefits; but few physicians considered it wise to imitate the saints to the letter. That said, in a society still feeling the effects of the Protestant and Catholic Reformations, both of which shared in a revived Augustinian sense of bodily self-discipline and spirituality, it is no surprise that the dietary works of the late sixteenth century are more ascetic in tone than previous ones. This moralizing element was already present in Galen, in his idea that to stay healthy one must live "rightly"; health and virtue were closely linked.[9] However, it becomes the raison d'être of works such as Alvise (Luigi) Cornaro's *Trattato de la vita sobria*, first published in 1558, which provided "sure and certain methods of attaining a long and healthful life," to quote the book's English title.[10] Cornaro advocated sobriety and "cheerful temperance." This was not the mortifying self-denial of the saints, but a balanced regimen providing the basis for virtuous living and thinking, benefiting body and mind. Cornaro was not a physician, but a high-ranking public official in Venice; nevertheless, his work became a favorite of European doctors. We also see the moralizing element in the widespread condemnation of courtly gluttony by the physician-authors. Courtiers were accused of avoiding food rules in their heady pursuit of pleasure, extravagance, exoticism, and excess. The dietary manuals make few explicit references to religion, but there is an underlying sense of guilt, of the need to avoid excess and indulgence, and of the mind being called on to control the body's baser, bestial instincts. There was a stress on what foods were good for one, not on what tasted good.

There was a golden mean, lying somewhere between abstinence and excess. Its exact location on the dietetical spectrum varied according to the context. A physician of Bergamo, who gave up the canonized men and women of Catholic Italy for the saints of Calvinist Basel, Guglielmo Gratarolo, realized that if public life was a duty, then staying in good health was necessary in the fulfillment of this. Gratarolo advocated moderation, but there is still plenty of meat and wine in his advice for magistrates, first published in 1555.[11] The Jesuits followed a similar model. Missionary and educational work required fit and healthy priests, which meant good, nourishing food, suitable for people who could consider themselves part of the privileged in society. Special occasions, such as the frequent visits of illustrious guests, were marked by equally special meals. The Jesuits rubbed shoulders with courtiers, noblemen, diplomats, and men of government—for whom public feasting and extravagance was seen as an obligation and a duty. Clearly, the Jesuits did not take it to the extent of "addicting themselves to voluptuousness and bellycheere," in Gratarolo's words; but there was a recognition that the *vita activa* pushed the boundaries of moderation and abstinence.

Around 1623 the natural philosopher and statesman Francis Bacon pushed the boundaries still further, arguing that within a balanced regimen, occasional "surfeit" might actually be beneficial, as it was "good for the irrigation of the body," especially if followed by a decent purge.[12] The Galenic system proved amazingly resilient: prudent and commonsensical, wary of extremes, novelty, and of advice applicable everywhere and to everyone, and founded on perceived experience. Most of all, it was flexible, allowing for a range of sometimes conflicting medical advice and interpretation.

If someone such as Bacon, credited with making a major contribution to the rise of experimental science, could stay within the Galenic framework, what else might try its resilience? The arrival of new foods from the Americas is one such test case. The first point is that they did not pose a problem to Galenic theory, even if they sometimes did in practice. Typical was Ludovico Bertaldi's 1620 additions to an older work by the Sienese Ugo Benzi. Not only are Bertaldi's comments entirely Galenic in tone and content, they also seamlessly integrate discussions of New World plants into this framework. This was most straightforward for those foodstuffs perceived as similar to those already present in the European diet, such as the turkey, soon widely eaten by the elites and praised by medical writers. Likewise, the chili pepper was adopted as a cheaper, colorful substitute to black pepper. It had the same virtues, "it warms the stomach, promotes the digestion of foods...and is used to correct the frigidity of foods," in the words of Bertaldi.[13] Even the most novel food items of the period—tobacco, coffee, tea, and chocolate—were all introduced first as medicinal goods. They were slotted into the Galenic paradigm, despite the fact that physicians did not always agree about where precisely to put them.[14]

This could take some time: Bertaldi's work came almost 130 years after Columbus's first voyage. Indeed, it is strange then that New World foods—even unproblematic turkeys and chilies—were seldom mentioned in sixteenth-century dietary manuals, whereas they quickly figured in botanical treatises. Scientific curiosity towards the new plants did not stretch as far as advising their consumption. On the contrary, when it came to maize, Bertaldi found it "gross [thick] and viscous" and so significantly harder to digest than wheat, but he did record, without too much disapproval, how maize had already entered the diet in certain mountainous parts of northern Italy. Elsewhere this dietary change had dire consequences. The reason why so many of the English colonists in Virginia succumbed to disease, according to the Spanish ambassador to the court of James I, writing in 1613, was that they were forced to subsist on maize and a little fish, with only water to drink, a diet "contrary to the English."[15]

## SAUCE RATHER THAN DIET

One area where culinary practice was at odds with dietary advice was in the shift in attitudes toward vegetables. This occurred first in Italy, and then in

France and England. Vegetables were criticized by every Renaissance physician worth his salt—and a lot of salt was just what was needed to counter their excessive moisture and coldness. Vegetables had previously had a marginal role in elite cookery, precisely for this reason; because they were considered earthy, gross, watery, and generally hard to digest, they were left to the urban and rural poor. Vegetables became attractive to the elites when they were rare, due to the development of novel and hard-to-obtain varieties, or by consuming them out of season. When it comes to vegetables, works of horticulture tell us more about actual diets than dietary manuals. In turn-of-the-century France, for example, Olivier de Serres described more than thirty plants which he considered highly desirable in the kitchen garden. Some fifty years later, in 1651, Nicolas de Bonnefons recommended forty-two different vegetables, in his very popular *Le jardinier françois*.[16] The place of vegetables in French cookery books also increased markedly, both in terms of the percentage of recipes devoted to vegetables and in terms of the varieties mentioned.

The seventeenth century was an intermediary period for medical dietetics. Galenism remained the dominant medical theory, especially at certain elite levels, in much of Europe, and continued to structure the manuals. However, new medical and scientific discoveries and theories made inroads, as they would throughout the rest of the early modern period, without yet offering a convincing alternative to Galenism, much less a unified medical paradigm.

Two main trends affected dietetics: iatromechanics and iatrochemistry. Iatromechanics (or mechanical medicine) offered a mechanical model of the body, including digestion, as this related to health. The Paduan physician Santorio Santorio, sometimes called the father of metabolism, first wrote about what he modestly called a new "art," that of "static medicine," in 1614.[17] Santorio identified "insensible perspiration" as the cause of health and disease. Through this hidden means the body excreted most of the food ingested, in addition to the usual, perceptible means of evacuation. Santorio identified the quantity of food thus excreted by means of his famous weighing chair, which he used to quantify the difference between food intake and evacuation (figure 8.2). The chair allowed one to determine the balance of the healthy body through correct, individual food intake. Underpinning Santorio's ideas was a vision of the body and its functions in terms of mathematical functions, rather than in terms of elements and qualities. Radical

FIGURE 8.2: The scientific eater. Santorio Santorio and his "weighing machine," engraving (London: Newton, 1718). © Wellcome Library, London.

the theory no doubt was, and certainly influential; but Santorio's dietary recommendations, as well as his view of the place evacuation had in the structure of the so-called non naturals, remained firmly Galenic.

The second medical trend to make an impact was the iatrochemistry (or chemical medicine) of Paracelsus. This saw disease and the processes of the body in chemical terms. However, even authors who followed Paracelsus in prescribing chemical drugs did not stray far from Galenic tradition. The structure of Joseph Duchesne's *Le pourtraict de la santé* was largely familiar, as was much of the advice, but the rationale was now chemical.[18] For instance, Duchesne regarded black pepper as least rather than most warming, its spicy quality coming from the "aromatic salt" it contained, which broke down all the incrustations and viscosity in the stomach and other organs. Yet his conclusion was the same: pepper was beneficial to digestion and good for combating a range of diseases.

Nor did Paracelsianism immediately affect perceptions of digestion. This came later, in the mid-seventeenth century, with the ideas of two of Paracelsus' followers. The Flemish physician and chemist, Jan Baptist van Helmont, explained digestion chemically as the decomposition of food by acids, or "ferments," in the stomach. This was but the first in a chain of six stages in the "transmutation" of food that took place in the body, involving different organs, including the heart and brain.[19] A pupil of his, François de la Boë, a French Huguenot refugee and physician in Leiden, took these concepts further. He paired iatrochemical theories with the latest anatomical explorations, regarding the glands of the digestive system, to present digestion as a series of chemical processes beginning with the exposure of food to saliva, and ending with the actions of the pancreatic juices in the intestines. The process ended when any imbalances between acids (such as pancreatic juice) and alkalines (such as bile) were neutralized, and gastronomic balance was restored.[20]

The relationship between medicine and cookery, previously symbiotic, changed as a result. Whether one viewed digestion and the body's other functions in mechanical or chemical terms—or, indeed, as a mixture of both, as Louis Lémery was bravely attempting to do (1702)[21]—the result was that dietetics was perceived as less important in the day-to-day maintenance of one's health. One might still speak of individual foods as being hot, cold, wet, or dry, in the Galenic manner; but achieving the right balance had less to do with preventing disease. As all bodies were now created the same, differing only in their size, use, and age, the main consideration now was not to overburden them. Medicine itself turned to focus more on treating and curing disease, on clinical medicine, and away from health maintenance and disease prevention. The first English history of medicine more or less separated dietetics from medicine in its survey, associating it instead with other arts such as cookery. The book's author, the physician and avid Newtonian John Freind, identified anatomy and chemistry as the most important and developing medical fields.[22] There was also a notable decline in the number of dietary works from the middle of the seventeenth century, which is not to say that they disappeared altogether.

Medical knowledge was less pertinent in determining the use of food ingredients and the planning of meals than it had been in the past. Or was it simply that the place of medicine in cookery had changed, had become more generalized, and less specific? Whereas *to season* (*assaisonner* in French) had meant both to temper or balance food, as well as to give flavor to it, the verb now lost the former connotation, as flavor became the more important consideration. The way foods were seasoned also changed. Gone were the strong flavors, heavy spices, and acidic tastes (of vinegar or verjuice) of late medieval and Renaissance cookery, replaced by an increasing use of butter, cream, gravies, and sauces. However, medicine was called on to justify this shift in elite cookery. When the physician Jacques-Jean Bruhier re-edited Lémery's *Traité des alimens* in 1755, he cited the then-influential Dutch physician and chemist Herman Boerhaave.[23] Boerhaave was opposed to condiments of any sort, arguing that they harmed even the healthiest of people. Spices were still used in cookery, but the amounts and the range of spices used both decreased. The cook's main considerations were now the aesthetic ones of taste and color, consistent with the physician's changing understanding of how the body worked.

The trend is evident in Bonnefons's *Délices de la campagne,* first published alongside his *Jardinier françois* in 1655. Bonnefons sought to capture the flavor, smell, and taste of the main ingredient in a dish. As he put it: "Il faut entretenir le goust naturel, le vrays goust," stressing the importance of maintaining the natural, true taste of the main ingredient. A cabbage soup should taste entirely of cabbage, leek soup of leeks, and so on.[24] This was no less than a revolution. It was no longer necessary to alter the natural properties of ingredients in order to make them healthy; it was enough to bring out the properties of the foods themselves. That said, there was nothing simple or natural about the natural taste advocated by Bonnefons. Rather, considerable refinement and artistry, not to mention cost, went into creating distinct but complementary flavors.

Medical concerns were certainly present in Bonnefons, but in a diminished measure and in a different guise. One traditionally minded contemporary rued that flavor had taken precedence over health: the new cookery was so much "sauce rather than diet."[25] The new French sauces were indeed not only different in consistency and taste: smoother, often rich in fats, made with cream, butter, bouillon, or wine. They were also different in function, no longer intended as dietary correctives to the main ingredient, but as a means of bringing out its perceived natural characteristics. However, this was just what was increasingly perceived of as healthy and digestible.

Cookery was becoming richer in another sense, too. The asceticism and restraint associated with, and advocated by the Reformations was losing cultural influence. By 1650, in England, for example, homilies against gluttonous eating were far less common than they had been. And if the Protestant rejection of fast days had once provided Catholics with the opportunity to evince in this the inherent gluttony of Protestantism, the number of fast days observed by Catholics declined significantly from its Counter-Reformation peak, especially over the course of the eighteenth century, as the example of Spain suggests.[26] Moreover, in their fast-day observance, Spanish religious orders increasingly shunned dried, salted codfish (*bacalao*) for fresh and daintier kinds of fish, if they could afford to. Drinking chocolate, once condemned by Catholic bishops for its lascivious nature and so prohibited during periods of abstinence, had outgrown its medicinal confines to become the arbiter of good taste and conspicuous consumption.[27]

During the eighteenth century, as part of a new sumptuous, Baroque aesthetic, the new cookery became firmly established in France, whence it spread throughout Europe, at least at elite levels. Menus changed, but courtly gourmandizing went on, even when the courts came to resemble learned salons, in the eighteenth century. Writing from the court of Frederick the Great at Potsdam, the cosmopolitan, widely travelled Francesco Algarotti bemoaned the dainty dishes whose only purpose was to stimulate already full diners to eat more. "Hélas! Les indigestions sont pour la bonne compagnie," Algarotti wrote, quoting his good friend Voltaire.[28] Not so much Augustinian ethics as the price of social networking.

## BETWEEN THINNESS AND FLUIDITY, AND LUXURIOUS ARTFULNESS

By the end of the seventeenth century, iatromechanics was the dominant medical theory in the ongoing tussle with iatrochemistry, against a backdrop of persistent Galenism. Drawing on the latest ideas of natural philosophers such as Isaac Newton, René Descartes, and Giovanni Alfonso Borelli, iatromechanics was used to explain all physiological and pathological processes. In Scotland, Archibald Pitcairne taught that digestion was strictly mechanical—the muscular motion of the stomach transforming food into chyle without chemical additions. A pupil of Pitcairne's, George

Cheyne, was prompted by his own obesity and poor health to turn theory into practice, developing dietary therapies consistent with iatromechanical principles. The body was composed of "solids" and "juices," the latter referring to blood, chyle, and other secretions. Chronic ailments, ranging from gout to nervous and mental complaints, were caused by obstructions in the tubes that carried the juices around the body, which occurred when the juices became glutinous, viscous, and thick. For Cheyne, "the grand secret and sole mean of long life is to keep blood and juices in a due state of thinness and fluidity," eating foods that were easy for the body to digest.[29]

The problem was that most people above the class of manual laborers simply ate too much, and too much of the wrong foods. "Made dishes, rich soop, high sauces, baking, smoking, salting, and pickling, are the inventions of luxury, to force an unnatural appetite and increase the load which nature, without incentives from ill habits and a vicious palate, will of itself make more than sufficient for health and long life," Cheyne wrote.[30] We should strive to be more like St Antony, who "liv'd to 105 years, on mere bread and water, adding only a few herbs at last," or "Lewis Cornaro, a Venetian nobleman," who "liv'd, by the mere force of his temperance, near to 100 years." More realistically, Cheyne settled for exact prescriptions of the amounts of food that were suitable for an ordinary person. He also discussed the relative merits of different foodstuffs, using a rationale radically different from the Galenic one, based as it was on ideas about glutinous particles and corrosive salts. The lightness of the regimen made it particularly suited to the "tender and valetudinary," especially women or men who cultivated the feminine emotions.

It all came down to this: eating one part meat to two parts "vegetable food," "at the great meal" of the day, washed down with "only water with a spoonful of wine, or clear small beer." Cheyne reduced diet to a simple framework, made up of simple rules. Gone was what Gratarolo had called "the diversitie that is in bodies," referring to the ancient idea of different bodily temperaments. Cheyne provided a standardized set of basic food rules, widely applicable, to avoid obesity, treat certain conditions, and stay healthy: in other words, a diet in the modern sense (as in, *The Cheyne Diet ®: A Healthier, Slimmer You through Abstinence*). Moderation and occasional abstinence had been a recommended part of diet at least since the School of Salerno in the eleventh century; now it *was* the diet.

For all its innovations, however, Cheyne's treatise is still traditional in structure. The focus is on the maintenance of health and the prevention of disease, by regulation of the six non naturals. It is directed at a specific class of people, "the studious" and "gentlemen of the learned professions," just as Gratarolo's treatise was two centuries earlier. There are some similarities in the actual advice, too, such as Cheyne's condemnation of "vegetables and animals of a strong, poignant, aromatick and hot taste." Cheyne is also Galenic in tone, singling out the great harm caused by "the luxurious artfulness of cookery." He wrote only for the "very learned, ingenious, and even religious persons" who had the "good sense" to want to follow a rule of diet and who were "willing to abstain from everything hurtful, deny[ing] themselves anything their appetites craved," for the sake of their health. As for everyone else, "the robust, the luxurious, the pot-companions, the loose, and the abandoned," they "have here no business; their time has not yet come." Note the biblical tone. Cheyne went further than most physicians in advocating an almost messianic reform of the individual as necessary for the pursuit of bodily and spiritual health, inextricably linked to one another.

Cheyne's diet was the source of some ridicule. What would happen to "all pamp'ring trades," "with nothing French, either in sauce or name," "no dish disguis'd by dear variety; nor owe an appetite to luxury?" asked one anonymous author. "For my physician I accept your book; but, by the gods!—you ne'er shall be my cook!" he cracked.[31] An easy slight, perhaps; but also an unintended recognition of the real dilemma confronted—between health and appetite.

Cheyne was not alone, however, but one of a spate of physicians interested in diet as the key to health during the middle decades of the eighteenth century. They were part of a revival in medical concern for hygiene, in the original sense of regulating health through diet, exercise, and so on; even if, in their interest in the effects of the environment, they owed more to Hippocrates than Galen. Their advice was couched in the latest medical and scientific theories. They also directed their fire at diseases that were then the subjects of much concern and investigation, such as scurvy and gout. Gout in particular was seen as a sign of the times, debauchery embodied, whose incidence increased "when luxury, intemperance, and indolence came in fashion."[32] For this reason gout became a point of convergence for

FIGURE 8.3: The overindulgent eater. "Comfort in the Gout," engraving by Thomas Rowlandson (1785 and 1802). Excess in food and drink (and perhaps something else), as a gouty diner is served his supper. © Trustees of the British Museum.

discussions relating to diet, health, and morality—especially that of rich, white men—during the latter half of eighteenth century (figure 8.3).

Some of this dietary writing revolved around the place of vegetables in a healthy diet. In 1743, the year Cheyne died, the Florentine physician and naturalist Antonio Cocchi advocated "an herbaceous, aqueous, sparing and tender diet," as part of a healthy regimen.[33] Cocchi, who put more trust in regimen than medicines, advocated a diet of fresh, uncooked vegetables and fruits, and clear water, avoiding meat and fish. Not only would it keep people healthy longer, it would also prevent diseases such as gout, elephantiasis, and rheumatism, and suppress "by temperance, our most noxious desires." This was all caused by an excess of crude, indigestible matter remaining in the body. By contrast, the presence of fluids carried throughout the body, as generated by vegetables, promoted insensible transpiration and, therefore, health. Cocchi did not refer to Cheyne, but both expressed a preference for herbs (good) over spices (bad), water over wine, fresh milk over aged cheeses. However, although Cocchi's diet was strict, there is little of Cheyne's moralizing, crusading tone. Instead, Cocchi argued that his "Pythagorean diet" was possessed of "a certain delicate voluptuousness, of a gentle and even splendid luxury, if we employ curiosity and art in the choice and abundance of the best fresh vegetable aliments" which nature had provided for us.

This revived interest in diet and regimen was more than merely academic. On the one hand, the medical reaction to Cocchi's work, at least in Italy, suggests how influential residual Galenism still was. For instance, the physician Giuseppe Pujati argued against an exclusively vegetable diet with reference to Boerhaave's writings on stomach acids; but Pujati's idea that vegetables were mainly suitable as correctives, with meat providing the main nourishment, was essentially Galenic.[34] On the other hand, at least one cook was inspired by the debate to produce a book of recipes. Vincenzo Corrado, a Celestine Benedictine in Naples, noted approvingly how "Pythagorean laws" were being increasingly put to effect in kitchens and on tables, and how people were "giving their bodies healthier, tastier and easier nourishment by means of vegetables."[35] Corrado's stated motive in writing his book was to provide ways of preparing "the simple Pythagorean foods" that were not only "pleasing to the palate" and able to "meet standards of luxury in setting sumptuous tables," but that were also able "to satisfy the delicate taste of noblemen and maintain the health of scholars." Corrado was no strict vegetarian: his various *colì* (from the French *coulis*), *purè* (from the French *purée*) and *brodi* (from the French tradition of *bouillons*) abound with beef, capon, veal, and ham. All these sauces were necessary in order to beef up—as we might say, and the pun *is* intended—the flavor of otherwise insipid vegetables.

## ELEGANT SIMPLICITY

In Paris during the late 1730s and 1740s the elites were caught up in a debate over cookery, involving arguments about health and disease, luxury and virtue, absolutism and equality. Brumoy and Bougeant's preface to *Les dons de Comus*, referred to in the introduction, was a part of this. Their praise of variety in food and its continual refinement, as part of the cultivation of a sense of taste, was a long way from St Augustine. The latest cookery was similar to chemistry in its artfulness, they wrote. This was evident in Marin's *bouillon:* a stock to be used as a base for sauces and virtually the only dish meriting a detailed recipe in the treatise. Galenic authors had praised meat broths, easier to digest than the meat itself because in some sense it was pre-concocted; but Marin's *bouillon* was of a different order entirely. The apparent lightness and simplicity of this complicated but harmonious preparation was not only the apogee of refinement, but was also in line with current medical thinking about what made for healthy foods. As Corrado drew on medical discussions of vegetable diets, so cookery books such as Marin's had shown some sign of being influenced by Cheyne's diet. When Marin's treatise was republished in a much-expanded edition in 1742, it contained an additional preface that praised the principles outlined by Cheyne. Marin's recipes even followed some of these principles, though the complexity that went into preparing apparently simple dishes would have astounded Cheyne. And Cheyne regarded beef broth as more harmful than beef itself.

The main thrust of Marin's cookery was to offer a radical departure from the cookery of Bonnefons and the increasingly complex Baroque cookery that had followed: a nouvelle cuisine without the pointless elaboration of the earlier style. By the middle of the eighteenth century, simplicity and moderation in cookery, as in art and literature, was seen as a virtue in itself—a sign of good taste. Throughout Europe the Enlightenment reform of the table followed the French lead (not without the occasional local grumble of protest). The shift to this nouvelle cuisine, perfectly suited to salon conversation, is described thus by the Milanese nobleman-philosopher Pietro Verri:

The cookery is as delicate as it can possibly be; the food is all healthy and easy to digest; there is no ostentatious over-abundance but everything necessary to give satisfaction. Heavy or viscous meats, garlic, onions, strong spices, salted dishes, truffles and other such substances poisonous to human nature are totally proscribed from this table. Their place has mainly been taken by the meat of fowl and chickens, by green vegetables, by oranges and their juice. The flavours of these foods are exquisite but not strong... Such is our meal, which we round off with an excellent cup of coffee, satisfied, sated and not oppressed by the kind of course nourishment that only puts the mind to sleep

and spreads boredom throughout our company, which, indeed, quite
to the contrary, after our meals seems to revive with general mirth.[36]

The new elite taste for elegant simplicity was more apparent than real,
however. "It takes a thousand ingredients for every dish, which has the
taste of none of them," rued the abbé Pietro Chiari.[37] During the latter half
of the eighteenth century the impulse towards artifice and sophistication
ran as deep as the contrary desire to simplicity and naturalness.

Delicate foods required someone—indeed a small army of someones—
in the kitchen to prepare them. Diet, likewise, presupposed the material
possibility of making choices. Put these together and we have an inescap-
able aspect of writing on dietetics that had plagued the genre since its
Renaissance revival. "To read over some specious systems of diet," the
London physician William Black wrote in 1782, "one could only conclude
that they were written for those who had a coach and six at their doors,
and a French cook at their kitchens." Whilst the privileged in society had
the luxury of being able to take the dietary advice, at least to the extent that
they wished to, and shape their habits accordingly, everyone else "must rest
satisfied with the food which is cheapest and easiest procured."[38] In chasing
after the privileged, medicine had shirked its social duties.

The sign of a new trend, inspired by the reforming ideals of the European
Enlightenment, is evident in William Buchan's seminal *Domestic Medicine,*
first published in Edinburgh in 1769 and the most successful general guide
to health of the late eighteenth century, widely translated and frequently
reprinted. Buchan advocated a kind of holistic environmentalism, in which
the well-balanced body interacted with the surrounding environment, as
guided by prudence and moderation. Food suggestions abound. Buchan
poured scorn on the idle and luxury-loving rich for adopting a way of living that damaged their own health, their "fat carcase[s], over-run with diseases occasioned by inactivity," and was sympathetic toward the humble
conditions of the urban and rural poor. Indeed, Buchan added a chapter to
the 1797 edition, describing the diet of the poor, particularly in England,
and offering recommendations for its improvement.[39] If England's poor ate
badly, it was because they knew no better—not because eating such foods
was somehow in keeping with their constitutions, as would have been ar-

gued earlier in our period. At the century's end, Enlightenment medical reformers such as Buchan claimed to offer the poor a dietary choice.

The tension between abstinence and appetite continued to influence both medical and cookery writing. From their close fit in the sixteenth century, medicine and cookery had both changed considerably by the end of the eighteenth, to the point of being almost unrecognizable. The two become quite separate disciplines. However, if cookery jettisoned the heavy spices and balancing agents of the Renaissance, so too did physic; if cookery became keen on vegetables, so too did physic (eventually, at least, and then with a vengeance); and if cookery sought simplicity and naturalness as an ideal, so too did physic. Elite cookery and medicine continued to mirror one another, to follow similar trajectories, sometimes distant and discordant, sometimes intersecting and harmonized, but always in communication with one another.

## CHAPTER NINE

# Food Representations in Early Modern Europe: Powerful Appetites

BRIAN COWAN

## INTRODUCTION: FOOD, GENRE, AND HISTORY

The biological necessities of eating and drinking have always been fraught with intense moral and social anxieties, and these anxieties have often been reflected in the ways in which food and drink were represented. What was particularly new and distinctive about the representation of food and drink in the early modern era was that the period also witnessed the proliferation of different media for disseminating these representations.

The introduction of the printing press was perhaps the most important innovation, which enabled not only the wide scale reproduction of printed books, treatises, and pamphlets, but also the reproduction of artists' images through printed engravings. While historians continue to debate about just how revolutionary the so-called early modern printing revolution was, few would demur from acknowledging that the press introduced a substantial quantitative increase in the number of titles and works that were made available to consumers.[1] The press was not the only method used for large-scale reproduction of representations: many painters used collaborative workshop techniques to produce large numbers of paintings efficiently for a broad-based consumer market. Ad van der Woude has estimated that somewhere between 5 and 10 million paintings were produced in the Dutch Republic between 1580 and the end of the eighteenth century.[2]

This substantial quantitative increase in the numbers and kinds of early modern media had a qualitative effect on the representations of food conveyed through them. It enabled the rise of new genres of representations of food. By genre, I refer to a conventional mode of representation in which certain formal characteristics are shared that is heuristically useful for understanding the ways in which certain modes of representation were similar to, or distinct from, one another.[3] Although some contemporaries might recognize the emergence of a new genre as it appeared, this was rarely the case. More often than not, genres only become recognizable after the fact. While today an art historian might look at a Dutch painting of silver vessels and recognize it as a *pronkstilleven* (luxury still life), a seventeenth-century viewer would have been content to call it a painting of silver vessels.[4] This anachronism does not detract from the heuristic value of the generic term, nor should it prevent us from acknowledging that seventeenth-century Dutch painters developed certain conventions for representing items of luxury consumption in recognizably similar ways that can help us understand what both the makers and the partakers of such representations thought was interesting about these items.

In both the visual and verbal media of early modern Europe, a number of new genres of food representation emerged. In painting and printed images, the still-life and the genre scene developed as distinct genres of visual representation after the late sixteenth century. In the realm of written texts, innovation in genres such as the cookbook, and early or proto-gastronomic writing developed somewhat later, in the later seventeenth and eighteenth centuries.

Food was central to these new genres. They were works which sought to represent food and its consumption realistically, rather than works in which food served primarily as a symbol for something else. Attempts to define and explain realism have resulted in a scholarly minefield, particularly when used to explain major representational changes such as the efflorescence of golden-age Dutch painting or the supposed rise of the eighteenth-century novel.[5] I use the term here in a relative (and needless to say, a value-neutral) sense: when compared with earlier representations of food, the new, early modern genres were relatively more concerned with representing food and its consumption in a realistic way. These new seventeenth and eighteenth-century food genres valued verisimilitude: Dutch pictures drawn *naer het leven* or *from life* were praised; cookbooks were meant to serve as practical guides for replicating their recipes. Realistic detail and precision were therefore key to their representative strategies. Realism also drove sales; consumers who bought paintings, prints, and books wanted and valued the verisimilitude they found in the new food genres. Thus, realism can also be understood to reflect the preferences and desires of early modern society more generally: it is best understood as "a mode of representation embedded in a specific…culture, rather than as a period style encompassing a characteristic choice of subject matter."[6]

These new genres were not solely concerned with gustatory matters— some still-lives and many genre scenes did not feature food or eating, for example—but alimentary concerns were nevertheless very common, and in some cases essential to these new genres. These new genres enabled the development of new fields of discourse and debates about dietary matters. Questions regarding issues such as how to properly prepare food, how it should be eaten, and what foods were delicious or healthy to eat were now often (although not exclusively) construed and discussed through the conventions of these fields. While these concerns had always existed, and indeed remain with us today, they were structured within the generic contours of representation and the debates within the fields of discourse generated by these new genres.[7]

The new alimentary genres did not fit well into pre-existing generic categories of early modern Europe, and thus their arrival on the scene was not immediately recognized. When it was, they were often disparaged. Despite their popularity with the purchasing public, genre scenes and still-life pictures were hardly recognized as valuable genres of painting until the eighteenth century, and even then they were always considered to be second-rate productions, especially when compared to the top-notch genre of history painting.[8] Gérard de Lairesse, one of the first art connoisseurs to recognize still-life painting, remarked in his *Groote Schilderboek* (1707) that still-lives of flowers were "the most choice," whereas "for cabbages, carrots, and turnips, as likewise codfish, salmon, herrings, smelts and such-like (which are poor and mean ornaments and not worthy of any apartment) he who is pleased with them may seek them in the markets."[9]

The situation with regard to the written word was perhaps even worse. Cookbooks have never really been recognized as an important genre of writing, despite the fact that they have remained bestsellers ever since at least the later seventeenth century. They have more often been studied by historians or sociologists than by literary critics.[10] Gastronomy emerged as a potentially promising new philosophy of food in the long eighteenth century, but its early promise was never fulfilled, notwithstanding Charles Perrault's recognition in his *Parallèle des Anciens et des Modernes* (1688–1696) that the "art of cooking" should be considered to be a form of modern science; nor did the remarkable notoriety accorded to post-revolutionary writers such as Grimod de la Reynière or Jean-Anthelme Brillat Savarin manage to elevate the status of food writing in the literary field as high as these gastronomers desired.[11] Although food writing gained increased prominence and cultural value over time, particularly in Francophone literary culture, it has never succeeded in becoming recognized as an elite genre on par with say, the novel, poetry, drama, or history.[12]

## FOOD IMAGERY: THE EMERGENCE OF STILL LIVES AND GENRE SCENES

Art historians have noticed that visual representations of food were transformed dramatically over the course of the sixteenth century.[13] For example, Kenneth Bendiner notes that whereas "in the fifteenth century food in art remained incidental to larger narratives," it was only in the sixteenth century that "food first became important" and the practice of food painting really took off only in the seventeenth century, especially with the work of Netherlandish still-life painting.[14] Sheila McTighe points out that northern Italian painters such as Vincenzo Campi (c. 1536–1591), Bartolomeo Passarotti (1529–1592), and Annibale Carracci (1560–1609) began to present images of food vendors such as butchers, fishmongers, and poultry sellers, as well as eaters in their genre paintings of the 1580s.[15] More generally, Elizabeth Honig has observed: "In almost every part of western

Europe, from Spain and Italy in the south to Germany and the Netherlands in the north, there arose at roughly the same time, around 1600, a strong and enduring practice of the pictorial representation of objects."[16] Among the most popular objects represented by these visual artists were foodstuffs, food markets, tableware, and table settings.[17]

Whereas late medieval images of food tended to subsume food into a larger narrative, and more often than not, a religious narrative, early modern artists began to delight in the representation of food as a subject and topic for study in its own right. These more traditional representative techniques did not disappear in the early modern era. The temptation of Adam and Eve by the forbidden fruit in the Garden of Eden remained a favorite theme in both art and literature, as did Biblical narratives such as the marriage at Cana, or Christ's Last Supper.[18] While food was important to these narratives, it could hardly be argued that they were works whose main subject was eating. The Fall and the Eucharist were central elements of Christian theology in which the forbidden fruit or the bread and wine were part of a much more important soteriological narrative.

Food could also figure prominently in secular narratives with moral themes. Consider, for example, Pieter Bruegel's (c. 1520–1569) famous rendition of the land of Cockaigne (figure 9.1). Four characters dominate this image: a knight who sits under a canopy covered with pancakes that slide from the roof to his mouth, and three men, a knight, a peasant, and a clerk, lying under a tree where various foods come to them fully prepared and ready to be eaten. The whole fantastic scene is based on the common medieval fantasy land of Cockaigne, "lubberland," or *luilekkerland,* where "they eat and drink the livelong day, And no one has to pay."[19] This is obviously a picture about food and the escapist fantasy of being able to eat without working for it. It makes no attempt, however, to portray food realistically. Its impact lies precisely in its fantastic representations of foods. The pig and the fowl have slain themselves, and even an egg has grown legs and offers itself up to be eaten without complaint. The picture's precise message remains ambiguous: Bruegel could be mocking the foolishness of those who really believe in a free lunch or he could be offering his viewers just this sort of escapist fantasy.[20] Either way, Bruegel's representation of food here, and indeed in most of his other well-known, food-oriented works such as the *Battle Between Carnival and Lent* (Kunsthistorisches

FIGURE 9.1: Attributed to Pieter van der Heyden (c. 1530–c. 1572), after Pieter Bruegel the Elder (c. 1525–1569), "The Land of Cockaigne" (1567–1569), engraving. British Museum, AN62108001; Dept. of Prints and Drawings, registration no. 1866,0407.21. 205mm x 275mm. © Trustees of the British Museum.

Museum, Vienna, 1559), his engraved satire on gluttony, "Gula" (1558), or his images of the "Fat kitchen" and the "Lean kitchen" (1563), is part of an exaggerated, sometimes fantastic, commentary about the contrasts between want and plenty, and the idleness or industriousness that lead to one or the other (figures 9.2, 9.3, and 9.4). This tradition would not die. Bruegel's works were reprinted again and again over the course of the seventeenth century, and some see William Hogarth's moralized 1751 pairing of Beer Street and Gin Alley as a late contribution to the genre, although Hogarth's works did adopt a relatively more realist technique.[21]

The emergence of a new way of representing food images can be observed in the growing popularity amongst late-sixteenth-century artists of creating compositions that combined traditional biblical scenes with realistic still-lives or genre scenes. The practice was prominent in the work of the late-sixteenth-century Antwerp artists Pieter Aertsen (1508–1575)

FIGURE 9.2: Pieter van der Heyden (1538–1572), after Pieter Bruegel the Elder, "Gula/ Gluttony" (Hieronymus Cock, 1558), engraving. British Museum, AN62097001, registration no. 1880,0710.638. 223mm x 294mm. © Trustees of the British Museum.

and his nephew Joachim Beuckelaer (1533–1574), and it was often imitated by other artists of the late sixteenth and early seventeenth centuries from the Spaniard Diego de Velázquez (1599–1660), and the Venetian painters Jacopo (1510/18–1592) and Francesco Bassano (1549–1592).[22] The Bassanos' paintings of the 1560s and 1570s included several kitchen scenes, which dominated compositions with biblical subjects such as the story of Lazarus and the rich man, or Christ's visit to the house of Martha and Mary.[23]

It would be extremely reductionist to interpret these images as just an excuse for the painter to indulge in representing "the Rabelasian pleasure of troweling on great heaps of comestible matter," for much of the power of these pictures lies in the way in which they juxtapose moral messages about the dangers of excessive consumption, such as that contained in the Biblical story of the rich man and Lazarus with the over-abundant display of luxurious edibles, along with the suggestion of sexual impropriety as

FIGURE 9.3: Pieter van der Heyden, after Pieter Bruegel the Elder, "The Fat Kitchen" (Johannes Galle, 1625–1670; originally by Hieronymus Cock, 1563), engraving. British Museum, AN62116001, registration no. 1868,0822.653. 221mm x 288mm. © Trustees of the British Museum.

well.[24] However, it is striking just how prominently the images of foodstuffs and kitchen work take centre stage in these images. It has been argued that many mannerist compositions of the age often deliberately relegate their "main event to a secondary place," such as in Andrea Boscoli's (c. 1560– 1607) drawing of Christ's Supper with his disciples at Emmaus, in which the kitchen scene also dominates, but it is unclear in these cases which aspect, the biblical or the gustatory, is really the main event.[25] So while it would be overly simplistic to claim that these works were only about food, it would be equally absurd to deny that they were *not* works in which food figures prominently as a subject.

The practice of juxtaposing biblical narratives with genre scenes or still-life images did not survive long into the seventeenth century. It is tempting to attribute this change to an inevitable generic telos in which the highly

FIGURE 9.4: Pieter van der Heyden, after Pieter Bruegel the Elder, "The Lean Kitchen" (Theodor Galle, 1610–1630; original by Hieronymus Cock, 1563), engraving. British Museum, AN62109001, registration no. 1868,0822.652. 223mm x 282mm. © Trustees of the British Museum.

descriptive work of artists such as Aertson and Beuckelaer ultimately laid the groundwork for the emergence and ultimate triumph of *true* still-life painting such as that of their fellow Antwerper, Frans Snyders (1579–1657) and later golden-age still-life painters, but this too would be overly simplistic. Still-life painting emerged in several national contexts around the turn of the seventeenth century, often without the peculiar so-called intermediate stage of juxtaposed compositions that one finds in the development of Flemish still-life paintings.[26]

Still-life pictures of foods and genre paintings of kitchen work and eating flourished in the seventeenth and eighteenth centuries. One of the most striking discoveries in recent scholarship on both genres has been the recognition that they demonstrate an awareness of the dietary recommendations found in early modern medical and dietetic literature. The meanings of early modern food imagery can be illuminated through an understanding

FIGURE 9.5: Jacob Matham after Peter Aertsen, "Kitchen Scene with the Rich Man and Lazarus" (Haarlem, 1603), engraving. British Museum, AN57476001; Department of Prints and Drawings, registration no. 1856,0209.291. 233mm (cut) x 330mm. © Trustees of the British Museum.

of contemporary food writing. Julie Berger Hochstrasser has compared the images of food in seventeenth-century Dutch still-life paintings in a way which "reveals countless points on which the laid tables of Dutch still life, for all their picturesque disarray, prove consistent with the rules of proper diet" articulated in the medical literature of the day.[27] Similarly, Sheila McTighe has demonstrated the extensive influence of Bartolomeo Pisanelli's (fl. 1559–1583) often republished natural history treatise of food and drink, the *Trattato della natura de' cibi et del bere* (1583) on the representation of foods in late Renaissance Italian genre paintings by artists such as Vincenzo Campi, Bartolomeo Passarotti, *and* Annibale Caracci.[28] These art historical studies fit well with the historian Ken Albala's conclusion upon an extensive reading of Renaissance dietetic literature that the social connotations of food became far more extensively considered in the sixteenth century than they had been previously, and "in the seventeenth century constitute an obsession."[29]

FIGURE 9.6: Jan Sadeler I (1550–1600?), after Jacopo Bassano (1510–1592), "Kitchen Scene with Lazarus, c. 1598", engraving. British Museum, AN446912001, Department of Prints and Drawings, registration no. W,9.131. 239mm x 298mm. © Trustees of the British Museum.

The convergence between early modern dietetic advice and visual representations of food and eating can help make sense of images such as Gerard van Honthorst's painting of a fashionable, early seventeenth-century ham-eater (figure 9.7), or Bernard Picart's rendering of an earlier and anonymous painter from the northern Italian school of Vicenzo Campi's image of a lentil-eating man next to a woman and a baby (figure 9.8).

Dried or cured meats, such as hams or sausages, were a food that transcended the traditional barriers of social class: while fresh meat was normally only affordable to social elites, preserved meat was still accessible to all, although presumably only on restricted occasions for the less well off.[30] Honthorst's ham-eater is also hard to place in the social order: his dress is neither ornate nor abject, although it is far too modest to be that of a wealthy merchant or nobleman, yet his feathered hat adds a touch of fashionability

FIGURE 9.7: Cornelis Bloemaert (1603?-84), after Gerard van Honthorst (1590–1656), "The Ham Eater" (1625), engraving. British Museum, AN454569001, registration no. 1868,0612.1388. 211mm x 156mm. Painted version: 8128mm x 6350mm. © Trustees of the British Museum.

that elevates him above a common laborer or peasant. The epigram at the bottom of the print reads: *Ick ben gesont, daer toe wat graeg / Dit syn recht pillen voor myn maeg,* or "I am healthy, that's what makes me happy. These are the right pills for my stomach." The connection between diet and health is made explicit here. It is less clear whether Honthort's image was designed to approve of, or criticize, his subject's proclaimed belief that eating ham kept him healthy. Early modern dieticians discouraged regular pork consumption and many warned against eating too much.[31]

The Campi School image of a lentil-eater is less ambiguous, for early modern dieticians were less equivocal about the social status and dietary value of beans: they were increasingly associated with the lower classes, especially peasants, and like the lower orders themselves, beans were coarse, rough,

FIGURE 9.8: Bernard Picart (1673–1733) after a late sixteenth-century painting from the school of Vincenzo Campi, "Le mangeur de lentille" (c. 1725–1733), etching, plate 55 of *Impostures innocentes* (Amsterdam, 1734). British Museum, AN561268001, registration no. 1861,1109.797. 172mm x 134mm. Painted version: 815mm x 625mm. © Trustees of the British Museum.

and fecund.[32] *Windy* foods that were prone to cause flatulence were also considered to have aphrodisiac effects as the gasses they produced diffused throughout the body, but especially towards extremities such as the genital organs.[33] In this picture, the lentil-eater's sexual prowess is emphasized again and again. If the smiling face of the woman next to him and the healthy baby on her lap were not clues enough, the wine, cheese, and garlic on the table, all of which were foods also associated with aphrodisiac effects, along with other sexualized symbols such as the cat and the bed-warming pan at the bottom of the image, all reinforce the same association between the lentil-eater and his lusty fertility.[34] The message expressed subtly in Carracci's *Bean Eater* painting (c. 1580–1590) is made explicit in this work.[35]

Although both pictures are no less normative than Bruegel's food imagery—both works seek to draw connections between good diet, good health, and good behavior—they diverge from Bruegel in their realism. While neither composition purports to represent a precisely lifelike scene from daily life, they do present images of realistic individuals engaged in activities which could be plausibly imagined by any contemporary witness. In their invocation of early modern dietetic dictates, these genre scenes also strive towards an even greater realism insofar as they attempt to present medical knowledge in a visual form.

Perhaps the best known and most striking form of early modern visual realism, however, is the still life. Emerging as a distinctive genre in the later sixteenth century, still-life painting came into its own as an established,

FIGURE 9.9: Robert Robinson (1674–1706 fl.), "*pronkstilleven* with fish, fruit and fowl" (1674–1706), mezzotint. British Museum, AN217501001, registration no. 1876,1111.58; 246mm x 193mm. © Trustees of the British Museum.

albeit sometimes slighted, genre in the seventeenth and eighteenth centuries.[36] Still-life pictures can be interpreted in a number of ways. They can be seen as complex texts filled with emblematic objects that demand to be read as something more than they first appear, as reflections on, and celebrations of the artist's ability to mirror reality, and as a product of the dramatic expansion of overseas trade and domestic consumption which began in early modern northwestern Europe. All of these readings are valuable, but none can overshadow the obvious fact that the vast majority of early modern still-life paintings represent images of food and drink, and that the most common setting for these compositions is the table. Still-life painters devoted an inordinate amount of their artistic effort to representing the minute details and visual beauty of edible foodstuffs and drinks. Given their subject matter, most still-life pictures could not help but be pictures about food first and foremost (figure 9.9).[37]

## EARLY MODERN FOOD WRITING: THE EFFLORESCENCE OF THE COOKBOOK

New genres of food writing took longer to develop than the innovations of still-life and genre pictures did in the visual media of the era. The widespread expansion of the printing press did not make an immediate impact on the development of new genres of culinary writing in the sixteenth and early seventeenth centuries. Many of the first printed works of cookery were copies of editions of well-known late medieval manuscripts such as the fourteenth-century *Le Viander* of Taillevant, which was first published in 1486. Bartolomeo Sacchi (1421–1481), better known as Platina, published his well-known dietetic manual and cookbook *De Honesta Voluptate et Valetudine* (c. 1470) based on the manuscript work of Martino of Como. The first cook books designed originally for print were published mostly in Italy and in England, but the numbers of new works produced are not impressive.[38] There were perhaps 139 different manuscript texts of cookery extent before the advent of print, whereas during the long sixteenth century from 1485 to 1620, only 29 new titles appeared. Although these works were often reprinted—at least 224 new editions were printed in 9 different European vernaculars—they did not initiate the flurry of imitators and detractors that later French and English books would stimulate.[39]

The food writing of the Renaissance remained on the whole quite conservative, and its main concern was dietetics—food writers were obsessed with explaining how to maintain a healthy diet that reconciled the medical knowledge of classical humanism with the expanding consumption possibilities opened up by the discovery of new worlds (and new foods) overseas, and the expansion of international trade more generally.[40]

The real generic innovations in food writing began in the mid-seventeenth century in France and in England when a number of innovative new publications began to appear. François Pierre (c. 1618–1678), best known by his pen name *La Varenne,* published his enormously influential *Le Cuisinier François* in 1651, and it was an immediate international best seller. An English translation appeared just two years later in 1653; a German edition was published in Hamburg in 1665 and an Italian book appeared in Bologna around 1670, which falsely purported to be a translation.[41] Including translations such as these, the work received at least forty-one different editions throughout the rest of the seventeenth century. It went through another ten editions in the eighteenth century, eight of which were published before 1750.[42]

La Varenne's work has been dubbed revolutionary by many culinary historians because he was relatively unconcerned with the dietetic aspect of cooking. Although his publisher, Pierre David, claimed that the book "aims only at keeping and maintaining a good, well-balanced state of health," La Varenne's work lacked the moralizing tone and references to classical authorities that were so common and distinctive of Renaissance food writing.[43] The kind of cooking he advocated also differed from earlier tastes: his recipes did not call for the heavy use of spices and strong flavors. He instead preferred to emphasize the natural flavors of the foods that a cook prepared, and to accentuate these tastes with rich sauces (more often than not butter or lard based) that created what he dubbed a *ragoust.*[44] One can call this new style of cooking a sort of culinary realism, and it would prove to be as central to subsequent European cuisine as literary realism would be in fictional genres such as the eighteenth-century novel.

La Varenne's *Cuisinier François* is also notable for its revolutionary new forms of presenting food writing. The title itself lent itself to a double meaning, as it could be understood to mean either "the cook (named) François" or else the more common translation "the French cook." The book referred to both its author and his nationality. La Varenne frequently refers to himself in the first person and his prose lends the text a distinctive and cohesive style.[45] His work and his pen name also came to represent French cooking to the rest of Europe as well, especially in its foreign translations.

Just as importantly, La Varenne's success established his work as an icon for a successful and influential cookbook writer. His book was not only reprinted and imitated, but it was also the object of critical attention for decades. The Marquise de Sablé (1599–1678), who claimed that no one's taste was as refined as her own, was known to rail publicly against La Varenne's cookery within years after the publication of his book, and her views would be repeated again and again by later commentators.[46] Perhaps most famously, La Varenne was denounced by the author of a later cookbook, *L'Art de Bien Traiter* (1674), known only by his initials L.S.R., who thought that La Varenne had imposed for too long upon "a foolish and ignorant populace by passing off his productions as infallible truths and doctrines in culinary matters approved throughout the world." Although even L.S.R. quickly admitted that "there are general rules," La Varenne's book contained "hardly any chapters where one cannot find bad taste, confusion and intolerable faults." The substance of L.S.R.'s criticism was that La Varenne had not gone far enough to purge his cuisine of old-fashioned, Arabic-style spices and vulgar artifice and did not emphasize enough the "exquisite choice of meats, the finesse of their seasoning," and the "politeness and propriety of their service."[47]

Despite, or even due to the criticism leveled against him, La Varenne and his writings reinvigorated food writing both in France, and in Europe more generally. After La Varenne, France would become the undisputed centre of European food writing, and henceforth the arbiter of culinary good taste throughout the continent and even beyond. Forty-four new cookery titles would be published by French authors in the later seventeenth and eighteenth centuries. If one counts the numbers of editions, the figures are even more impressive: at least 230 new editions were published in French between 1650 and 1789.[48] Only Great Britain could rival French production in cookery titles. The highly developed British print trade managed to produce 168 new cookery titles and 374 reprinted editions between 1650 and 1800.[49]

Despite their greater output, British writers struggled to contend against an enduring presumption of French hegemony in matters of good taste: few English works on cookery were translated into French, but many French culinary writings were eagerly translated into English from La Varenne

onward. One major exception proves the rule: the French chef Vincent
La Chapelle, who had been employed in London by Philip Stanhope, the
Fourth Earl of Chesterfield, first published his book *The Modern Cook* in
English in 1733 and it was later translated into French in 1735. As with
L.S.R., La Chapelle began his work by denigrating that of a predecessor,
François Massialot (1660–1733), whose *Le Cuisinier Roïal et Bourgeois*
(1698) had been published in many editions and had also been translated
into English. Although nearly one-third of La Chapelle's recipes were borrowed from Massialot, he felt compelled to distinguish his own work from
that of earlier writers.[50] By the eighteenth century, food writing had become
a competitive domain and every new author had to stake out a claim to
originality and superiority.[51]

A robust culinary discourse thus emerged in late-seventeenth-century
Europe, with its cultural capital in Paris.[52] Even when food writers wrote
in their vernaculars, the vocabulary for discussing food and cooking was
almost always French. Beginning with La Varenne's table of "hard and
strange words," many English works included a glossary of French cooking terms for their readers.[53] French hegemony in this new field of culinary
writing mirrored similar developments in other fields of literature and culture in which the lingua franca replaced Latin and became a commonly
accepted medium for polite communication amongst European elites.[54]
French cooking, like the manners of the French court, the French language,
and French fashions, became the standard for polite society throughout
old-regime Europe.[55] In the works of French food writers, their haute cuisine was presented to the world as both cosmopolitan and universal, yet it
was also undeniably a national cuisine.[56]

There were nationalist reactions to the hegemony of French haute cuisine.[57] Hannah Glasse's 1747 exhortation that "so much is the blind folly
of this age, that they would rather be imposed on by a French booby, than
give encouragement to a good English cook" was a typical expression of
English frustration with the continued dominance of French taste in the culinary domain. However, even Glasse's work contained a number of French
recipes and she drew heavily on the work of preceding French cookery
writers such as Massialot and La Chapelle, although almost entirely at
second- or third-hand and in translation.[58] The writer Giambattista Roberti
(1719–1786) complained that his Italian contemporaries all agreed that the

only good cooks were French cooks, "or at the very least Piedmontese."
The first Italian cookery book of the long eighteenth century was *Il Cuoco
Piemontese Perfezionato a Parigi* (Turin, 1766), or "the Piedmontese cook
made perfect in Paris."[59] The culinary hegemony of French haute cuisine
that was achieved during the reign of Louis XIV has persisted to a certain
degree to the present day, although its position today is more precarious
than ever and it may not survive for much longer.[60]

## CONCLUSION: REALISM AND POWER

Power also shaped the representations of food in early modern Europe.[61]
The media revolutions of the age, and particularly the rise of the printing
press and commercial art markets, offered new venues for the production,
sale, and consumption of these representations, and they allowed for the
widespread reproduction and dissemination of these works to a broader
audience. The new realist genres of food representation such as still-life and
genre pictures, as well as cookbook writing were no less moralistic, or less
partisan for all of their realistic detail. If anything, the proliferation of these
representations only served to exacerbate and to exaggerate the national or
class prejudices of their creators.

Food and eating gained a greater prominence in the early modern media
than they had ever had before. Despite the centrality of food to the new
genres of early modernity, it was never autonomous from the larger con-
figurations of state power, wealth, and class privilege. Netherlandish food
imagery flourished during the golden age of Dutch commerce in the seventeenth century; where Renaissance Italian food writing had once been
preeminent, it was increasingly eclipsed by the French haute cuisine, which
came to dominate European culture during the *âge classique* of Louis XIV
and his Bourbon successors; British writers and artists borrowed freely
from all of these traditions, and supplemented them with their own domestic and imperial influences. Throughout Europe, the impulse to distinguish
between local, popular eating habits and cosmopolitan, elite cuisines became stronger, although a clear and fast distinction was never possible to
maintain. The media revolutions and generic innovations of early modernity could not satiate the powerful appetites of the age, but they did shape
their representations.

## CHAPTER TEN

# World Developments: The Early Modern Age

FABIO PARASECOLI

The previous chapters in this volume have illustrated many aspects of food culture during the so-called Age of Enlightenment in Western Europe and the new colonies in the Americas. This chapter does not claim to offer new insights based on original material, but it is rather an overview of the research on the products, food-related behaviors and concepts, economic and productive dynamics, techniques, and social structures in other parts of the world during the same period. The material is organized around the areas that played a relevant role at the time and interacted systematically with the emerging Western states.

## THE BIOLOGICAL EXPANSION
## OF THE WESTERN EMPIRES

The period following the appearance of Western European powers in the Indian Ocean and in the Americas saw the expansion of empires that were mostly based on the production, the control, and the trade of valuable commodities: gold from Mexico, silver from Peru and Bolivia, spices from Eastern Asia, and a new category of stimulant substances that could be smoked, drunk, or eaten, destined to turn into the most valuable global commodities. However, at least initially, many of these crops constituted natural monopolies. China, for instance, was the sole producer of tea, while cocoa originally grew only in Mexico, Central America, and the Amazon basin, coffee in Yemen, coca in the Andes, and tobacco in the Americas.

To avoid the hurdles connected with these natural monopolies, the burgeoning European empires focused on transferring those cultivations to their own colonies. The new scientific approach to nature that was changing European mentalities proved to be the perfect partner of imperial expansion. In fact, great efforts were dedicated to studying tropical and exotic crops not only in their natural habitats, but also in botanical gardens, where seeds and young plants were nurtured to then be redistributed across far-flung territories in the hope that they would adapt and expand.[1]

Some of these plants did not require much to prosper in the new environments. Sugarcane, for instance, introduced by the Spaniards to Caribbean islands, was planted by the Dutch in the northeast of Brazil in the short period in which they controlled those territories at the beginning of the seventeenth century, and then transferred to the French and English islands, in particular Jamaica, Trinidad, Martinique, and Guadeloupe. While initially sugarcane was grown by European small-holders and indentured servants, over time the possibility of enormous revenues favored the establishment of large plantations, modeled on the Spanish and Portuguese cultivations in the Azores and Cape Verde Islands, manned by large numbers of African slaves in a production system that was highly organized, time-sensitive, and requiring relevant investment of capital.[2]

Traditional spices were introduced in the New World to break the East Asian monopolies, which had caused excesses such as the 1621 massacres in the Bandas Islands by the Dutch *Vereenigde Oost-Indische Compagnie* (VOC; East India Company) to maintain control over the production of nutmeg.[3] Over time, Grenada became a major provider of cloves and nutmeg, while the French introduced pepper in Mauritius, Réunion, and French Guyana. While cacao originally grew only in Mesoamerica and in the upper Amazon basin, once it became a highly demanded product the Spaniards, who had a monopoly on it, expanded the cultivation to Venezuela, Brazil (under Spanish control in the first half of the seventeenth century), and the Philippines. The Dutch then transferred seeds from Venezuela to Curaçao in 1634, thus breaking the Spanish monopoly.[4] The French introduced the plant to their Caribbean islands, while the Dutch brought it to Ceylon and Indonesia. Over time, the cultivation also spread to West and Central Africa.[5] In this period, tea remained a Chinese monopoly. The Portuguese first got acquainted with the drink when they encroached on the Indian Ocean trade routes, followed by the British, the French, and the Dutch. However, it is not until the eighteenth century that European demand grew to the point that the Chinese monopoly came to be perceived as a hurdle to free commerce, so much so that the situation eventually led to a series of devastating wars in the nineteenth century.[6]

Coffee, in its Arabica variety, had been domesticated in Ethiopia and brought to Yemen, from where it acquired cultural relevance among increasingly larger strata of the population in Western Asia.[7] The drink, consumed hot, unsweetened, and dense, was sold under a tight monopoly controlled by the Indian and Arab traders in the Yemeni port of Mocha.[8] All over the Ottoman Empire, coffee drinking became associated with consumption in public places where men could gather and discuss current matters, to the point that coffee houses were at times considered as suspect—as possible hotbeds of sedition.[9] From the seventeenth century, the presence of Ottoman diplomats and merchants also made the drink popular in Europe. As demand grew, the Dutch managed to introduce some plants to Ceylon and Java, and to bring coffee plants to the Amsterdam Botanical Gardens in 1706. From there, the French transferred the crop to Martinique, Haiti, and French Guyana, from where it spread to Brazil, thus eliminating the remnants of the Ottoman monopoly by the end of the eighteenth century.[10]

Other plants were transferred not because of their commercial value, but because of their potential as a source of nourishment. This is the case for the breadfruit, the high-yielding tree in the mulberry family, with a single plant producing more than 150 fruits per season. Rich in starch and used as a staple, either roasted or baked, in 1789 it was famously brought from Tahiti (recently discovered in 1767) to the Caribbean by Captain William Bligh in order to feed the slaves, in spite of the fact that the local crops would have provided enough sustenance if they had been taken into consideration by the plantation owners.[11]

## THE AMERICAS

The areas that felt the most widespread consequences of the political and biological expansion of the Western empires were the new American colonies. The disappearance of the natives, decimated by the diseases carried by the Europeans, often contracted before any direct contact—as in the aftermath of the 1539–1542 expedition of Hernando De Soto into North America (whose pigs also introduced diseases in areas that were not explored by the Spaniards)—deeply affected ecosystems and food production all over the Americas.[12]

In North America, due to the lack of containment through fire that had been applied by the native populations, forests occupied areas previously kept open for hunting and agriculture. However, the plains were still so extensive that European horses and cattle, introduced by the first explorers as a source of food, tallow, and hides, had gone wild and expanded, both towards the pampas of Argentine and Uruguay, and into the prairies from Mexico to Canada, where the bison also thrived because of the lack of human predators. By the time they actually met the colonizers, the tribes living in the Great Plains such as the Sioux, the Barefoot, and the Cheyenne had already adopted the horse as their main means of transportation and had become bison hunters.[13] The Europeans would often describe the native males as shifty and lazy, only concerned with hunting, fishing, and fighting while the women toiled to produce, gather, and cook food. However, this negative perception was probably connected to the fact that in the Old World hunting was mostly a leisurely activity for the upper classes and did not constitute a way of living.

After the short-lived attempt by Ponce de León to create an outpost in Florida between 1513 and 1521, in 1565 Pedro Menéndez de Avilés founded the Spanish colony of St Augustine, also in Florida. Long-lasting settlements of Europeans in North America developed at a later date compared to the ones in the Southern continent. After Queen Elizabeth I chartered the East India Company in 1600, in 1606 James I of England granted a charter to the Virginia Company to establish a colony in the Mid-Atlantic called Virginia. This was to be controlled directly by investors in England, supposedly to spread Christianity, but in fact it was a commercial enterprise, with incentives such as monopolies on trading rights. In 1607 the first colonists from England settled in Jamestown. As tobacco soon became the crop of choice, grown following the plantation model that was already successful in the Caribbean colonies, slaves were brought over to work the fields. Only from the end of the seventeenth century did local colonists switch sizable parts of their land to the cultivation of wheat, hemp, and flax. However, outside the larger estates, farming was often devoted to pure self-sufficiency, especially among the European farmers who were brought over at first as indentured servants and later turned independent.

Further south, the agricultural product that quickly assumed a fundamental importance for Georgia and the Carolinas, settled at the end of the seventeenth century, was rice, especially the variety known as Carolina Gold.[14] The soils near the coast, often occupied by lagoons and freshwater marshes, were suitable for its cultivation. Slaves from the coastal areas of West Africa and the Gulf of Guinea, traditionally rice farmers, brought with them experience and techniques that allowed for the growing of rice in areas very close to salt water.[15] Although the crop lost its relevance from the nineteenth century, rice is still the main ingredient in traditional dishes such as Hoppin' John (with beans and salt pork). In Louisiana, too, where New Orleans was founded in 1718 as a form of publicity stunt to raise money for a new colony that was supposed to thrive on sugarcane plantations, rice still plays an important role in specialities such as gumbo (a soup with okra and other ingredients such as shrimp and andouille sausage) and jambalaya (meat cooked with vegetables and often with tomatoes).

The cuisine that developed in the southern English colonies initially grew out of the combination of the material culture of the natives with the legacy of the new immigrants. The various local tribes instructed the settlers in the use of raw materials and cooking techniques unknown to them. The extensive use of corn was reflected in the popularity of cornbread and grits. The list of crops whose production the colonists borrowed from the local tribes is impressive. Pumpkins, beans, other local vegetables, and berries were consumed with game, opossum, and various types of fish, and oysters. For their part, settlers introduced European cooking techniques and pork, which over time became the most important source of meat in the south. With the increasing presence of black slaves from Africa, new ingredients such as okra, black-eye peas, collard greens, and yams enriched southern cuisine.[16] Many of the enslaved blacks had spent long periods in the Caribbean colonies, where they probably absorbed some elements of the local cuisines, spicy and full of flavor, and learned to use products from the Spanish colonies such as tomatoes, peanuts, and sweet potatoes.

In the northern areas of the continent, Samuel de Champlain founded Quebec, the capital of the French colony of New France, in 1608, while one year later Henry Hudson, sent by the Dutch, discovered the river that was named after him, and the Dutch started settling on Manhattan Island. The French expanded their control over the Great Lakes, and from there, following the Mississippi and the Ohio rivers they reached the Gulf of Mexico, where they encountered the Spanish expansion north of Mexico that reached from Louisiana all the way to today's California.

In 1620 a group of English religious dissenters, often referred to as the Pilgrim Fathers, landed in Plymouth and laid the basis for the future Commonwealth of Massachusetts. Since they arrived in late fall, by spring many of them were starving: they were not farmers, and the wheat and rye they had brought from England could not grant high yields under the new conditions. Over time, the colonists learned from the local natives how to grow and cook the local products, mainly maize, beans, and squash, but also berries, seafood, fish, game, and venison. Many cooking techniques were also borrowed from the natives, including pit cooking and barbecuing. A local cuisine soon developed, with dishes such as baked beans and chowder, a stew that often included cream, bacon, and seafood. Due to the limited productivity of agriculture, fishing—especially cod—acquired increasing economic relevance, especially in the cold season. By the end of the century, the Massachusetts colonists were importing salt, first from Spain and then from the Caribbean, to cure the cod that they sold in the West Indies, where plantation owners used it as an important ingredient for the slaves' nutrition. In exchange, the traders bought molasses that spurred the production of rum in many of the northern colonies, which thrived thanks to the noticeable local consumption and to the development of public spaces of sociability such as taverns.[17]

After the Civil War, which disrupted the trade between England and the Americas, Oliver Cromwell issued the Act of Navigation in 1651, which reaffirmed the British monopoly on the commerce with its colonies, including commodities such as tobacco and sugar. The act jeopardized the commercial exchanges between the English colonies and the Low Countries, causing a war that England won in 1654 that ensured its possession of New Amsterdam (from then on New York) and Jamaica. Protected by the imperial system, the colonies prospered, especially when in the eighteenth century the demand for rice and wheat increased as a consequence of European population growth, which allowed the colonists to boost their participation in the transatlantic trade and in the exchanges with the Caribbean (including non-English colonies).[18] The English Crown did not exert much control over these trade routes until 1733, when it decided to impose heavy import duties over molasses, also to profit from the growing rum industries in the colonies. To deal with the debt it had incurred during the Seven Years' War, in 1764 the Crown imposed stricter enforcement on the taxes levied on molasses, and new import duties on Madeira, thus hoping to push colonists to increase their consumption of port, whose commerce was controlled by English merchants. The following year, England introduced the first direct tax on the colonists through the Stamp Act, which was soon replaced by the Townshend Acts, a series of laws that imposed import duties on some items, including tea, which had become a popular beverage in the colonies, and a visible element in the burgeoning consumer culture that provided colonists with status and comfort. As a matter of fact, it has been suggested that precisely the English attempt to deprive colonists of their consumer goods was, together with economic and political issues, at the root of the revolution.[19] Tea became the symbolic focus of the first act of rebellion against the Crown with the Boston Tea Party in 1773. As a reaction, in 1775 the English Parliament passed the Restraining Act, which precluded New England fishermen from access to the North Atlantic cod fisheries, while leaving them open for the fishermen of Nova Scotia and Newfoundland, which remained faithful to the Crown.[20] The following years saw the colonists' rebellion turn into a full-fledged revolution that also exerted a powerful ideological influence across the Atlantic.

In South America, the presence of the Spaniards and the Portuguese led to the development of cuisines that adopted and appropriated ingredients and techniques from the local cultures, but also maintained many features of the Old World foodways. In fact, European crops such as wheat thrived in northern Mexico, although adopted skeptically by local populations, while olive trees and vineyards did better in Peru and California.[21] Furthermore, culinary customs connected with Christianity and its ceremonies, considered inherently superior, were imposed as a way for the natives to reach salvation. European foodways and ingredients also penetrated in the areas with higher concentrations of native people, signifying prestige and a superior social status.[22] As much as they wanted to distance themselves from the natives by displaying conspicuous consumption and by sticking to bread and wine, for instance, instead of maize, potatoes, *pulque,* and *chica,* the

Creole upper classes adopted a hybrid material culture that expressed itself in dishes such as mole.[23] At the same time, the African slaves developed their own distinctive cuisines, with specialities that still survive, such as the Peruvians' *antichucos* (beef-heart skewers), the Caribbean *callalloos* (soups with taro leaves and other greens), and the Brazilian *moquecas* (coconut-milk stews seasoned with palm oil).

## AFRICA

At the beginning of the European explorations in the fifteenth century, Africa had been considered as a source of gold and other luxury items, and secondarily, especially in the case of Egypt and the East Africa Coast, as a trade relay for the spices from the Far East. The climate and tropical diseases constituted a very strong deterrent to direct control of the hinterland.

The Europeans limited their presence to coastal trading posts where the slaves were brought from the interior and foreigners sold their merchandise, very often as advances for future deliveries of slaves. However, with the boom of plantation agriculture in the New World in the seventeenth and eighteenth centuries, Africa's manpower became the main commodity. While initially the black slaves brought to the Spanish and Portuguese colonies (known as *ladinos*) had either lived in Europe or had been born there from *ladino* parents, later on they were taken directly from Africa (and were called *bozales*).[24] While in the sixteenth century the slave trade had been mainly under Portuguese control, in the following two centuries the lucrative commerce passed to the Dutch and the British.

The presence of European posts on the coasts allowed the introduction into Africa of many New World crops, such as manioc, sweet potato, and cocoyam (*Xanthosoma sagittifolium*). Before the end of the seventeenth century, millet and sorghum, the locally domesticated grains that constituted the main staples for a large part of the population in large, arid areas of West Africa, were partly substituted by maize, especially in its floury and flint varieties, the latter introduced via Egypt and the Nile following the caravans heading to Mecca. However, in the West African regions where rice was the main staple, maize was grown in more limited ecological niches; in Ethiopia, it never achieved the status of a staple.[25]

While most Europeans limited their presence to the coasts, in the seventeenth century the Dutch East India Company settled Dutch and German farmers, known as Boers, on the tip of the continent. These communities, constituting the first actual European colony in African territory, greatly affected the local cultures of the San hunter-gatherers, the Khoi herdsmen (who consumed great quantities of milk and fresh meat), and further east, the Xhosa agriculturalists, who had lived in symbiotic relationships built on the exchange of their diverse food production.[26] The colony, seized by the British in 1795, developed its own food traditions based on European customs such as stewing, *barbacoa* meat grilling—an ancestor of the present-day barbecue—and sausage making.

The cross-Atlantic slave trade profoundly changed the traditional, black African slavery system, where slaves, often captives, were integrated in the local societies as the only private property that could produce wealth, since land was not privately owned.[27] Furthermore, the contact with the Europeans and with the Ottoman Empire led to the diffusion of various types of feudal exploitation where individuals such as merchants or state officials, at times connected with the slave trade, directly controlled the population in large sections of the countryside. In Ethiopia, for instance, domestic landed elites exploited farmers as serfs, while the traditional social structure was shaken by the massive mass migration of Galla herdsmen, known for the very close, almost emotional, connection with their animals, and of the Islamized Somali cattle-rearing nomads. In the Great Lake region, herdsmen gave cattle to the farmers in exchange for their service and the service of their descendants.[28] In general, the slave trade depleted local agriculture of labor, causing a decline in rural activities, especially around the European trading posts. When they could, farmers moved inland toward the forest, where, however, the environment limited production. In the long run, the slave trade contributed to the agricultural decline of the continent, since little or no international interest was shown toward local crops, investments were non-existent, and most of the production was geared toward subsistence.[29] The situation changed in the nineteenth century with the boom of palm oil and groundnut cultivation, and the actual establishment of colonial control.[30]

## THE OTTOMAN EMPIRE

As the Europeans started their pillage of Africa, the Ottoman Empire entered a troubled period that eventually led to its demise. The systems of food provision, distribution, and market control that had been among the main instruments of the political establishment, ensuring legitimacy and avoiding famines, became increasingly inefficient as the Empire reached the limits of its geographical expansion, and regional authorities acquired greater autonomy from Istanbul.[31] Since lands and titles attributed by the sultan to his followers were not hereditary, with the lack of central control the local lords took advantage of their temporary positions to extract as much as they could from their subjects during their tenure, as well as in terms of crops and food products, often causing unrest.[32] Some of the public soup kitchens (*imaret*), established by charitable endowments in previous centuries to provide food to the poor, fell into disrepair, while a few stopped functioning altogether. At the same time, the kitchens in the sultan's residence in Istanbul increased in size, refinement, complexity, and number of employees (up to almost 1,400 in the mid-seventeenth century).[33] Some food customs and techniques spread from the Balkans to Anatolia, so that to this day similar dishes and ingredients, such as yogurt, meat skewers, vine leaves, or anise-based liquors can be found in Serbia, Greece, and Turkey.[34] At the same time, many European nations, starting with France, managed to obtain from the sultan the so-called capitulations—treaties that conferred rights and privileges to Western subjects who were resident or trading in the Ottoman Empire. These agreements facilitated cultural contacts and the spread in Western Europe of traditions such as coffee drinking, while they increased the European influence in the East.

## INDIA

Western powers and their culinary cultures also penetrated southern India, where the Portuguese had established strongholds in the sixteenth century and had left their culinary traces in the introduction of chili peppers, in many dishes of the cuisine of Goa, and in the use of *chhana* in Bengala (a product of acid coagulation of hot milk and the draining out of whey, similar to fresh cottage cheese).[35] Over time, the British replaced the Portuguese in the hegemony over the sea routes, by occupying Surat, a major Mughal port in Gujarat, founding Madras on the east coast, settling in Calcutta in Bengal, and acquiring Bombay from the Portuguese themselves. In doing so, they clashed with the Dutch for the control of the spice trade from the East. In the British colonies, the occupants tried to maintain their culinary customs as much as possible, which included eating meat and drinking imported alcohol, but it was inevitable that the newcomers got accustomed to some of the dishes that their cooks, often Muslims, prepared for them.

In the north of the subcontinent, the descendants of the Mughal emperors increasingly adopted local customs and opened their courts to Persian administrators, who introduced many elements from their culture and their foodways. Spices such as saffron and asafoetida, sorbets, and dishes such as *byriani* and *pilau* rice, now considered Mughal classics, became common among the upper classes. The court expenses on food grew, as did the refinement, and the use of banquets as conspicuous consumption for political reasons.[36] The diffusion of desserts was also stimulated by the adoption of sugarcane as a cash crop. Fruits such as apples, melons, and peaches, which did not grow in India, were also popular, but as the Mughals adapted to the new environment, they added mango to the list of the favorite fruits of the court.

At the same time, elements from local traditions were integrated into imperial cooking, creating dishes like *rogan josh,* based on a Kashmiri speciality, that consisted of meat cooked in clarified butter over intense heat, enriched with plenty of garlic and onion to please the Central Asian taste.[37] The splendor of the court, reflected in buildings such as the Taj Mahal, also trickled down to the culinary world of the lower classes, who also gained from the urban development and the growth of markets and bazaars that were connected with the rest of the Muslim world.

## CHINA

During the penetration of the European empires in the Indian Ocean, China maintained its distance from the West under the new Qing dynasty that Manchu tribes from today's North-Eastern China established in 1644. After the stagnation that marked the end of the Ming dynasty, the early Qing emperors, despite their foreign origins, proved to be relatively open-minded and innovative. The Chinese Empire expanded to include many provinces in Central Asia, Tibet, and Mongolia. The Kangxi Emperor reopened all the ports in 1685, only to close them again for good in 1715. With strict regulations on foreign merchants, the single exception was Canton, which became the only market for tea, silk, and porcelain in the whole world.[38]

A change in the weather, to warmer and wetter, favored an overall expansion of agricultural production, which, in turn, determined a further increase of the population (from 150 million in the early 1700s to 450 million in the mid-1800s).[39] The mid-eighteenth century marks the beginning of prosperity and economic growth that gave way to an increase in consumption, especially under the Qianlong Emperor (1736–1795). At its inception, the new dynasty supported the development of smallholdings against the estates of the landed elites, who were considered as politically dangerous and connected with the Ming establishment. However, over time, large estates became common. The absentee landlords often rented their lands to well-off tenants who, in turn, rented to poor peasants.

Despite these shortcomings, the Qing dynasty established a system of granaries run by civil functionaries to avoid scarcity and turmoil in areas where the market alone was not able to guarantee sufficient provisioning.[40] Thanks to this system, which remained efficient during the whole eighteenth century, farmers could borrow grain and then give it back at the time of the harvest. Furthermore, emergency grain could be sent to areas struck by famine.[41]

Although New World crops were introduced under the Ming via the Spanish possessions in the Philippines, it is under the Qing that they took hold. Local authorities saw in the new plants a means to sustain the population growth and allow an intensive use of marginal lands: sweet potatoes in the south, maize in Yunnan and Sichuan, potatoes in Shanxi and Hebei. Products were commercialized from the local to the national level, generating an expansion in cash crops and an increase of wealth and power for the merchant class. Small peasant farmers, too, tried to take advantage of the market by differentiating production, focusing on commercially valuable crops, and relocating to the frontier where the government was more likely to help them in terms of seed, irrigation, and land management. This growth, however, implied an increased pressure on the agricultural lands, which were already suffering from the flooding created by weather changes and deforestation. However, the Qing did not allow ethnic Chinese to relocate either to Manchuria, their ancestral homeland, to protect the harvest of ginseng root, a very profitable state monopoly, or to Taiwan—at least in the period after the island was taken from the Dutch.[42]

Unlike the Mongols, who had invaded China in the thirteenth century, the Manchu Qing quickly absorbed many of the Chinese habits, especially the use of dazzling and extravagant court meals with dozens of dishes, spectacular vessels and containers, and complex table etiquette as a symbol of power, which required complicated purchase systems and a huge staff.[43] In spite of his Manchu origins, the Qianlong Emperor apparently enjoyed Chinese cuisine and as a Buddhist he consumed vegetarian meals on special occasions.[44] However, it was the landed elite, especially in the area around the cities of Nanjing, Suzhou, and Yangzhou, who maintained and expanded the culinary heritage based on the traditions of the ethnic Han culture as it had developed under the Song and Ming dynasties. It reflected the cultural pride and aesthetic refinement which emerge from cookbooks such as the famous *Recipes from Sui Garden* by the celebrated poet and artist Yuan Mei (1716–1797).[45]

## JAPAN AND KOREA

In Japan, the local lords, or *daimyō,* recognized the central power of the shoguns, the military representatives of the emperors, but in reality the actual national leaders. In 1600, Tokugawa Ieyasu seized power, establishing the domination of the Togukawa family as shoguns, with Edo (now Tokyo) as its capital.

Society was rigidly divided (in ascending order) into merchants, artisans, farmers, and warriors, who often had access to privileges, including higher status foods. The ideology of agrarian Japan, sustained by a taxation system based on rice, became prevalent, with agricultural production considered as the core of the national identity. The cultural relevance of rice became transparent in prints and poetry, where seasons were connoted by the various phases in the rice-growing cycle.[46] The Tokugawas also introduced agricultural innovations and commercial crops such as sugar and tea, while the local lords established profitable forms of production, developing local specialities to compete with one another on the market.

In 1635 the shogun closed Japan to foreign trade, with the exceptions of ships coming from China, Korea, and the Netherlands, from where a few new ingredients and dishes were introduced, such as *yakidofu* (broiled tofu), *goren,* inspired by the Javanese *goreng,* referring to food cooked or stir-fried in oil or fat, and *furu-gasuteru,* something similar to the Dutch *frikandel,* a fried minced-meat snack. Overall, due to its isolation, Japanese cuisine developed independently from outside influences.

While Kyoto remained a cultural center that witnessed fine cuisine and further development of the *chakaiseki,* the refined meals that accompanied the tea ceremony in the monasteries, Edo became a major artisanal and trading hub due to the presence of the shogun and the *daimyōs,* who were obliged to spend long periods at the court, and who required their local specialities in the capital.[47] The urban population, which was overwhelmingly male, determined the growth of commercial restaurants catering mostly to urban dwellers, merchants, and samurai. Street food and peddlers, who for many foods were not expected to carry a license, also played an important role in feeding the commoners. The Edo food culture saw a growing consumption of warm *sake,* the alcoholic beverage brewed from rice which, due to technical innovations, was now produced also in its clear, filtered version), and the diffusion of the use of *bentō,* the box-shaped wooden trays containing a complete meal for one person, to provide easy and fast lunches.[48] It also became common to acidify the rice that was used to maintain fish in what was known as *narezushi,* not through lactic fermentation but by mixing it with vinegar.[49] Sushi, in the style now known as *nigirizushi,* gradually became a dish to be prepared immediately prior to eating it, opening the way for variations that included vegetables, tofu, and seaweed.

The shogun palace boasted several kitchens, and the meals tended to be very complex and lavish, based on a sequence of various courses served on trays. The shogun expected a similar treatment during his visits to the *daimyōs.* The enormous food-related expenses often led the authorities to introduce sumptuary laws, reminding citizens of the cultural value of frugality. Various schools of cuisine prospered, each of them with a set of dishes, cutting styles, and techniques that were passed on secretly.[50]

While Japan was developing a lively urban cuisine, despite attempts by the shoguns to curb excesses and extravagance, neighboring Korea was recovering from a series of attacks from the Manchus and from Japan, which brought devastation at the beginning of the sixteenth century. A group of scholars, known as *sirhak,* cooperated with the Choson dynasty to introduce innovations in various fields, including agriculture. While new irrigation techniques, double cropping, and the introduction of cash crops as well as new plants from the Americas increased the rural output, the government reduced taxes on farmers, and allowed the growth of markets, and of a merchant class.[51]

## CONCLUSION

In the period following the Portuguese exploration of the African Coast and the Indian Ocean, the establishment of Western bases in Asia, and the arrival of the Europeans in the Americas, large areas of the world became connected like never before, forming a complex network of trade routes, cultural contacts, and colonial control. The most direct consequence of these historical developments was the diffusion of American plants (such as corn, tomatoes, peppers, squashes, beans, and chocolate) all over the world on the one hand, and the introduction of Old World plants and animals into the Americas on the other. Some regions in China, Japan, and the interior of Africa, which somehow managed to maintain a certain political and commercial isolation from the budding Western empires, saw the rapid adoption of American plants (allowing the expansion of agriculture into lands that had previously been underexploited or ignored), or the substitution of local cultivars due to higher yields and adaptability. While spices diminished in commercial value in the long run, stimulants such as coffee, tea, and chocolate (together with sugar) gained growing popularity, becoming the focus of trade and political exchanges (often in the forms of slavery, exploitation, and war) between Europe and the producing areas. Furthermore, the growing Western empires initiated voluntary transfers of plants into their territories to acquire greater control over production, or to provide nourishment to local workers engaged in growing the new cash crops. Together with new products and patterns of consumption, food-related cultures and traditions changed all over the world to accommodate these transformations at the agricultural, social, and commercial levels. This period provided the basis for the political and cultural dynamics characterizing food production, distribution, and consumption throughout most of the nineteenth century, with consequences that continue to be felt to the present day.

# NOTES

*Introduction*

1. Paraphrased from Hidber 1858, 18–19.
2. Gercken 1784, 138, 150.
3. Reinach 1790, 93.
4. Starn 2002.
5. For introductory surveys see Kamen 2000 and Kümin 2009.
6. Hagen 2002; Te Brake 1998.
7. Brady, Oberman, and Tracy 1995.
8. Blockmans and Genet 1995–2000; Henshall 1992; Adamson 1999.
9. Rogers 1995; Black 2002.
10. Musgrave 1999; Ogilvie and Cerman 1996.
11. Brown 1999; Burke 1994; Outram 1995; Kaplan 2007.
12. Behringer 2006; Mączak 1995.
13. See volume 3 in this series. The recipes appear in Scappi [1570] 2008. On gastronomic debates see Laurioux 2006.
14. Abel 1980.
15. Jenisch 1995, 278; Hagn 1993, 25.
16. Albala 2003, 245–46. For further surveys see Applebaum 2006, Thirsk 2007, and, most recently, Meyzie 2010.
17. Cowan 2007; for specialized studies on public dining in Tudor England cf. Carlin 2008, on the Burgundian nobility, see Janssens and Zeischka 2008, and on the rise of French cuisine see Pinkard 2009.
18. Toussaint-Samat 2009, 403–544.
19. See Houston 2001, 161 and chapter 2 in this volume.
20. Raeff 1983, 97–98, 112–16.
21. See the digital collection of European culinary and dietetic texts from the Middle Ages to 1800 in Gloning 2000.

22. Hsia 1989.
23. Goldgar 2007.
24. Moryson [1617] 1971, 91 (part 3, book 2, chapter 3); Pezzl 1784, 222.
25. Tilly 1971, and most recently Bohstedt 2010.
26. Ludington 2004. In terms of food, meat became much less affordable com-
    pared to the late Middle Ages, and periods of dearth could put lower social
    groups under enormous strain (see chapter 3 in this volume).
27. Pulz 2007, 185.
28. Tlusty 2001, chapter 7.
29. One potentially significant factor, the relationship between household struc-
    ture and food security, remains largely unexplored, in contrast to the functions
    of the (extended) family as a welfare agency more generally: Viazzo 2003.
30. Teuteberg 1997.
31. Smyth 2004; Camporesi [1980] 1989.
32. Assél and Huber 2009, 115.
33. While the cover image is charged with sensual connotations (oysters were consid-
    ered an aphrodisiac), the artist also alludes to key aspects of early modern food
    history, where processes such as urbanization (especially in the Dutch Republic),
    expanding trade network's (facilitating the import of wine as well as overseas
    spices) and growing prosperity (including many members of the middling sort)
    allowed consumers to refine and differentiate their dining experiences.
34. Martin 2001.
35. In addition to the works cited above, see also Blickle 2008, Rosseaux 2007,
    Glanville 2007, Tomasik and Vitullo 2007, and North 2008.
36. A strong rejection of the view that the diet of ordinary people was monoto-
    nous is made in Thirsk 2007.

## Chapter 1

1. Kriedte 1983, 41; Braudel 1981–84, 127.
2. Van Zanden 1991, 219, 226. Most estimates of pre-nineteenth-century agricultural labor forces are perforce extrapolations and are therefore subject to
   very considerable uncertainty. Estimates for c. 1800 may be found in Allen
   2003, 403–43, but note that Allen's figure for the English agricultural labor
   force (35%) now seems slightly low. Compare it to the online report of Shaw-
   Taylor and Wrigley 2008, which is based on extensive soundings in militia lists
   for the 1750s and parish register data for the 1810s.
3. Jones, Montanarella and Jones 2006.
4. Ibid.
5. For temperature and precipitation data from the 1930s see Bacon et al. 1948,
   8–11.
6. Semple 1928, 65–66.

7. Estimates in Reis 2000, 21, 27, suggest that in c. 1850, animal production was 46–54 percent of agricultural production in Scandinavia, but only 26–35 percent in the Mediterranean, even though per capita income in the two regions was about the same. Stocking densities from the period 1935–1937 mapped in Bacon et al. 1948, 48–55.

8. Braudel 1981–1984, 145–63; Parthasarathi 1998, 103–4; Pomeranz 2002, 542–44.

9. Pomeranz 2000 and Wong 1997 have been especially influential in the rapidly growing literature on this subject.

10. Cipolla 1974, 26, 125–26 and 464 (contributions by Aldo de Maddalena, Walter Minchinton and Kristof Glamann); Albala 2003, 26; Livi-Bacci 1991, 95–98; Slicher van Bath 1963, 266–71. For the data on Italian agricultural output in 1914 see O'Brien and Toniolo 1991, 394.

11. Thirsk 1978, 177.

12. Braudel 1981–1984, 134 estimates the composition of grain and grain-equivalent consumption in Piedmont c. 1750 as 34.7 percent wheat, 33.6 percent rye, 15.1 percent other grains, and 16.6 percent chestnuts.

13. Weiss Adamson 2002, 163; Thirsk 2007, 34.

14. It is no longer clear, as was once thought, that Dutch gardeners were the first to develop the orange carrot, since an unmistakably orange carrot is pictured in a sixth-century illustrated Byzantine herbal: Heywood 1983, 51–65; Banga 1963, 357–70.

15. This was partially due to the global cooling trend during the early modern period commonly known as the Little Ice Age. For a recent overview of this episode in climatic history see Parker 2008, 1053–79.

16. Pounds 1979, 41; Lamb 1985, 279.

17. A range of estimates are helpfully collected in Livi-Bacci 1991, 92–94. Note that Wilhelm Abel's widely quoted figure for annual meat consumption in late medieval Germany of 100 kg per capita (cf. Abel 1980, 71) seems quite implausible, since it suggests that fifteenth-century Germans ate as much meat as late-twentieth-century Americans. Data on fish consumption are much less reliable than for livestock consumption, but see Mitchell 1977, 172–78 and Braudel 1981–1984, 216–20. Mitchell cites Andrzej Wyczanski's estimate that calories from fish made up 8–16 percent of early modern meat consumption in Poland and Italy.

18. The intensive/extensive distinction is from Slicher Van Bath 1977, 90–92.

19. Orrman 2003, 271–77; Melton 1998.

20. For an excellent overview of the subject see Shiel 1991, 51–77.

21. Abel 1980, 116–17 and table 1, 304–5.

22. Semple 1928, 77–80; Slicher Van Bath 1963, 62–63; Pounds 1994, 193–97.

23. Long 1979, 459–69.

24. Fussell 1935, 1–21 and Fussell 1969, 538–551; Kerridge 1951, 14–36; Campbell 1983, 379–404.

25. Wrigley 1991, 326–30.
26. Grantham 1993, 484; Clark 1991, 226–28.
27. For recent assessments of an enormous literature, see the articles collected in Van Bavel and Thoen 1999.
28. Gragnolati et al. 2006. Per capita income data for India available at the United Nations' data website: http://data.un.org (accessed 23 September 2010).
29. Livi-Bacci 1991, 23–78; see also the chapter by Pier Paolo Viazzo below.
30. Sen 1981, 1.
31. The most exhaustive work on this subject is Meuvret 1977–1988, helpfully discussed in Grantham 1989, 184–200.
32. Lee 1981, 356–401; Weir 1984, 17–47.
33. On food circulation see the chapter by Anne Radeff in this volume.
34. Livi-Bacci 1999, 8, table 1.1.
35. These data have been widely republished, for example, in Slicher van Bath 1977, 81.
36. For a recent comparative overview of rural property regimes, see the essays collected in Scott 1998.
37. In addition to Shiel 1991 see Overton 1991, 284–322.
38. Fussell 1972; more recently Ambrosoli 1997.
39. Allen and Ó'Gráda 1988, 93–116; also Van Zanden 1991, 227–30.
40. O'Brien and Prados de la Escosura 1992, 514–36.
41. Shaw-Taylor and Wrigley 2008 estimate the proportion of the English, adult male population in the primary sector (agriculture, fishing, and mining) at 47 percent in c. 1755 and 40 percent in c. 1820. Mining and fishing represented a very small share of primary employment; Shaw-Taylor and Wrigley estimate agricultural employment at 41.3 percent in 1801 compared to a total, primary employment share of 43 percent in 1801. All of this makes Clark's claim of an English agricultural population smaller than 50 percent by 1570 most implausible: Clark 1991, 228.
42. Sources quoted above at note 2; see also Crafts 1984, 438–58.
43. Wrigley 1991, 326–30.
44. O'Brien and Prados de la Escosura 1992; Reis 2000.
45. Grantham 1993, 486–88.
46. For a thoughtful discussion of the long-term consequences of the precocious shedding of labor in English agriculture see O'Brien 1996, 213–49. O'Brien is not able to come up with a compelling explanation for this precocity; see especially 226–27, 239–41.
47. Aston and Philpin 1985, especially Cooper 1985, 458–77.
48. Simpson 2004, 69–85, especially 79–81.
49. De Vries 1984.
50. Wrigley 1967, 44–70; Ringrose 1983.
51. For a useful overview see Ogilvie and Cerman 1996.

## Chapter 2

Translated from the French original by Anne McBride.

1. Examples include Everitt 1968, 57–71; Thirsk 1978; Chartres 1990; Radeff 1996; Montenach 2009; Reininghaus 1993; Cavaciocchi 1998 and 2001; Meyzie 2010. Pioneering works appeared from the early twentieth century.
2. Flandrin and Montanari 1996. Some recent works, however, discuss this aspect: Montanari 2006, 19–21, 83–85, 134–37; Quellier 2007, 142–57.
3. Estienne 1562, 3–4; Orlin 2000, 1.
4. Robert Burton, *The anatomy of melancholy*, 1621, cited by Reed 1996, 78.
5. Defoe [1724] 2001, 12 (vol. 1); Chartres 1986, 181 on the exaggerations of Defoe.
6. Cited by Abad 2002, 804.
7. Clark and Lepetit 1996. London examples: Overton 2001, 299–308; Sacks 2000, 40–43. Paris examples: Le Roux 1996; Roche 1997, 241, 259, 267.
8. Orlin 2000, 12, 106; Chartres 1986, 190.
9. Thirsk 2000, 97. Also see Everitt 1990, 63–65 or Pennell 2000, 228–29.
10. Radeff 1996.
11. Radeff 1996, 421–24.
12. Radeff 1996, 116–19; Montenach 2009, 339–50; Fontaine 2008, 49–76, 148–56; Kümin 2007, 123; Denzel 1994, 479–80, 532–34.
13. See, for example, the pioneering work of Abel 1973, which was first published in 1935.
14. Smith 2002, 41 (quote), 47.
15. Smith 2002, 37.
16. Vertecchi 2009. *Fondachi* were storehouses used for commercial purposes.
17. Radeff 1996, 366.
18. Margairaz 1988, 65.
19. Everitt 1990, 48–49; Dyer 2000, 429.
20. Dyer 2000, 437.
21. Kaplan 1988, 71–73, 502–3.
22. Smith 2002, 36.
23. Zahedich 2001, 365; Backouche 2000, 112 ff.
24. Archer 2000, 175.
25. Coquery 1998, 45.
26. Reed 1996, 69.
27. Everitt 1990, 60–61, 69, 102–11.
28. Chartres 1990, 220 ff.
29. Kaplan 1988, 81, 180–82, 453.
30. Moriceau 1994, 645 ff., 779; Kaplan 1988, 79–81.
31. Vogt 1992, 93.
32. Chartres 1986, 187.
33. Smith 2002, 43–44.

34. Quellier 2003, 346–62.
35. Thirsk 2000, 99–101.
36. Michel 1993, 146; Radeff 1996, 102.
37. Smith 2002, 43; Pennell 2000, 235.
38. Roche 1998a, 333.
39. Radeff 1996, 446–47.
40. Biloghi 1998, 401 ff.; Kroener 1987, 328–30; Bérenger 1994, 303–20; Fayard Duchêne and Riedmatten 1997, 117.
41. Magagna 1991, 65–68.
42. Radeff 1996, 102.
43. Schneider 1998, 555–68; Denzel 1997.
44. Jahier 1998, 796 ff.
45. Westermann 1979.
46. Pickl 1993, 92–94.
47. Fussell and Goodman 1936, 214–36.
48. Everitt 1990, 109.
49. Oberpenning 1996.
50. Vogt 1987, 281–97.
51. Radeff 2007a.
52. Radeff 1996, 165–66.
53. Quellier 2003, 349–62.
54. Pickl 1993; Oberpenning 1996, 73–74.
55. Radeff 2007a.
56. Abad 2002, 397–456.
57. Defoe [1724] 2001, 57 (vol. 1).
58. Radeff 1996, 104.
59. Everitt 1990, 79.
60. Calculations based on Bairoch, Batou, and Chèvre 1988, 255, 271.
61. Saupin 2006, 18.
62. Waddesdon Manor trading cards collection: The Rothschild Collection, Accession no. 3686.3.28.68 (see online resources in the bibliography section).
63. Coquery 1998, 300.
64. Waddesdon Manor trade cards no. 3686.3.19.50.
65. Willesme 1996, 39, 54, 64.
66. Waddesdon Manor trade cards, nos. 3686.1.28.46 (Clomeny) and 3686.3.4.11.
67. Pelet 1962, 121.
68. Kümin 2007, 117; Radeff 1993, 125–37.
69. Christaller 1933; Radeff 2000 (online).
70. Radeff 2007b.
71. Adam, Nicolas and Radeff, forthcoming.
72. Radeff 1996, 421–24; Montanari 2006, 83–85.
73. Barnes 1996, 218.
74. Krugman 1997, 53, 107; Barnes 1996, 197.

## Chapter 3

1. Laslett 1965, 113.
2. Cunningham and Grell 2000, 4–7.
3. Cunningham and Grell 2000, 15.
4. Malthus [1798] 1970, 109.
5. Camporesi 1995.
6. Walter 1989, 75.
7. Cunningham and Grell 2000, 15.
8. Livi-Bacci 1990, 1.
9. McEvedy and Jones 1978; Biraben 1979. McEvedy and Jones's estimates for Europe between 1500 and 1800 are basically accepted, and compared to Biraben's, by Dupâquier 1997, 250–51.
10. Following the procedure adopted by Dupâquier 1997, 251, Biraben's estimates have been adjusted by adding to his figures (which exclude European Russia) three-quarters of the population of the territories corresponding to the former USSR.
11. Cf. Dupâquier and Lepetit 1988, 55–98 (France), and Wrigley, Davies, Oeppen, and Schofield 1997, 614 (England).
12. Pfister 1997, 515–26.
13. Cf. Del Panta, Livi-Bacci, Pinto, and Sonnino 1996, 275.
14. Bickel 1947, 48–49.
15. McEvedy and Jones 1978, 86.
16. Mattmüller 1987, 347–82.
17. Pfister 1997, 519–20.
18. Breschi, Pozzi, and Rettaroli 1994, 42–43.
19. Nadal 1988, 39–47.
20. Galloway 1986, 12.
21. Burke1985, 179–80.
22. Casey 1985, 212.
23. Galloway 1986, 9.
24. Cunningham and Grell 2000, 207–8.
25. Clark 1985a, 4.
26. Quoted by Clark 1985b, 44. *Cleanness of teeth* is a Biblical expression used for famine (Amos 4:6).
27. Cunningham and Grell 2000, 234–6.
28. Cunningham and Grell 2000, 216.
29. Galloway 1986, 12.
30. Le Roy Ladurie 1972, 144.
31. Greengrass 1985, 111.
32. See Guichonnet 1980, 282–87, and also Viazzo 1989, 132–35.
33. Davidson 1985, 158.
34. Alfani 2007, 674–79; see also Alfani 2010, 214–23.
35. Davies 1985, 200.

36. Braudel 1972, 599.
37. Clark 1985a, 9.
38. Pullan 1985, 289–90. See also Casey 1985, 222, and Davidson 1985, 170–1.
39. Cunningham and Grell 2000, 239.
40. Souden 1985, 292.
41. Appleby 1978, 1.
42. Ibid.
43. Meuvret 1946.
44. Most notably Goubert 1960.
45. Meuvret 1965, 510–13.
46. Appleby 1978, 97.
47. As shown by Galloway 1988, mortality was high in France between 1677 and
    1734 (the period of great famines studied by Meuvret), but in the same years
    the relationship between mortality and food shortages appears to have been
    much weaker in England.
48. Lunn 1989, 131–45.
49. Livi-Bacci 1990, 115. For similar views see e.g. Souden 1985, 237, and Per-
    renoud 1997, 295–300.
50. Livi-Bacci 1990, 63.
51. Cunningham and Grell 2000, 201.
52. Gian Battista Segni, *Trattato sopra la carestia e fame* (Bologna: Eredi di Giovanni
    Rossi, 1602), quoted by Zanetti 1963, 62. See also Clark 1985a, 10–11.
53. Flinn 1974. See also Biraben 1975, 118–26, and Del Panta 1980, 179–219.
54. McKeown 1976.
55. See Wrigley and Schofield 1981, 236–48, and also Breschi, Pozzi, and Rettaroli
    1994, 86–89.
56. See Livi-Bacci 1990, 97–99.
57. Flinn 1974, 309–10.
58. Livi-Bacci 1990, 22.
59. Appleby 1978, 133–54.
60. Walter and Schofield 1989, 2.
61. In a controversial book on *Famine in Peasant Society*, Seavoy has claimed
    that "peasant societies, past and present, are governed by similar social values
    and institutions that control food production and fertility behavior" (1986, 1)
    and encourage neither population limitation nor the production of assured
    food surpluses. Since low per capita food production inevitably results, when
    coupled with high fertility, in periodic peacetime famines, whenever there are
    consecutive poor crop years, the only way to get rid of this recurring threat
    would be, for peasant societies, to turn into commercial societies producing
    food primarily for the market rather than just for subsistence.
62. Cunningham and Grell 2000, 243–46.
63. On the modernization of English and Dutch agricultural economies as a refu-
    tation of Malthus, see Grigg 1980, 147–89.

64. See Crosby 1972.
65. Salaman [1949] 1985, 100–125.
66. Salaman [1949] 1985, 115; Viazzo 1989, 185–86; Livi-Bacci 1990, 95.
67. Post 1977.
68. Viazzo 1989, 212.
69. Livi-Bacci 1990, 96.
70. Connell 1950, 160.
71. Viazzo 1989, 183.
72. Grigg 1980, 232; Livi-Bacci 1990, 96.
73. Grigg 1980, 232.

## Chapter 4

1. For general works on food production and distribution in Europe and a comparative perspective see Blum 1982; Braudel 1981–1984; Goldstone 1990; Howell 2010; Magagna 1991; Wong 1997, 13–32.
2. On the importance of kinship in early modern Europe see Gottlieb 1993. For the idea of the stakeholder household I am indebted to several insights in Netting 1993, 58–101. Cf. Hagen 2002 and Sabean 1984, 1990, and 1998.
3. Blickle 1981 and 1997; Magagna 1991.
4. For constructive critiques of moral economy (Thompson 1971) see Goldstone 1990; Magagna 1991; Root 1994.
5. The best detailed study of the regulation of food supply and regulation in any period or area in early modern Europe remains Kaplan 1976. For country studies that touch on food supplies in a largely narrative context see Hoppit 2000; Howell 2010, 1–144; Langford 1989; Roche 1998b, 11–173.
6. Kaplan 1976; Magagna 1991; Wong 1997, 73–153, 207–30.
7. Goldstone 1990; Magagna 1991. For violent rural protest in England see Charlesworth 1983.
8. Root 1994.
9. For psychological factors such as credit, social capital, and reputation see Langford 1989, 59–182; Root 1994.
10. Magagna 1991.
11. Braudel 1981–1984; Sabean 1984, 1990, and 1998.
12. For culture and the modern context see Howell 2010; Roche 1998b, 11–173, 251–319; Strauss 1989, 56–96.
13. The discussion of sacred and secular commensality is inspired by Braudel 1981–1984; Taylor 2007; Wong 1997.
14. For the rise and role of the state in early modern Prussia see Clark 2006. A good overview of state-building from a comparative European perspective in Bonney 1999, 1–18.
15. Wilson 2010.

16. On this issue see especially Clark 2006, 145–82.
17. For the role of nobilities and rulers in German state-building see Blackbourn 1997, 1–44 and Sheehan 1989, 72–206.
18. The discussion of serfdom in this section relies heavily on Hagen 2002, 183–279.

## Chapter 5

1. Heinrich Julius [1594] 1996, 37–39.
2. Kaemena 1999, 41; Earnshaw 2000, 13.
3. Heinrich Julius [1594] 1996, 13.
4. This excludes the grey area of mass catering in institutions such as alms-/workhouses, prisons and monasteries, all of which constituted (at least temporary) homes for their residents.
5. Spang 2000; Teuteberg 2003.
6. The varieties of food provision in inns are examined in Kümin 2003a/2003b and Carlin 2008. At Wolfenbüttel in 1748, guests had a choice between two types of eating establishments, with the better one offering five varieties of lunch (from 3 to 8 dishes apart from bread, cheese, and beer) in three different settings (dining hall, budget lounge, bedroom): *Serenissimi Verordnung wegen der Gastho(e)fe in dero Residenz = Stadt Wolfenbu(e)ttel* (November 28, 1748): Wolfenbüttel, Herzog August Bibliothek, Gn Sam. Bd. 96 (38).
7. Pennell 2000; O'Callaghan 2004.
8. Carlin 1998; Handel 2002; see the large-size ovens on house plans in London's pie-corner near Smithfield *c*. 1600, where a cluster of cook shops catered for visitors to the nearby market: Schofield 1987, 25 and plate 7.
9. Kahl 1961.
10. Hoerner 1999: 90–94.
11. Schulz 1983.
12. The Abbey of Melk in Austria enjoyed a particularly high reputation in the late eighteenth century: Meiners 1791, 98–99.
13. Teply 1980; Bologne 1993; Ellis 2004; Cowan 2005.
14. Spang 2000.
15. See the series of contemporary illustrations of specialized street traders with attractive stalls, carts, baskets, and dispensers in Furnari 1980, chapter *Il commercio*.
16. *De regimine iter agentium* is discussed in Albala 2003, 113.
17. Pennell 2000, 233–39.
18. Beier 1985.
19. Lawson 1986.
20. Krug-Richter 1994, 141, 232, 326.
21. Tanzer 1992, 186.
22. Tanzer 1992, 186, 195; Schulz 1983, 221–22.

23. Latham 1993, 608, 66, and passim.
24. Misson 1719, 146–47.
25. Printed copy in Wolfenbüttel, Herzog August Bibliothek, Gm 4° 1066, Nr. 11.
26. Krug-Richter 1994, 317–20.
27. Turner 1984, 37, 55.
28. Turner 1984, 114, 292, 302.
29. Erasmus [1523] 1997, 368–80; when dining at an inn at Borgo San Donnino (Duchy of Parma, Italy) in the early eighteenth century, Jean-Baptiste Labat, a Dominican friar, was brought a typical meal of "a pea soup, a stew, calf sweetbreads and a large roast pigeon.... Then I had artichokes with salt and pepper, then strawberries and excellent cheese, with chilled white and red wine." (Labat 1927, 133); on the highly problematic billeting of soldiers in inns see Tlusty 2002.
30. Tappert 1967.
31. Hersche 1997, 326.
32. On dining at princely courts see Albala 2007b, on the stagecoach revolution see Beyrer 2006.
33. Moritz [1782] 1985, 175.
34. Spazier 1790, 248–49.
35. Kümin 2003c; meal evidence from Ebel 1793, 22; Arnold 1985, 500; Meiners 1788–90, 423 (pt. 1), 258 (pt. 2).
36. Giebmeyer 2000, 563–81, see especially the appendix.
37. Further insights into the wide range of inn dishes, which included exotic victuals as well as fresh vegetables, fruit, and salads, e.g. in Hagn 1993; Roth-Lochner 1991.
38. Fenton 1998; Kellenbenz 1983.
39. Brennan 1999, 188, 127.
40. Noted e.g. by Italian Antonio de Beatis during a visit to Flanders: Pastor 1905, 71.
41. Ehlert 1997, 131–47.
42. Breakfasts with coffee were served in inns from England to the Swiss provinces by the 1780s: Moritz [1782] 1985, 181 (Dunstable); Gercken 1783–84, 206 (Wiedlisbach).
43. Tlusty 1998; Clark 1988. By 1800, a town such as Hannover also offered chocolatiers, restaurants, and confectioneries: Hoerner 1999, 158–59.
44. Borsay 1991; Cowan 2007; Carlin 2008, 216–17.
45. Rageth-Fritz 1987, 85, 202–3. On culinary developments see the essays by Brian Cowan and Sara Pennell in this volume.
46. Waddesdon Manor (Buckinghamshire), Trading Cards Collection, 3686.4.008.14 and 3686.4.013.20 (cf. the contribution of Anne Radeff to this volume). In the French quote, Lippert recommends himself as "an expert cook [who] will provide the most exquisite meals [and] the best local and foreign wines."
47. Tanzer 1992, 194–96. "Even when a group of twenty people eats at the same table, each is served separately": Röder 1789–93, 332 (vol. 1).

48. *Oxford Dictionary of National Biography* 2008: article "Verral, William" by Gilly Lehmann; Collingwood and Woollams 1792, title-page.
49. Family Archive Weiß, Calendar notes of Franz Jakob Weiß for 1740, 74; Hagger 1719, 121 (see also figure 0.1 in the introduction).
50. Brennan 1984–85; Rosseaux 2007; Tanzer 1992, 142, 160 (Viennese parks).
51. Marfany 1997; North 2008.

## Chapter 6

1. May 1660, sigs. A4v, A8r; *Oxford Dictionary of National Biography* [hereafter: ODNB] 2008, article "May, Robert (b. 1588?, d. in or after 1664)" by Tom Jaine.
2. Lehmann 2003, 40–41.
3. The London Cooks' Company was incorporated in 1482, but earlier fourteenth-century regulations refer explicitly to cooks or the "mystery of cooks": Phillips 1966, 9–20.
4. Herbage 1982; Wheaton 1983, 72–73; MacKenney 1987.
5. Quoted in Messent 2001.
6. Guildhall Library, London, Records of the Worshipful Company of Cooks, MS 3111/1: Cooks' Company Court Minute Book, 1663–1682; citing order made April 15, 1670, f. 105r.
7. Pennell 2000.
8. Cited in Phillips 1966, 124.
9. Wheaton 1983, 75–77; Spang 2000, 7–11; Montenach 2009, 169–71.
10. Montenach 2009, 208; Wheaton 1983, 72–73.
11. Montenach 2009, 210–13.
12. Gore [1766] 1907, passim.
13. Fisher 1954; Pardailhé-Galabrun 1988, 258, 293; Pennell 2000; Voth 2000; Montenach 2009, 167–68.
14. Meldrum 2000, 142–46; Brears 2008.
15. Michel 1999; Albala 2007b, 139–45.
16. Verral 1759, xxx–xxxi (cited in Lehmann 1999, 75).
17. *ODNB* 2008, article "May"; *ODNB* 2008, article "Verral, William (1715–1761)" by Gilly Lehmann.
18. Wheaton 1983, 73.
19. Cited in Meldrum 2000, 143.
20. Letters of 1651 and 1653 mention the tuition given by a "pastryman": Isham 1955, 29, 60; Hecht 1956; Lehmann 1999, 78.
21. Brown 2001, 49.
22. David 1994, 111–24, 310–11; Lehmann 1999; British Museum, Prints & Drawings, Heal Trade Cards, 48.43: engraved trade card for Domenico Negri (c. 1760–65).
23. May 1660, sigs B2r–B5v; Day 2001, 37–39; Mitchell 2001, 28.

24. Anon. 1685, 63.
25. Hardwick 1998, 88 (citing the case of Jeanne Chavreau against her stepmother, Isabel Dubois, March to April 1639).
26. Wheaton 1983, 113–28; Lehmann 2003, 40–41, 57; Peterson 2006, 185–202.
27. *ODNB* 2008, article "Lamb, Patrick (c. 1650–1708/9)" by S. M. Pennell.
28. Peterson 2006; La Varenne 1651, sigs A2r–A3v; La Varenne [1653] 2001, vi–vii. Scappi's text trumpets him as Pope Pius V's "cuoco secreto" and Rumpolt served as head cook to Daniel Brendel von Homburg (1555–82), elector of Mainz: Scappi [1570] 2008; Rumpolt 1581.
29. Rabisha 1661, sig. A4r.
30. Mennell 1996, 94. La Chapelle 1733 and 1735. La Chapelle served as chef to Philip Dormer Stanhope (1694–1773), 4th Earl of Chesterfield, in the Hague between c. 1728–32: *ODNB* 2008, article "La Chapelle, Vincent (fl. 1733–36)" by Philip Hyman and Mary Hyman.
31. Wheaton 1983, 167–69; La Varenne [1653] 2001.
32. Barnes and Rose 2002, 34, 36.
33. *Verstandige kok* 1667; see also Rose 1989.
34. Briggs 1788, "To the reader"; *ODNB* 2008, article "Briggs, Richard (fl. 1788)" by Fiona Lucraft.
35. I thank my Masters' student Sandra Rugea for bringing this source to my attention: Rugea 2009.
36. The figure of the Steward is believed to represent William Talbot, 1st Earl Talbot (1710–82), George III's much-hated Lord Steward between 1761 and 1782; British Museum, Prints & Drawings, BM Satires 3989, "The kitchin Metamorphoz'd" (c. 1762?); Mennell 1985, 124–25.
37. Llopis 1995, 348; Parasecoli 2004, 27–28.
38. Scappi's plates, however, also reveal items peculiar to the Italian kitchen, such as the macaroni iron (*ferro da maccaroni*); Scappi [1570] 2008: unpaginated plate *Diversi Coltelli*.
39. La Varenne [1653] 2001, "An Alphabeticall Table for the explaining of the hard and strange words used in this book." See also Pinkard 2009, 110.
40. Feild 1984, 76 (plate 55); see also Pardailhé Galabrun 1988, 289–90.
41. London Metropolitan Archives, Guildhall MS 9186/4.
42. The *Opera* also depicts manually-operated spits; Scappi 1570: unpaginated plates *Cucina per Campagna* and *Cucina principale*.
43. London Metropolitan Archives, AM/Pi 1688/17, Archdeaconry Court probate inventory of Roger Parks (taken February 21, 1688); Pardailhé-Galabrun 1988, 288; Pennell 1997, table 10, and chapter 7 in this volume; Lehmann 2003, 120–21.
44. Illustrated in Wheaton 1983, 109.
45. Cooper 1999, 129, 136; Chatelain 2001, 132–33.
46. Pennell 2002, 68–71.
47. Flandrin 2007, 57–89. See also Lehmann 2003, 324–36.

48. Pinkard 2009, 92–94.
49. Albala 2002a, 105–6, 206–8.
50. Coutts and Day 2008.
51. Trade card for Domenico Negri (c. 1760–65); Coutts and Day 2008.
52. Ogilvie 2003, 170; van den Heuvel 2008; Montenach 2009.
53. Guildhall Library, London, Records of the Worshipful Company of Cooks, MS 9994/vol. 3, Cooks' Company Court Minute Book, 1693–1707, f. 24v (minute dated January 16, 1694/5): "noe girle…shall be bounde as an apprentice for the future"; cf. ibid., MS 11,764A, f. 3r-4r: "Admission of Freemen [to the Cooks' Company], excerpts by C.M. Phillips" (c. 1899), noting the admission of three female apprentices on May 13, 1701.
54. Lehmann 1999, 78; Field 2010, 8–10. See also British Museum, Prints and Drawings, 1856, 1208.890, *A Macaroni French Cook* (published by Matthew Darly, 1772?); and Lewis Walpole Library, Yale University, ref. 799.625.2, *High Life Below Stairs* (engraving, c. 1799).
55. Eales 1718; *ODNB* 2008, article "Eales, Mary (d. 1717/18?)" by S. M. Pennell.
56. Potter 1999.
57. Sarti 2002, 162.
58. *ODNB* 2008, article "Wolley, Hannah (b. 1622?, d. in or after 1674)" by John Considine; *ODNB* 2008, article "Glasse, Hannah (bap. 1708, d. 1770)" by A.H.T. Robb-Smith.
59. Sarti 2002, 161.
60. Erickson 2008; Van den Heuvel 2008; Montenach 2009, 178–87, 243–47.
61. London Metropolitan Archives, MS 9186/4, Commissary Court probate inventory of Mary Rabson (taken May 30, 1739); British Museum, Prints & Drawings, 1871, 1209.3368, Marcellus Laroon II, "Colly Molly Puff", from *The Cryes of London Drawne After the Life* (1688).
62. Simonton 1991.
63. Montenach 2009, 244.
64. London Metropolitan Archives, MS 3041/6/i, entry for June 16, 1699 and following; Hecht 1956, 141–42.
65. The 1690 second edition is given as "Printed for the author at her House in Lime Street, 1690": M.H. 1690, titlepage. See also Spiller 2008.
66. Illustrated in Day 2004, 130.
67. One surviving manuscript copy of Kidder's receipts suggest he was operating as early as 1702; Varey 1991, 48.
68. *ODNB* 2008, article "Kidder, Edward (1665/6–1739)" by Simon Varey; Targett 1989, 41; Potter 2000.
69. Scott-Moncrieff 1911, xxxiii–iv.
70. Wellcome Library, MS 1176.
71. Ibid., f. 2v (my emphasis).
72. See the essay by David Gentilcore in this volume.
73. See the essay by Beat Kümin in this volume; Black 2003, 149–65.

74. Spang 2000, 10.
75. For example Spang 2000; Kelly 2003. See also London Metropolitan Archives, MS 3041/6/i.

## Chapter 7

1. For example, Hardwick 1998, 85–100; Ogilvie 2003; van den Heuvel 2008; Steedman 2009; Whittle with Griffiths forthcoming.
2. Voth 2000, 82–83; Ogilvie 2003, 141–52.
3. Pennell 1998; Hardwick 1998, 93; Pennell 2004.
4. Faussett 1757, unpaginated.
5. For example, Markham [1615] 1994.
6. Ezell 1987, 36–61.
7. Hardwick 1998, 87, 91; Pennell 1998, 213–14; Wall 2002, 18–58; Ajmar-Wollheim 2006, 153; Harvey forthcoming.
8. Oxfordshire Archives, Dorchester Poor Accounts, f. 68r.
9. For full publication details of *The English Housewife* see Poynter 1962; Smith 1727, sig. A4r.
10. Wall 2002, 37–41.
11. Markham [1615] 1994, i–viii, 5–8, 60–62; Smith 1727, preface; Haywood 1745, 177; Wall 2002, 18–58.
12. Wall 2002, 189–220.
13. For example, Mennell 1985.
14. Gloning 2000 (online); Meijer 1982; Mennell 1987, 203; Hyman and Hyman 2001.
15. Hunter 2002, 531.
16. Lehmann 2003, 81–166.
17. Lehmann 2003, 101–28, 420–21, 442, 450–51.
18. McKenzie and Ross 1968, 254.
19. Amussen 1988, 67.
20. Mennell 1985, 130–32; Lehmann 2003, 161–66.
21. Rose 1989; Lehmann 2003; Rankin 2007; Gloning 2000.
22. Lehmann 2003, 53.
23. Bodleian Library, Cartwright MS, f. 73v; Library of Congress, MS Ac. 5963, 2.
24. Wellcome Library, Fanshawe MS, f. 154v, 157r; Potter 2006.
25. Field 2007.
26. Wellcome Library, Lisle MS, f. 43r; Folger Shakespeare Library, Pudsey MS 1675, f. 57r. See also Pennell 2004, 247–50.
27. Wellcome Library, Lomas MS, f. 74r–79v.
28. Cumbria Record Office, Kendal, Browne MSS, MS recipe book c. 1699, 12, 62; and WD/TE/box 8/1/3–8, 8/2/1, accounts 1714–37; Pennell 2004.
29. See Turner 1984 and Bodleian Library, Oxford, Turner Diary.

30. Lehmann 2003, 44, 230–31; Bod. Lib. Thirsk 2007, 185–86, 284–94.
31. Turner 1984, 220–21, 232; Turner Diary, vol. 70 (July 29, 1761).
32. Turner 1984, 60, 331; White 1951, 252.
33. Lehmann 2003, 44; Thirsk 2007, 293–304; Hassell et al. 1984, 268.
34. For example, Miller 1988. See also the current doctoral research of Victoria Yorke-Edwards on obesity in eighteenth-century London: http://www.ucl.ac.uk/archaeology/research/student-research/topics.htm (accessed January 4, 2010).
35. For example, Sarti 2002, plates 52–55.
36. Schama [1987] 1988, 375–480; Barnes and Rose 2002, 148.
37. Pardailhé-Galabrun 1988, 289; Ogilvie et al. 2009, 150.
38. Van Koolbergen 1997; Pennell 2004; Guerzoni 2006, 149; Ogilvie et al. 2009.
39. Pardailhé-Galabrun 1988, 338–40; Barnes and Rose 2002, 82.
40. Pardailhé-Galabrun 1988, 288; Overton et al. 2004, 99.
41. Pardailhé-Galabrun 1988, 289.
42. Ibid., 290; Pennell 1997, ch. 4.
43. Pardailhé-Galabrun 1988, 289–90; Pennell 1997, table 8; Overton et al. 2004, 102.
44. And the Parisian, if *égrugeoir* is translated as dredger rather than mill: Pardailhé-Galabrun 1988, 289.
45. Markham [1615] 1994, 84; Wolley 1684, 176; Bradley 1760, frontispiece.
46. Pennell 1997, table 13; Hardwick 1998, 80–81; Pardailhé-Galabrun 1988, 257–58 (my translation).
47. Pennell 2000, 230; Overton et al. 2004, 130.
48. Guillery 2004, 31, 40, 43, 232.
49. Pardailhé-Galabrun 1988, 249.
50. Pennell 1998; Overton et al. 2004, 126–27; Pardailhé-Galabrun 1988, 258.
51. Pardailhé-Galabrun 1988, 258–59.
52. Shaw 1904, 689.
53. Steedman 2009, 276–303, 345.
54. For example, Ogilvie 2003, 140–205.
55. Ogilvie 2003, 170–71; Overton et al. 2004, 57–64, 131; De Vries 2008, 71.
56. Sarti 2002, 101.
57. The National Archives, ASSI 45/11/17, Deposition of Thomas Stamper August 25, 1675.
58. Latham and Matthews 1970–83, 29 (vol. 4); Glasse [1747] 2005, ch. 9.
59. Pardailhé-Galabrun 1988, 238; Pennell 2000, 240–41.
60. Wall 2002, 189, 192–201.
61. Dolan 1994, 24, 30–32.
62. *Gentleman's Magazine* 1731, 130.
63. Hunt 1992, 18; Ogilvie 2003, 182.
64. Richards 1853, 100; Latham and Matthews 1970–83, 238 (vol. 2).
65. Thompson 1991, 490, 499–503.
66. Weatherill 1988, 142–46; Wall 2002, 219.

67. Barnes and Rose 2002, 130; Latham and Matthews 1970–83, 409 (vol. 9) and 147 (vol. 10).
68. May 1660, 218–20.
69. Ogilvie et al. 2009, 151.
70. Weatherill 1990, 9, 12, 15–16, 20, 24. For earthenware posset pots, see Victoria and Albert Museum, no. C.32&A-1972, London-made posset pot c. 1630–1635 (online at http:// collections.vam.ac.uk/ote/O20991/posset-pot/; accessed May 25, 2010).
71. Cumbria Record Office, Browne MSS, WD/TE box 1, vol. III, f. 41, 46a.
72. Hardwick 1998, 104, 106. See also Weatherill 1988, 156.
73. Turner 1984, 331; Turner Diary, vol. 73.
74. Turner 1984, 60, 66, 69.
75. Quoted in David 1983, 55, 57.
76. Weatherill 1988, 153; Clifford 2002, 54; Young 2002, 90–91; cf. Pardailhé-Galabrun 1988, 300–308.
77. Richards 1999, 127–76.
78. Pennell 2010; Stobart and Van Damme 2010.
79. For example, Lister 1699, 148–62.

## Chapter 8

1. Letter from Ignatius Loyola to Adrian Adriaenssens, May 12, 1556, in Gioia 1977, 758–59, and discussed in Gentilcore 2010.
2. Marin 1758, vii–xlviii (for all quotations in this paragraph). Discussed in Pinkard 2009, 159–62.
3. St Augustine [397–98 AD] 1991, 204–7 (bk. 10, ch. 31).
4. For full treatments of the theory of humoral physiology as it related to diet and regimen see Eden 2008, 9–22; Pinkard 2009, 3–28; Albala 2002a, 48–77; Flandrin 1999a; Mikkeli 1999, 70–115.
5. The saying is quoted by Cheyne [1724] 1725, 2.
6. Mercurio [1603] 1645, 511.
7. Cited in Ercolani 2001, 143.
8. Bernini 1768, 22–23.
9. Edelstein 1967, 303.
10. Cornaro 1558; Cornaro 1702.
11. Gratarolus [1558] 1574.
12. Bacon [1623] 1857–58, 304.
13. Bertaldi 1620, 428.
14. For a discussion of seventeenth-century difficulties in categorizing the humoral qualities of chocolate see Alaba 2007a.
15. In Eden 2008, 60.
16. de Serres 1600 and de Bonnefons 1651.

17. Santorio [1614] 1676.
18. Duchesne 1606.
19. Pagel 1982, 79–86.
20. King 1970, 93–112.
21. Lémery [1702] 1755.
22. Friend 1725–26.
23. Lémery [1702] 1755.
24. "One should strive to keep the natural taste, the real taste." *Aux maistres d'hotels. Epistre,* in de Bonnefons 1655, 108–16.
25. May 1660, preface (unpaginated).
26. Grafe 2004, 17–18.
27. Camporesi [1990] 1994; Forrest and Najjaj 2007; Albala 2007b.
28. Letter from Francesco Algarotti to Francesco Maria Zanotti (1750) in Algarotti 1794, 164.
29. Cheyne [1724] 1725, 114.
30. Ibid., 15–16.
31. Pillo-Tisanus 1725, 9.
32. Drake 1758, 169.
33. Cocchi 1743.
34. Pujati 1751; Pujati [1762] 1768.
35. Corrado [1781] 2001, 11–12.
36. Verri 1947, 50–51.
37. Roberti 1785, i–xviii; Chiari 1751, 210.
38. Black 1782, 225.
39. Buchan 1797.

## Chapter 9

I would like to thank Bronwen Wilson and Angela Vanhaelen for sharing their expertise and bibliographic suggestions for further reading in Italian and Netherlandish art history with me; thanks also to James Amelang, Beat Kümin, and Benjamin Madley for their insightful readings and corrections of early drafts of this essay. All remaining errors are mine alone.

The images chosen to illustrate this essay are all taken from early modern prints and engravings, many of which were based on painted originals. I have tried to identify the paintings upon which these prints were based in some, but not all, of the selections. Differences and discrepancies are often apparent when one compares the paintings and the prints upon which they are based. The widespread duplication and imitation of these images reinforces the argument that the era saw the articulation of new genres of food representation.

1. See Eisenstein 2002, 87–105, 106–25, 126–28. For the methodological problems inherent in quantifying the expansion in the book trade see Raven 1993, 5–19.

2. Honig 1998a, 174–89; Van der Woude 1991, 310.

3. McKeon [1987] 2003 and 2005 both offer influential accounts of genre formation in early modern English literary culture.

4. Honig 1998b, 170; Hochstrasser 2007, 312 (n. 3).

5. Some key and controversial works include Auerbach [1946] 2003; Alpers 1983; Watt 1957. The various meanings attributed to golden-age Dutch realism are explored in Boombaard 1999, 166–83 and Westermann 1996, 71–98.

6. McTighe 2004, 322 (n. 7).

7. Ferguson 2004, 104–9 explains the development of the gastronomic field in France from the mid-eighteenth century. The culinary writing upon which this field was based emerged a century earlier, after the 1650s, for which see Charbonneau 2008. There was also an even older tradition of learned dietetic writing, which is sometimes called gastronomic, as in Laurioux 2006.

8. Jansen 1999, 51–58.

9. Lairesse [1707] 2000, 306.

10. A notable exception is Appelbaum 2006.

11. Peterson 1994, 175–76; on Romantic gastronomic writing, see Gigante 2005b and for its eighteenth-century background Gigante 2005a.

12. Ferguson 2004 and Charbonneau 2008 detail the rise of modern Francophone food writing; for a recent attempt to elevate the artistic status of cooking, see This and Gagnaire 2008.

13. Varriano 2009 was published too late to be taken into account here.

14. Bendiner 2004, 224.

15. McTighe 2004. See also McTighe forthcoming.

16. Honig 1998b, 165.

17. Schneider 2003; Malaguzzi 2008.

18. Appelbaum 2006, 192–200; Prest 1981.

19. "Rhyming Text L" (late fifteenth century) in Pleij 2001, ll. 55–56, 34. For the persistence of this theme in early modern imagery, see O'Connell 1999, 120–22, 160.

20. Bendiner 2004, 212–13.

21. Paulson 1993, 24. On Hogarth's realism see Donald 2001, 163–91.

22. Brown 1998, 108–10; Pignatti 1979, 142–43.

23. Luke 16:19–31; Luke 10:38–42; John 12:1–8. For an extended discussion of this particular genre see McKeon 2005, 423–35.

24. Schama 1987, 155. On the sexual anxieties provoked by similar images see Honig 2001, 294–315.

25. Turner 1986, 235; on Bascoli's drawing of the Supper at Emmaus, BM, Prints and Drawings, 1946,0713.22.

26. Honig 1998a, 151.

27. Hochstrasser 2000, 74.

28. McTighe 2004.

29. Albala 2002a, 190.

30. Albala 2002a, 188. The availability of fresh meat to more than just elites may have varied over time and place. For an argument for the widespread availability of meats see Rebora 2001; fresh meat does seem to have been widely available in early modern Spain, for example. The question deserves further research. I am grateful to James Amelang for discussing this matter with me.

31. Albala 2002a, 70, 168; Hochstrasser 2000, 77 notes that Dutch dietary literature recommended ham as fit for workers. On early modern ham production see Rebora 2001, 80–84.

32. See Paliaga 1997, 203–4 (n. 89), for the association of this image with Campi's studio and its many copies and imitations. Picart's etching was reprinted in Dutch (1734) and English (1756) editions.

33. Albala 2002a, 148.

34. On the sexual significance of feline imagery see Darnton 1985.

35. McTighe 2004, 317–18.

36. Stoichita 1997.

37. Hochstrasser 2007; Pinkard 2009, 64.

38. Scappi [1570] 2008 was a landmark, late Renaissance publication, but it was only one of four Italian cookbook titles published in the sixteenth century.

39. Appelbaum 2006, 74; Girard 1982, 112. Girard seems to have overlooked the Danish *Koge Boge* (Copenhagen, 1616), which is discussed in Gold 2007.

40. Albala 2002a; Cowan 2007, 196–231.

41. La Varenne 2006, 23, 119 (n. 167).

42. Flandrin, Hyam, and Hyman 1983, 62–63.

43. La Varenne 2006, 27.

44. Pinkard 2009; Peterson 1994; Flandrin 2000, 403–17; Flandrin, Hyman, and Hyman 1983, 14–31; La Varenne 2006, 94–95.

45. La Varenne 2006, 23; Hyman and Hyman 2000, 396–97.

46. La Varenne 2006, 67 (n. 79).

47. L.S.R. 1995, 22–23, 21 (my translation). See also Mennell [1986] 1996, 73–74.

48. Charbonneau 2008, 59, 147 (n. 2); Girard 1977, 497–523.

49. Lehmann 2003, 383 (and cf. 65).

50. Lehmann 2003, 101–2, 437–38; Pinkard 2009, 143–44.

51. See e.g. Mennell 1981.

52. Cowan 2007, 226–30.

53. La Varenne [1653] 2001, 13–18; Massialot 1702, sigs. b2r–cr.

54. Casanova 2004; Blanning 2002.

55. DeJean 2005 offers a simplified account of this phenomenon; see also Jones 2004.

56. The term *haute cuisine* itself appears to have been a product of early nineteenth-century gastronomic discourse. The earliest use of the term that I have identified is in Grimod de La Reynière 1808, 170.

57. Rogers 2003. Britain's global empire offered an entirely different source of culinary inspiration, although it is telling that these influences never developed into a tradition of British imperial haute cuisine: Bickham 2008, 71–109; Collingham 2006.
58. Glasse [1747] 2005, ii [bis], xxv–xxviii.
59. Camporesi [1990] 1994, 33.
60. Drouard 2007, 263–300; Steinberger 2009.
61. Although I emphasize here the effects of social stratification and international cultural competition on the shaping of early modern food representations, it is worth recognizing that there were other influences as well, not least of which was the endurance of a Rabelaisian celebration of gustatory and especially bibulatory indulgence. See O'Callaghan 2007 and the classic account in Bakhtin 1984.

## *Chapter 10*

1. Sheller 2003, 13–35. Brockway 2002, 34–60.
2. Mintz 1986; Curtin 1998.
3. Villiers1981; Milton 1999.
4. Brockway 2002, 53.
5. Pomeranz and Topik 1999, 83.
6. See chapter 10 of volume 5 in this series.
7. Pendergrast 1999; Wild 2005.
8. Pomeranz and Topik 1999, 87–89.
9. Komecoğlu 2005.
10. Brockway 2002, 51.
11. Spary and White 2004; DeLoughrey 2008.
12. Mann 2005, 97–99.
13. Curtin 1984, 207–29.
14. Hess 1992.
15. Carney 2001.
16. Mintz 1996, 33–49.
17. Salinger 2002.
18. McCusker and Menard 1991.
19. Breen 2004.
20. Kurlansky 1997.
21. Dunmire 2004; Pilcher 2006, 21–23.
22. Bauer 2001, 87–104.
23. Laudan and Pilcher 1999.
24. Ogot 1999, 1–12.
25. McCann 2005, 26–30.
26. Ogot 1999, 335–44.

27. Thornton 1998, 72–97.
28. Ogot 1999, 25–38.
29. Ogot 1999, 13–24.
30. Ade Ajayi 1998.
31. Murphey 1988; Özveren 2003.
32. Roux 1984.
33. Singer 2002, 136.
34. Yerasimos 2005.
35. Achaya 2000, 87–100; Banerji 2007, 29–44; Collingham 2006, 47–80.
36. Achaya 2000, 64–73; Banerji 2007, 106–40.
37. Collinghman 2006, 13–46.
38. Martin 2007, 127–33.
39. Chang 1977, 263.
40. Li and Dray-Novey 1999.
41. Will and Wong 1991.
42. Pomeranz and Topik 1999, 59–62.
43. Chiu 1995.
44. Waley-Cohen 2007, 124.
45. Waley 1958; Yuan 2000.
46. Ohnuki-Tierney 1994, 86–90.
47. Ishige 2001, 105–33.
48. Harada 2006.
49. See chapter 10 of volume 3 in this series.
50. Nishiyama and Groemer 1997, 144–80.
51. Pettid 2008, 17–19.

# BIBLIOGRAPHY

## ARCHIVAL MATERIALS

Bodleian Library, Oxford, MS.Don.e.6: MS recipe collection of the Cartwright family (c. 1632–58).

Bodleian Library, Oxford, MSS Film 1673–75: Thomas Turner diaries (1755–64; microfilm of originals kept at Sterling Memorial Library; special collections, Yale University).

British Museum, London: Prints and drawings.

Cumbria Record Office, Kendal: Browne MSS/Browne of Troutbeck family papers (c. 1650–1750), WD/TE/box 16/1: MS recipe book (c. 1699); WD/TE/box 8/1/3–8, 8/2/1: Accounts (1714–37).

Family Archive Weiß, Fürstenfeldbruck, Bavaria: Calendar notes of Franz Jakob Weiß (1740).

Faussett, Bryan. 1757. *MSS notes on Kent church inscriptions, c. 1756–70.* London: Society of Antiquaries.

Folger Shakespeare Library, MS V.a.450: Attributed to Lettice Pudsey (c. 1675).

Guildhall Library, London: Records of the worshipful company of cooks.

Lewis Walpole Library, Yale University: Engravings.

Library of Congress, MS Ac. 5963: Anonymous MS recipe collection (early eighteenth century).

London Metropolitan Archives, AM/Pi 1688/17: Archdeaconry Court probate inventory of Roger Parks (taken February 21, 1688).

London Metropolitan Archives, MS 3041/6/i: Thomas Bowrey of Stepney (c. 1650–1713), miscellaneous accounts (1699–1715: Expenses at Bath 1699).

London Metropolitan Archives, MS 9186/4: Commissary Court probate inventory of Mary Rabson (taken May 30, 1739).

London Metropolitan Archives, Guildhall MS 9186/4: Commissary Court probate inventory of Jonathan Carter (taken March 1735–36).

Oxfordshire Archives, MS D.D. Par. Dorchester b.10: Overseers of the poor accounts (1680–1744).

The National Archives (TNA), ASSI 45: Northern circuit assizes depositions.

Waddesdon Manor, Buckinghamshire: Trading cards collection, 3686.4.008.14, 3686.4.013.20, 3686.3.19.50, 3686.3.28.68, 3686.1.28.46, and 3686.3.4.11.

Wellcome Library, London, MS 1176: Manuscript recipe collection attributed to Hannah Bisaker (fl. 1692–1713).

Wellcome Library, London, MS 3294: Manuscript recipe book attributed to Anne Lisle (c. 1748).

Wellcome Library, London, MS 7113: Manuscript recipe book attributed to Lady Ann Fanshawe (c. 1651–early eighteenth century).

Wellcome Library, London, MS 7726: Manuscript recipe book attributed to the Lomas family (c. 1799–1807).

Wolfenbüttel, Herzog August Bibliothek, Gm 4° 1066, Nr. 11: Wedding ordinance of the Imperial free city of Strasbourg (1664).

Wolfenbüttel, Herzog August Bibliothek, Gn Sam. Bd. 96 (38): *Serenissimi Verordnung wegen der Gastho(e)fe in dero Residenz = Stadt Wolfenbu(e)ttel* (November 28, 1748).

## PRINTED PRIMARY SOURCES

Algarotti, Francesco. 1794. "Lettere varie." In *Opere del conte Algarotti edizione novissima.* Vol. 9. Venice: Palese.

Anon. 1685. *The Compleat Servant-maid, or Young Maidens Tutor.* 4th ed. London: no publisher given.

Bacon, Francis. [1623] 1857–58. "The history of life and death..." In *The Philosophical Works of Francis Bacon,* ed. J. Spedding, R. L. Ellis, and D. D. Heath. Vol. 5. London: Longman.

Bernini, Domenico. 1768. *Vita di S. Giuseppe da Copertino sacerdote professo dell'Ordine de' Minori Conventuali di S. Francesco.* Florence: Stamperia Bonducciana.

Bertaldi, Ludovico. 1620. *Regole della sanità et natura de' cibi.* Turin: Gio. Domenico Tarino.

Black, William. 1782. *An Historical Sketch of Medicine and Surgery.* London: J. Johnson.

Bradley, Martha. 1760. *The British Housewife: Or, the Cook, Housekeeper's and Gardiner's Companion.* London: S. Crowder and H. Woodgate.

Brennan, M. G., ed. 1999. *The Travel Diary of Robert Bargrave, Levant Merchant, 1647–56.* London: Hakluyt Society.

Briggs, Richard. 1788. *The English Art of Cookery, According to the Present Practice.* London: G.G.J. and J. Robinson.

Buchan, William. 1797. "Observations Concerning the Diet of the Common People, Recommending a Method of Living Less Expensive, and More Conducive to Health, than the Present." In *Domestic Medicine: Or, a Treatise on the Prevention and Cure of Diseases by Regimen and Simple Medicines*, 647–79. London: A. Strahan.

Cheyne, George. [1724] 1725. *An Essay of Health and Long Life*. Reprint, Dublin: George Ewing.

Chiari, Pietro. 1751. "De' cibi appruovati e disappruovati dall'uso." In *Lettere scelte di varie materie piacevoli, critiche ed erudite scritte ad una dama di qualità*, 206–14. Vol. 2. Venice: Angelo Pasinelli.

Cocchi, Antonio. 1743. *Del vitto pitagorico per uso della medicina: discorso*. Florence: Francesco Moücke. (English translation 1745: *The Pythagorean diet of vegetables only, conducive to the preservation of health and the cure of diseases*. London: R. Dodsley; and French translation 1762: *Régime de Pythagore*, trans. P. Puisieux. Paris: La Haye.)

Collingwood, Francis, and John Woollams. 1792. *The universal cook*. London: R. Noble.

Cornaro, Luigi. 1558. *Trattato de la vita sobria*. Padua: Gratioso Perchacino.

Cornaro, Luigi. 1702. *Sure and certain methods of attaining a long and healthfull life: With means of correcting a bad constitution...made English by W. Jones*. London: Tho. Leigh.

Corrado, Vincenzo. [1781] 2001. *Del cibo pitagorico ovvero erbaceo per uso de' nobile e de' letterati*. Reprint, Rome: Donzelli.

De Bonnefons, Nicolas. 1651. *Le jardinier françois, qui enseigne à cultiver les arbres et les herbes potagères*. Paris: Des-Hayes.

De Bonnefons, Nicolas. 1655. *Les délices de la campagne suitte du Jardinier françois*. Amsterdam: Raphael Smith.

De Serres, Olivier. 1600. *Le théâtre de l'agriculture et mesnage des champs*. Paris: Métayer.

Defoe, Daniel. [1724–26] 2001. *A tour thro' the whole island of Great Britain*. Reprint, London: Pickering and Chatto.

Drake, Richard. 1758. *An essay on the nature and manner of treating the gout*. London: Self-published.

Duchesne, Joseph. 1606. *Le pourtraict de la santé*. Paris: Claude Morel.

Eales, Mary. 1718. *Mrs Mary Eales's receipts*. London: Printed by H. Meere.

Ebel, Johann G. 1793. *Anleitung, auf die nützlichste und genussvollste Art in der Schweitz zu reisen*. Zurich: Orell.

Erasmus, Desiderius. [1523] 1997. "Diversoria (public houses)." In *Colloquies: Collected works of Erasmus*, ed. C. R. Thompson, 368–80. Vol. 39. Reprint, Toronto: Toronto University Press.

Ercolani, Gian Luca. 2001. *Il pane dei santi. Storia e curiosità sull'alimentazione dei santi*. Lugano: Todaro.

Estienne, Charles. 1562. *La guide des chemins de France.* Paris: Chez Charles Estienne.

Freind, John. 1725–26. *The history of physick, from the time of Galen to the beginning of the sixteenth century.* 2 vols. London: J. Walthoe.

Furnari, Mario, ed. 1980. *'700 napoletano: Cultura popolare a Napoli nel diciottesimo secolo.* Napoli: A. Gallina.

*The Gentleman's Magazine.* 1731. Vol. 1 (3).

Gercken, Philipp W. 1783–84. *Reisen durch Schwaben, Baiern, angränzende Schweiz.* 2 parts. Stendal: Franzen.

Gioia, Mario, ed. 1977. *Gli scritti di Ignazio di Loyola.* Turin: UTET.

Glasse, Hannah. [1747] 2005. *The art of cookery made plain and easy...by a lady.* Reprint, Totnes: Prospect.

Gore, J. [1766] 1907. *Liverpool's first directory,* ed. George T. Shaw and Isabella Shaw. Reprint, Liverpool: Henry Young and Co.

Gratarolus, Gulielmus [Guglielmo Grataroli]. [1558] 1574. *A direction for the health of magistrates and students,* trans. Thomas Newton. Reprint, London: William How.

Grimod de La Reynière, Alexandre-Balthazar-Laurent. 1808. *Manuel des Amphitryons.* Paris: Capelle et Renand.

H., M. 1690. *The Young Cooks Monitor: or Directions for Cookery and Distilling.* 2nd ed. London: Printed for the author.

Hagger, Conrad. 1719. *Neues Saltzburgisches Koch-Buch.* Augsburg: Johann Jakob Lotter.

Haywood, Eliza. 1745. *The female spectator.* Vol. 3, book 13. London: T. Gardner.

Heinrich, Julius. [1594] 1996. *Tragica Comoedia. Von einem Wirthe oder Gastgeber,* ed. H. Blume. Reprint, Braunschweig: Literarischer Verein.

Isham, Giles, ed. 1955. *The correspondence of Bishop Brian Duppa and Sir Justinian Isham, 1650–1660.* Northampton: Northamptonshire Record Society.

Kidder, Edward. c. 1720. *Edward Kidder's receipts of pastry and cookery, for the use of his scholars.* London.

L.S.R. 1995. "L'Art de Bien Traiter." [1674] In *L'Art de la Cuisine Française au XVIIe Siècle.* Paris: Payot.

La Chapelle, Vincent. 1733. *The modern cook.* 3 vols. London: Self-published.

La Chapelle, Vincent. 1735. *Cuisinier moderne.* 3 vols. The Hague: Self-published.

La Varenne, François Pierre de. 1651. *Le Cuisinier François.* Paris: no publisher given.

La Varenne, François Pierre de. [1653] 2001. *The French cook,* ed. Philip Hyman and Mary Hyman, trans. I.D.G. Reprint, Lewes: Southover.

La Varenne, François Pierre de. 2006. *La Varenne's cookery: The French cook; the French pastry chef; the French confectioner,* trans. Terence Scully. Trowbridge: Prospect Books.

Labat, Jean Baptiste. 1927. *La comédie ecclésiastique: Voyage en Espagne et en Italie.* Paris: Grasset.

Lairesse, Gérard de. [1707] 2000. "The great book on painting." In *Art in theory 1648–1815: An anthology of changing ideas,* ed. Charles Harrison, Paul Wood, and Jason Gaiger. Reprint, Oxford: Blackwell.

Latham, Robert, ed. 1993. *The shorter Pepys.* London: Penguin.

Latham, Robert, and William Matthews, eds. 1970–83. *The diary of Samuel Pepys: A new and complete transcription.* 12 vols. London: Bell and Hyman.

Lémery, Louis. [1702] 1755. *Traité des alimens...augmenté...par Jacques Jean Bruhier.* Reprint, Paris: Durand.

Lister, Martin. 1699. *A journey to Paris in the year 1698.* London: Jacob Tonson.

Marin, François. 1758. *Les dons de Comus, ou l'art de la cuisine réduite en pratique.* Paris: Pissot.

Markham, Gervase. [1615] 1994. *The English housewife, containing the inward and outward virtues which ought to be in a complete woman,* ed. Michael R. Best. Reprint, Montreal/Kingston ON: McGill-Queen's University Press.

[Massialot, François?]. 1702. *The court and country cook.* London: W. Onley.

May, Robert. 1660. *The accomplisht cook, or the art and mystery of cookery.* London: Nathaniel Brooke.

McKenzie, D. F., and J. C. Ross, eds. 1968. *A ledger of Charles Ackers, printer of the London magazine.* Oxford: Oxford Bibliographical Society.

Meiners, Christoph. 1788–90. *Briefe aus der Schweiz.* 2nd ed. 4 parts. Berlin: Spener.

Meiners, Christoph. 1791. *Kleinere Länder- und Reisebeschreibungen.* Berlin: Spener.

Mennell, Stephen, ed. 1981. *Lettre d'un Pâtissier Anglois et Autres Contributions à une Polémique Gastronomique du XVIIIème Siècle.* Exeter: University of Exeter Press.

Mercurio, Scipione. [1603] 1645. *De gli errori popolari d'Italia.* Reprint, Verona: Francesco Rossi.

Misson, Henri. 1719. *Memoirs and observations in his travels over England,* ed. Mr Ozell. London: D. Browne.

Moritz, Philip. [1782] 1985. *Journeys of a German in England in 1782.* Reprint, London: Cape.

Moryson, Fynes. [1617] 1971. *An itinerary...containing his ten yeeres travell throvgh the twelve domjnions of Germany, Bohmerland, Sweitzerland...England etc.* Facsimile ed. 3 parts. Reprint, Amsterdam: Theatrum Orbis Terrarum.

Pastor, Ludwig, ed. 1905. *Die Reise des Kardinals Luigi d'Aragona durch Deutschland, die Niederlande, Frankreich und Oberitalien 1517–18.* Freiburg: Herder.

Pezzl, Johann. 1784. *Reise durch den Baierschen Kreis.* 2nd ed. Salzburg: Orell.

Pillo-Tisanus [pseud.]. 1725. *An epistle to Ge—ge Ch—ne, M.D. F.R.S. upon his essay of health and long life. With notes, physical and metaphysical.* London: J. Roberts.

Pujati, Giuseppe. 1751. *Riflessioni sul vitto pitagorico.* Feltre: Odoardo Foglietta.

Pujati, Giuseppe. [1762] 1768. *Della preservazione della salute de' letterati e della gente applicata e sedentaria.* Reprint, Venice: Antonio Zatta.

Rabisha, William. 1661. *The whole body of cookery dissected, taught and fully manifested*. London: R. W. for Giles Calvert.

Reinach, J.W.F. 1790. *Kleine Schweizerreise von 1788*. Heidelberg: Pfähler.

Richards, John. 1853. "Extracts from the diary of John Richards, esquire, of Warmwell in Dorsetshire; from March 1697 to March 1702." *Retrospective Review* 1: 97–101, 201–5, 408–18.

Roberti, Giovambattista. 1785. "Lettera a sua eccellenza Pietro Zaguri sopra la semplicità elegante." In *Raccolta di varie operette*. Vol. 4. Bologna: Lelio della Volpe.

Röder, Philipp. 1789–93. *Reisen durch das südliche Deutschland*. 3 vols. Leipzig: Crusius.

Rumpolt, Marx. 1581. *Ein New Kochbuch*. Frankfurt am Main: Rumpolt.

Santorio, Santorio. [1614] 1676. *Medicina statica, or rules of health, in eight sections of aphorisms*, trans. J. D. Reprint, London: John Starkey.

Scappi, Bartolomeo. [1570] 2008. *The opera of Bartolmeo Scappi: L'arte Et Prudenza D'un Maestro Cuoco*, trans. Terence Scully. Reprint, Toronto: University of Toronto Press.

Schofield, John, ed. 1987. *The London surveys of Ralph Treswell*. London: London Topographical Society.

Scott-Moncrieff, Robert, ed. 1911. *The household book of Lady Grisell Baillie, 1692–1733*. Edinburgh: Scottish History Society.

Segni, Gian Battista. 1602. *Trattato sopra la carestia e fame*. Bologna: Eredi di Giovanni Rossi.

Shaw, W.A., ed. 1904. *Calendar of treasury books 1660–67*. Vol. 1. London: Public Record Office.

Smith, E.S. 1727. *The compleat housewife: Or accomplished gentlewoman's companion*. London: J. Pemberton.

Spazier, Karl. 1790. *Wanderungen durch die Schweiz*. Gotha: Ettinger.

Spiller, Elizabeth, ed. 2008. *Seventeenth century English recipe books: Cooking, physic and chirurgery in the works of Queen Henrietta Maria and Mary Tillinghast*. Aldershot: Ashgate.

St Augustine of Hippo. [397–98 AD] 1991. *Confessions*, trans. Henry Chadwick. Reprint, Oxford: Oxford University Press.

Tappert, Theodore G., ed. 1967. *Table talk, Luther's works*. Vol. 54. Philadelphia: Fortress Press.

Tillinghast, Mary. 1690. *Rare and excellent receipts, experienc'd and taught by Mrs Mary Tillinghast and now printed for the use of her scholars only*. 2nd ed. London: Self-published.

Turner, Thomas. 1984. *The diary of Thomas Turner 1754–1765*, ed. David Vaisey. Oxford: Oxford University Press.

Verral, William. 1759. *A complete system of cookery*. London: Self-published.

Verri, Pietro. 1947. *Articoli tratti dal Caffè*. In *Opere varie*, ed. Nino Valeri. Vol. 1. Florence: Le Monnier.

*Verstandige kok.* 1667. *De Verstandige kok, of Sorghvuldige Huyshoudster.* Amsterdam: Doornick.

Weatherill, Lorna, ed. 1990. *The account book of Richard Latham 1724–67.* Oxford: Oxford University Press.

Witteveen, Joop, ed. [1668] 1993. *Der Verstandige Kock, of Sorghvuldige huys houdster.* Reprint, Amsterdam: de KAN.

Wolley, Hannah. 1684. *The Queen-like closet, or rich cabinet stored with all manner of rare receipts.* 5th ed. London: printed for R. Chiswell and T. Sawbridge.

## SECONDARY LITERATURE

Aaronson, Béa. 2006. "La civilisation du goût: savoir et saveur à la table de Louis XIV." *FLS: Civilization in French and Francophone Literature* 33: 85–114.

Abad, Reynald. 2002. *Le grand marché. L'approvisionnement alimentaire de Paris sous l'Ancien Régime.* Paris: Fayard.

Abel, Wilhelm. 1973. *Crises agraires en Europe: XIIIe–XXe siècles.* Paris: Flammarion.

Abel, Wilhelm. 1980. *Agricultural fluctuations in Europe: From the thirteenth to the twentieth centuries.* London: Methuen.

Achaya, K. T. 2000. *The story of our food.* Hyderabad: Universities Press.

Adam, Sylvie, Georges Nicolas, and Anne Radeff. Forthcoming. *Hexagones et centres.*

Adamson, John, ed. 1999. *The princely courts of Europe: Ritual, politics and culture under the ancien régime 1500–1750.* London: Weidenfeld and Nicolson.

Ade Ajayi, J. F. 1998. *Africa in the nineteenth century until the 1880s.* Paris: UNESCO.

Ajmar-Wollheim, Marta. 2006. "Housework." In *At home in Renaissance Italy,* ed. Marta Ajmar-Wollheim and Flora Dennis, 152–63. London: V&A Publications.

Albala, Ken. 2002a. *Eating right in the Renaissance.* Berkeley: University of California Press.

Albala, Ken. 2002b. "Insensible perspiration and oily vegetable humor: An eighteenth-century controversy over vegetarianism." *Gastronomica* 2: 29–36.

Albala, Ken. 2003. *Food in early modern Europe.* Westport, Conn.: Greenwood Press.

Albala, Ken. 2007a. "The use and abuse of chocolate in seventeenth-century medical theory." *Food and Foodways* 15 (1–2): 53–74.

Albala, Ken. 2007b. *The banquet: Dining in the great courts of late Renaissance Europe.* Urbana and Chicago: University of Illinois Press.

Alfani, Guido. 2007. "Population et environnement en Italie du Nord au XVIᵉ siècle." *Population* 62 (4): 667–706.

Alfani, Guido. 2010. *Il Grand Tour dei Cavalieri dell'Apocalisse. L'Italia del "lungo Cinquecento" (1494–1629).* Venice: Marsilio.

Allen, Robert C. 2003. "Progress and poverty in early modern Europe." *Economic History Review* 56 (3): 403–43.

Allen, Robert C., and Cormac Ó'Gráda. 1988. "On the road again with Arthur Young: English, Irish and French agriculture during the Industrial Revolution." *The Journal of Economic History* 38 (1): 93–116.

Alpers, Svetlana. 1983. *The art of describing: Dutch art in the seventeenth century.* Berkeley: University of California Press.

Ambrosoli, Mauro. 1997. *The wild and the sown: Botany and agriculture in Western Europe, 1350–1850.* Cambridge: Cambridge University Press.

Amussen, Susan Dwyer. 1988. *An ordered society: Gender and class in early-modern England.* Oxford: Oxford University Press.

Applebaum, Robert. 2006. *Aguecheek's beef, Belch's hiccup, and other gastronomic interjections: Literature, culture, and food among the early moderns.* Chicago: University of Chicago Press.

Appleby, Andrew B. 1978. *Famine in Tudor and Stuart England.* Liverpool: Liverpool University Press.

Archer, Ian W. 2000. "Material Londoners?" In *Material London c. 1600,* ed. L. C. Orlin, 174–92. Philadelphia: University of Pennsylvania Press.

Arnold, Renato. 1985. "Gasthof- und Wirtshauswesen im Wallis des 18. Jahrhunderts." *Blätter aus der Walliser Geschichte* 18 (4): 489–500.

Assél, Astrid, and Christian Huber. 2009. *München und das Bier.* Munich: Volk.

Aston, T. H., and C.H.E. Philpin, eds. 1985. *The Brenner debate: Agrarian class structure and economic development in pre-industrial Europe.* Cambridge: Cambridge University Press.

Auerbach, Erich. [1946] 2003. *Mimesis: The representation of reality in western literature,* trans. Willard Trask. Reprint, Princeton: Princeton University Press.

Backouche, Isabelle. 2000. *La trace du fleuve. La Seine et Paris (1750–1850).* Paris: EHESS.

Bacon, Lewis Bigelow. 1948. *Agricultural geography of Europe and the Near East.* Washington: U.S. Government Printing Office.

Bairoch, Paul, Jean Batou, and Pierre Chèvre. 1988. *La population des villes européennes. Banque de données et analyse sommaire des résultats, 800–1850.* Geneva: Droz.

Bakhtin, Mikhail. 1984. *Rabelais and his world,* trans. Helene Iswolsky. Bloomington: Indiana University Press.

Banerji, Chitrita. 2007. *Eating India.* New York: Bloomsbury.

Banga, O. 1963. "Origin and distribution of the western cultivated carrot." *Genetica Agraria* 17: 357–70.

Barnes, Donna, and Peter G. Rose, eds. 2002. *Matters of taste: Food and drink in seventeenth-century Dutch art and life.* Albany: Albany Institute of History and Art/Syracuse University Press.

Barnes, Trevor J. 1996. *Logics of dislocation: Models, metaphors, and meanings of economic space.* New York/London: The Guilford Press.

Bauer, Arnold J. 2001. *Goods, power, history: Latin America's material culture.* New York: Cambridge University Press.

Behringer, Wolfgang. 2006. "Communications revolutions: A historiographical concept." *German History* 24: 333–74.

Beier, A. L. 1985. *Masterless men: The vagrancy problem in England 1560–1640.* London: Methuen.

Bendiner, Kenneth. 2004. *Food in painting: From the Renaissance to the present.* London: Reaktion.

Bérenger, Jean. 1994. "Samuel Oppenheimer (1630–1703), banquier de l'empereur Léopold I$^{er}$." *Dix-septième siècle* 46: 303–20.

Beyrer, Klaus. 2006. "The mail-coach revolution." *German History* 24: 375–86.

Bickel, Wilhelm. 1947. *Bevölkerungsgeschichte und Bevölkerungspolitik der Schweiz.* Zurich: Büchergilde Gutenberg.

Bickham, Troy. 2008. "Eating the Empire: Intersections of food, cookery and Imperialism in eighteenth-century Britain." *Past and Present* 198: 71–109.

Biloghi, Dominique. 1998. *Logistique et Ancien Régime. De l'étape royale à l'étape languedocienne.* Montpellier: PULM.

Biraben, Jean-Noël. 1975. *Les hommes et la peste en France et dans les pays européens et méditerranéens.* Vol. 1. Paris: Mouton.

Biraben, Jean-Noël. 1979. "Essai sur l'évolution du nombre des hommes." *Population* 34 (1): 13–25.

Black, Jeremy. 2002. *European warfare in a global context: 1660–1815.* New York: Routledge.

Black, Jeremy. 2003. *The British abroad: The Grand Tour in the eighteenth century.* Pbk. ed. Stroud: History Press.

Blackbourn, David. 1997. *The long nineteenth century: A history of Germany 1780–1918.* Oxford: Oxford University Press.

Blanning, T.C.W. 2002. *The culture of power and the power of culture: Old regime Europe 1660–1789.* Oxford: Oxford University Press.

Blickle, Peter. 1981. *The revolution of 1525: The German peasants' war from a new perspective.* Baltimore: Johns Hopkins University Press.

Blickle, Peter. 2008. *Das alte Europa: Vom Hochmittelalter bis zur Moderne.* Munich: Beck.

Blickle, Peter, ed. 1997. *Resistance, representation and community.* Oxford: Oxford University Press.

Blockmans, Wim, and Jean-Philippe Genet, eds. 1995–2000. *The origins of the modern state in Europe.* 7 vols. Oxford: Oxford University Press.

Blum, Jerome. 1982. *Forgotten past: Seven centuries of life on the land.* Oxford: Oxford University Press.

Bohstedt, John. 2010. *The politics of provisions: Food riots, moral economy, and market transition in England c. 1550–1850.* Farnham: Ashgate.

Bologne, Jean-Claude. 1993. *Histoire des cafés et cafetiers.* Paris: Larousse.

Bonney, Richard, ed. 1999. *The rise of the fiscal state in Europe 1200–1815.* Cambridge: Cambridge University Press.

Boombaard, Jeroen. 1999. "Sources and style: From the art of reality to the reality of art." In *The golden age of Dutch painting in historical perspective,* ed. Frans Grizenhout and Henk van Veen. Cambridge: Cambridge University Press.

Borsay, Peter. 1991. *The English urban renaissance.* Oxford: Clarendon Press.

Brady, Thomas A., Heiko Oberman, and James Tracy, eds. 1995. *Handbook of European history 1400–1600: Late Middle Ages, Renaissance and Reformation.* Leiden: Brill.

Braudel, Fernand. 1972. *The Mediterranean and the Mediterranean world in the age of Philip II,* trans. S. Reynolds. London: Collins.

Braudel, Fernand. 1981–1984. *Civilization and capitalism, 15th–18th Century.* Vol. 1: *The structures of everyday life;* Vol. 2: *The wheels of commerce;* Vol. 3: *The perspective of the world.* London: Collins.

Brears, Peter. 2008. *Cooking and dining in medieval England.* Totnes: Prospect Books.

Breen, T. H. 2004. *The marketplace of revolution: How consumer politics shaped American independence.* Oxford: Oxford University Press.

Brennan, Thomas. 1984–85. "Beyond the barriers: Popular culture and Parisian guinguettes." *Eighteenth-Century Studies* 18: 153–69.

Brennan, Thomas. 1988. *Public drinking and popular culture in eighteenth-century Paris.* Princeton: Princeton University Press.

Breschi, Marco, Lucia Pozzi, and Rosella Rettaroli. 1994. "Analogie e differenze territoriali nella crescita della popolazione italiana, 1730–1911." *Bollettino di Demografia Storica* 20: 41–94.

Brockway, Lucile H. 2002. *Science and colonial expansion.* New Haven: Yale University Press.

Brown, Alison. 1999. *The Renaissance.* 2nd ed. London: Longman.

Brown, Jonathan. 1998. *Painting in Spain 1500–1700.* New Haven: Yale University Press.

Brown, Peter, 2001. "Dining by design." In *British cutlery,* ed. Peter Brown, 43–51. London: Philip Wilson.

Burke, Peter. 1985. "Southern Italy in the 1590s: Hard times or crisis?" In *The European crisis of the 1590s,* ed. Peter Clark. London: Allen and Unwin.

Burke, Peter. 1994. *Popular culture in early modern Europe.* Rev. ed. Ashgate: Scolar.

Campbell, Bruce M. S. 1983. "Arable productivity in medieval England: Some evidence from eastern Norfolk." *Economic History Review* 43 (2): 379–404.

Campbell, Bruce M. S., and Mark Overton, eds. 1991. *Land, labour and livestock: Historical studies in European agricultural productivity.* Manchester: Manchester University Press.

Camporesi, Piero. [1983] 1988. *The incorruptible flesh: Bodily mutation and mortification in religion and folklore,* trans. T. Croft-Murray. Reprint, Cambridge: Cambridge University Press.

Camporesi, Piero. [1980] 1989. *Bread of dreams: Food and fantasy in early modern Europe,* trans. D. Gentilcore. Reprint, Cambridge: Polity Press.

Camporesi, Piero. [1990] 1994. *Exotic brew: The art of living in the age of enlightenment,* trans. C. Woodall. Reprint, Cambridge: Polity Press.

Camporesi, Piero. 1995. *The land of hunger,* trans. Tania Croft-Murray and Claire Foley, Italian dialect and Latin text trans. Shayne Mitchell. Cambridge: Polity Press.

Capatti, Alberto, and Massimo Montanari. [1999] 2003. *Italian cuisine: A cultural history,* trans. A. O'Healy. Reprint, New York: Columbia University Press.

Carlin, Martha. 1998. "Fast foods and urban living standards in medieval England." In *Food and eating in medieval Europe,* ed. Martha Carlin and J. T. Rosenthal, 27–51. London: Hambledon.

Carlin, Martha. 2008. "'What say you to a piece of beef and mustard?': The evolution of public dining in medieval and Tudor London." *Huntington Library Quarterly* 71 (1): 199–217.

Carney, Judith. 2001. *Black rice: The African origins of rice cultivation in the Americas.* Cambridge, MA: Harvard University Press.

Casanova, Pascale. 2004. *The world republic of letters,* trans. M. B. DeBevoise. Cambridge: Harvard University Press.

Casey, James. 1985. "Spain: A failed transition." In *The European crisis of the 1590s,* ed. Peter Clark. London: Allen and Unwin.

Cavaciocchi, Simonetta, ed. 1998. *Prodotti e tecniche d'Oltremare nelle economie europee, secc. XIII–XVIII.* Florence: Le Monnier.

Cavaciocchi, Simonetta, ed. 2001. *Fiere e mercati nella integrazione delle economie europee secc. XIII–XVIII.* Florence: Le Monnier.

Chang, Kwang-chih. 1997. *Food in Chinese culture: Anthropological and historical perspectives.* New Haven: Yale University Press.

Charbonneau, Frédéric. 2008. *L'École de la Gourmandise: De Louis XIV à la Révolution.* Paris: Éditions Desjonquères.

Charlesworth, Andrew. 1983. *An atlas of rural protest in Britain 1548–1900.* London: Croom Helm.

Chartres, John A. 1986. "Food consumption and internal trade." In *London 1500–1700. The making of the metropolis,* ed. A. L. Beier and Roger Finlay, 168–96. London/New York: Longman.

Chartres, John A., ed. 1990. *Agricultural markets and trade, 1500–1750.* Cambridge: Cambridge University Press.

Chatelain, Jean-Marc. 2001. "L'art de bien traiter." In *Livres en bouche: cinq siècles d'art culinaire français.* Paris: Bibliothèque nationale de France/Hermann.

Chiu, Che Bing. 1995. "La Table Imperiale sous la dynastie Qing." In *Asie III: Savourer, Gouter,* ed. Flora Blanchon, 357–71. Paris: Presses de l'Université de Paris-Sorbonne.

Christaller, Walter. 1933. *Die zentralen Orte in Süddeutschland. Eine ökonomisch-geographische Untersuchung über die Gesetzmässigkeit der Verbreitung und Entwicklung der Siedlungen mit städtischen Funktionen.* Jena: Fischer.

Cipolla, Carlo M., ed. 1974. *The Fontana economic history of Europe, Vol. 2: The sixteenth and seventeenth centuries.* Glasgow: Collins.

Clark, Christopher. 2006. *Iron kingdom: The rise and downfall of Prussia 1600–1947.* Cambridge, MA: Harvard University Press.

Clark, Gregory. 1991. "Labour productivity in English agriculture, 1300–1860." In *Land, labour and livestock: Historical studies in European agricultural productivity,* ed. B.M.S. Campbell and M. Overton. Manchester: Manchester University Press.

Clark, Peter. 1983. *The English alehouse: A social history 1200–1830.* London: Longman.

Clark, Peter, 1985a. "Introduction." In *The European crisis of the 1590s,* ed. Peter Clark. London: Allen and Unwin.

Clark, Peter, 1985b. "A crisis contained? The condition of English towns in the 1590s." In *The European crisis of the 1590s,* ed. Peter Clark. London: Allen and Unwin.

Clark, Peter. 1988. "The 'mother gin' controversy in the early eighteenth century." *Transactions of the Royal Historical Society* 5 (38): 63–84.

Clark, Peter, and Bernard Lepetit, eds. 1996. *Capital cities and their hinterlands in early modern Europe.* Aldershot: Scolar Press.

Clifford, Helen. 2002. "Knives, forks and spoons 1600–1830." In *Elegant eating: Four hundred years of dining in style,* ed. Philippa Glanville and Hilary Young, 54–57. London: V&A Publications.

Collingham, Lizzie. 2006. *Curry: A tale of cooks and conquerors.* Oxford: Oxford University Press.

Connell, K. H. 1950. *The population of Ireland, 1750–1845.* Oxford: Clarendon Press.

Cooper, J. P. 1985. "In search of agrarian capitalism." In *The Brenner debate: Agrarian class structure and economic development in pre-industrial Europe,* ed. T. H. Aston and C.H.P. Philpin, 458–77. Cambridge: Cambridge University Press.

Cooper, Nicholas. 1999. *Houses of the gentry 1480–1680.* London/New Haven: Yale University Press/Paul Mellon Centre for British Art.

Coquery, Natacha. 1998. *L'hôtel aristocratique. Le marché du luxe à Paris au XVIIIe siècle.* Paris: Publications de la Sorbonne.

Coutts, Howard, and Ivan Day. 2008. "Sugar sculpture, porcelain and table layout, 1530–1830." Paper given at Henry Moore Institute, Leeds, October 8. Available at: http://www.henry-moore.org/hmi-journal/homepage/view-occasional-papers/sugar-sculptire/intro. Accessed April 1, 2010.

Cowan, Brian. 2005. *The social life of coffee: The emergence of the British coffeehouse.* New Haven: Yale University Press.

Cowan, Brian. 2007. "New worlds, new tastes: Food fashions after the Renaissance." In *Food: The history of taste,* ed. Paul Freedman, 196–231. London: Thames and Hudson.

Crafts N.F.R. 1984. "Patterns of development in nineteenth-century Europe." *Oxford Economic Papers* N. S. 36 (3): 438–58.

Crosby, Alfred W. 1972. *The Columbian exchange: Biological and cultural consequences of 1492.* New York: Greenwood Press.

Cunningham, Andrew, and Ole Peter Grell. 2000. *The four horsemen of the Apocalypse: Religion, war, famine and death in Reformation Europe.* Cambridge: Cambridge University Press.

Curtin, Philip D. 1984. *Cross-cultural trade in the world history.* Cambridge: Cambridge University Press.

Curtin, Philip D. 1998. *The rise and fall of the plantation complex.* Cambridge: Cambridge University Press.

Darnton, Robert. 1985. *The great cat massacre: And other episodes in French cultural history.* New York: Vintage.

David, Elizabeth. 1983. "The John Trot fault: An English dinner table in the 1750s." *Petits Propos Culinaires* 15: 55–59.

David, Elizabeth. 1994. *Harvest of the cold months: The social history of ice and ices.* London: Michael Joseph.

Davidson, Nicholas S. 1985. "Northern Italy in the 1590s." In *The European crisis of the 1590s,* ed. Peter Clark. London: Allen and Unwin.

Davies, Timothy B. 1985. "Village-building in Sicily: An aristocratic remedy for the crisis of the 1590s." In *The European crisis of the 1590s,* ed. Peter Clark. London: Allen and Unwin.

Day, Ivan. 2001. "The honours of the table." In *British cutlery,* ed. Peter Brown, 32–42. London: Philip Wilson.

Day, Ivan. 2004. "From Murrell to Jarrin: Illustrations in British cookery books, 1621–1820." In *The English cookery book: Historical essays,* ed. Eileen White, 98–150. Totnes: Prospect Books.

De Vries, Jan. 1984. *European urbanization, 1500–1800.* London: Methuen.

De Vries, Jan. 2008. *The industrious revolution: Consumer behaviour and the household economy 1650 to the present.* Cambridge: Cambridge University Press.

DeJean, Joan. 2005. *The essence of style: How the French invented high fashion, fine food, chic cafes, style, sophistication and glamour.* New York: Free Press.

Del Panta, Lorenzo. 1980. *Le epidemie nella storia demografica italiana.* Turin: Loescher.

Del Panta, Lorenzo, Massimo Livi-Bacci, Giuliano Pinto, and Eugenio Sonnino. 1996. *La popolazione italiana dal Medioevo a oggi.* Rome: Laterza.

DeLoughrey, Elizabeth. 2008. "Globalizing the routes of breadfruit and other bounties." *Journal of Colonialism and Colonial History* 8 (3). Available at: http://muse.jhu.edu/journals/journal_of_colonialism_and_colonial_history/toc/cch8.3.html. Accessed February 15, 2010.

Denzel, Markus A. 1994. '*La practica della cambiatura.*' *Europäischer Zahlungs-verkehr vom 14. bis zum 17. Jahrhundert.* Stuttgart: Franz Steiner Verlag.

Denzel, Markus A. 1997. *Der Preiskurant des Handelshauses Pelloutier & Cie aus Nantes (1763–1793).* Stuttgart: Franz Steiner.

Dolan, Frances E. 1994. *Dangerous familiars: Representations of domestic crime in England 1550–1700.* Ithaca: Cornell University Press.

Donald, Diana. 2001. "'This truly natural and faithful painter': Hogarth's depiction of modern life." In *Hogarth: Representing nature's machines,* ed. David Bind-man, Fréderic Ogée, and Peter Wagner. Manchester: Manchester University Press.

Drouard, Alain. 2007. "Chefs, gourmets and gourmands: French cuisine in the nineteenth and twentieth centuries." In *Food: The history of taste,* ed. Paul Freedman. London: Thames and Hudson.

Dunmire, William. 2004. *Gardens of new Spain: How Mediterranean plants and foods changed America.* Austin: University of Texas Press.

Dupâquier, Jacques. 1997. "Les vicissitudes du peuplement (XV$^e$–XVIII$^e$ siècles)." In *Histoire des populations de l'Europe,* ed. Jean-Pierre Bardet and Jacques Dupâquier. Vol. 1. Paris: Fayard.

Dupâquier, Jacques, and Bernard Lepetit. 1988. "Le peuplement." In *Histoire de la population française,* ed. Jacques Dupâquier. Vol. 2. Paris: Presses Univer-sitaires de France.

Dyer, Alan. 2000. "Small market towns 1540–1700." In *The Cambridge urban history of Britain, Vol. 2: 1540–1840,* ed. P. Clark, 425–50. Cambridge: Cam-bridge University Press.

Earnshaw, Steven. 2000. *The pub in literature: England's altered state.* Manches-ter: Manchester University Press.

Edelstein, Ludwig. 1967. "The dietetics of antiquity." In *Ancient medicine: Se-lected papers of Ludwig Edelstein,* ed. Oswei Temkin and Lilian Temkin, 303–16. Baltimore: Johns Hopkins University Press.

Eden, Trudy. 2008. *The early American table: Food and society in the new world.* Dekalb, Ill.: Northern Illinois University Press.

Ehlert, Trude. 1997. "Regionalität und nachbarlicher Einfluss in der deutschen Rezeptliteratur des ausgehenden Mittelalters." In *Essen und kulturelle Iden-tität,* ed. Hans-Jürgen Teuteberg and Eva Barlösius, 131–47. Berlin: Akademie.

Eisenstein, Elizabeth. 2002. "An unacknowledged revolution revisited." *American Historical Review* 107 (1): 87–105, 126–28.

Ellis, Markman. 2004. *The coffee house: A cultural history.* London: Weidenfeld.

Erickson, Amy Louise. 2008. "Married women's occupations in eighteenth-century London." *Continuity and Change* 23 (2): 267–307.

Estes, J. Worth. 1996. "The medical properties of food in the eighteenth century." *Journal of the History of Medicine and Allied Sciences* 51: 127–54.

Everitt, Alan. 1968. "The food market of the English towns, 1660–1760." In *Third international conference of economic history, Munich 1965,* 57–71. Paris/La Haye: Mouton.

Everitt, Alan. 1990. "The marketing of agricultural produce, 1500–1640." In *Agricultural markets and trade, 1500–1750,* ed. J. Chartres, 15–156. Cambridge: Cambridge University Press.

Ezell, Margaret. 1987. *The patriarch's wife: Literary evidence and the history of the family.* Chapel Hill: University of North Carolina Press.

Fayard Duchêne, Janine, and Louiselle de Riedmatten. 1997. "La compagnie valaisanne de Joseph Augustin de Riedmatten au service de Sardaigne pendant la Révolution française (1793–1794) ou la critique d'une source d'histoire militaire." *Vallesia* 52: 69–142.

Feild, Rachel. 1984. *Irons in the fire: A history of cooking equipment.* Marlborough: Crowood Press.

Fenton, Alexander. 1998. "Receiving travellers: Changing Scottish traditions." In *Food and the traveller: Migration, immigration, tourism and ethnic food,* ed. Patricia Lysaght, 70–80. Nicosia: Intercollege Press.

Ferguson, Priscilla Parkhurst. 2004. *Accounting for taste: The triumph of French cuisine.* Chicago: University of Chicago Press.

Field, Jacob F. 2010. "Service, gender and wages in England, c. 1700–1860." Unpublished paper presented at Economic History Society Conference, Durham.

Field, Catherine. 2007. "'Many hands hands': Writing the self in early modern women's recipe books." In *Genre and women's life writing in early modern England,* ed. M. Dowd and J. Eckerle, 49–64. Aldershot: Ashgate.

Fisher, F. J. 1954. "The development of the London food market, 1540–1640." In *Essays in economic history,* ed. E. M. Carus-Wilson, 135–51. Vol. 1. London: Edward Arnold.

Flandrin, Jean-Louis. 1999a. "Dietary choices and culinary technique, 1500–1800." In *Food: A culinary history,* ed. Jean-Louis Flandrin and Massimo Montanari, 403–17. New York: Columbia University Press.

Flandrin, Jean-Louis. 1999b. "From dietetics to gastronomy, the liberation of the gourmet." In *Food: A culinary history,* ed. Jean-Louis Flandrin and Massimo Montanari, 418–33. New York: Columbia University Press.

Flandrin, Jean-Louis. 2000. "Dietary choices and culinary technique, 1500–1800." In *Food: A culinary history,* ed. Jean Louis Flandrin and Massimo Montanari. New York: Penguin.

Flandrin, Jean-Louis. 2007. *Arranging the meal: A history of table service in France,* trans. Julie Johnson. Berkeley: University of California Press.

Flandrin, Jean-Louis, Philip Hyman, and Mary Hyman, eds. 1983. "La Cuisine dans la Littérature de Colportage." In *Le Cuisinier François.* Paris: Montalba.

Flandrin, Jean-Louis, and Jane Cobbi, eds. 1999. *Tables d'hier, Tables d'ailleurs: Histoire et ethnologie du repas.* Paris: Jacob.

Flandrin, Jean-Louis, and Massimo Montanari, eds. 1996. *Histoire de l'alimentation.* Paris: Fayard.

Flinn, Michael W. 1974. "The stabilisation of mortality in pre-industrial Western Europe." *Journal of European Economic History* 3 (2): 285–318.

Fontaine, Laurence. 2008. *L'économie morale: pauvreté, crédit et confiance dans l'Europe préindustrielle.* Paris: Gallimard.

Forrest, Beth Marie, and April Najjaj. 2007. "Is sipping sin breaking fast? The Catholic chocolate controversy and the changing world of early modern Spain." *Food and Foodways* 15 (1–2): 31–52.

Fussell, George Edwin. 1935. "Farming methods in the early Stuart period, 1." *The Journal of Modern History* 7 (1): 1–21.

Fussell, George Edwin, and Constance Goodman. 1936. "Eighteenth century traffic in livestock." *Economic History* 3: 214–36.

Fussell, George Edwin. 1969. "The classical tradition in West European farming: The sixteenth century." *Economic History Review* 22 (3): 538–51.

Fussell, George Edwin. 1972. *The classical tradition in West European farming.* Rutherford: Farleigh Dickinson University Press.

Galloway, Patrick R. 1986. "Long-term fluctuations in climate and population in the preindustrial era." *Population and Development Review* 12 (1): 1–24.

Galloway, Patrick R. 1988. "Basic patterns in annual variations in fertility, nuptiality, mortality, and prices in pre-industrial Europe." *Population Studies* 42 (2): 275–303.

Gentilcore, David. 2010. "The *Levitico,* or how to feed a hundred Jesuits." *Food and History* 8: 87–120.

Giebmeyer, Angela. 2000. "'Die übertriebensten und schändlichsten Forderer'? Wirte und Wirtshäuser in Wesel am Ende des 18. Jahrhunderts." In *Das Wichtigste ist der Mensch,* ed. Helga Schnabel-Schüle, 563–81. Mainz: Zabern.

Gigante, Denise. 2005a. *Taste: A literary history.* New Haven: Yale University Press.

Gigante, Denise, ed. 2005b. *Gusto: Essential writings in nineteenth-century gastronomy.* London: Routledge.

Girard, Alain. 1977. "Le Triomphe de 'La Cuisinière Bourgeoise': Livres Culinaires, Cuisine et Société en France aux XVIIe et XVIIIe siècles." *Revue de l'Histoire Moderne et Contemporaine* 24: 497–523.

Girard, Alain. 1982. "Du Manuscrit à l'Imprimé: Le Livre de Cuisine en Europe aux 15e et 16e Siècles." In *Pratiques et Discours Alimentaires à La Renaissance,* ed. Jean-Claude Margolin and Robert Sauzet. Paris: G.-P. Maisonneuve et Larose.

Glanville, P., ed. 2007. *The art of drinking.* London: V&A Publications.

Gold, Carol. 2007. *Danish cookbooks: Domesticity and national identity 1616–1901.* Seattle: University of Washington Press.

Goldgar, Anne 2007. *Tulipmania: Money, honor, and knowledge in the Dutch golden age.* Chicago: University of Chicago Press.

Goldstone, Jack A. 1990. *Revolution and rebellion in the early modern world.* Berkeley: University of California Press.

Gottlieb, Beatrice. 1993. *The family in the Western world from the Black Death to the Industrial Age.* Oxford: Oxford University Press.

Goubert, Pierre. 1960. *Beauvais et le Beauvaisis entre 1600 et 1730*. Paris: S.E.V.P.E.N.

Grafe, Regina. 2004. "Popish habits vs. nutritional need: Fasting and fish consumption in Iberia in the early modern period." *University of Oxford: Discussion Papers in Economic and Social History* 55.

Gragnolati, Michelle, Caryn Bredenkamp, Meera Shekar, Monica Das Gupta, and Yi-Kyoung Li. 2006. *India's undernourished children: A call for reform and action*. Washington DC: World Bank.

Grantham, George W. 1989. "Jean Meuvret and the subsistence problem in early modern France." *The Journal of Economic History* 49 (1): 184–200.

Grantham, George W. 1993. "Divisions of labour: Agricultural productivity and occupational specialization in pre-industrial France." *The Economic History Review* N.S. 46 (3): 478–502.

Greengrass, Mark. 1985. "The later wars of religion in the French Midi." In *The European crisis of the 1590s*, ed. Peter Clark. London: Allen and Unwin.

Grigg, David B. 1980. *Population growth and agrarian change: An historical perspective*. Cambridge: Cambridge University Press.

Guerrini, Anita. 1999. "A diet for the sensitive soul: Vegetarianism in eighteenth-century Britain." *Eighteenth-Century Life* 23: 34–42.

Guerzoni, Guido. 2006. "Servicing the *casa*." In *At home in Renaissance Italy*, ed. Marta Ajmar-Wollheim and Flora Dennis, 146–51. London: V&A Publications.

Guichonnet, Paul, 1980. "Le partage politique des Alpes aux XVII$^e$–XIX$^e$ siècles." In *Histoire et civilisations des Alpes*, ed. Paul Guichonnet. Vol. 1. Toulouse: Privat and Lausanne: Payot.

Guillery, Peter. 2004. *The small house in eighteenth-century London*. London: English Heritage/Yale University Press.

Hagen, William. 2002. *Ordinary Prussians: Brandenburg Junkers and villagers, 1500–1840*. Cambridge: Cambridge University Press.

Hagn, Herbert. 1993. "Ein Münchner Gaststättenbetrieb in der früheren Neuzeit: Abfallgrube als Spiegel vergangener Alltagskultur." *Kunst und Antiquitäten* 3: 22–26.

Handel, Günther. 2002. "Die historische Wurstküche in Regensburg." *Verhandlungen des Historischen Vereins für Oberpfalz und Regensburg* 142: 127–31.

Harada, Nobuo. 2006. "A peek at the meals of the people of Edo." *Kikkoman Institute for International Food Culture Bulletin* 12: 2–6 and 13: 8–12.

Hardwick, Julie. 1998. *The practice of patriarchy: Gender and the politics of household authority in early modern France*. University Park, PA: Penn State Press.

Harvey, Karen. Forthcoming. *Domesticating patriarchy: Male authority in the eighteenth-century English home*. Oxford: Oxford University Press.

Hassell, T. G., C. E. Halpin, and M. Mellor. 1984. "Excavations at St Ebbe's, Oxford, 1967–76, Part II." *Oxoniensa* 49: 153–276.

Hecht, J. J. 1956. *The domestic servant class in eighteenth-century England.* London: Law Book Co.

Henshall, Nicholas. 1992. *The myth of absolutism: Change and continuity in early modern European monarchy.* London: Longman.

Herbage, P. F. 1982. *The cooks and the city of London: A history of the worshipful company of cooks.* London: Worshipful Company of Cooks.

Hersche, Peter. 1997. "Die Lustreise der kleinen Leute—zur geselligen Funktion der barocken Wallfahrt." In *Geselligkeit und Gesellschaft im Barockzeitalter,* ed. Wolfgang Adam, 321–32. Wiesbaden: Harrassowitz.

Hess, Karen. 1992. *The Carolina rice kitchen: The African connection.* Columbia, SC: University of South Carolina Press.

Heywood, V. H. 1983. "Relationships and evolution in the Daucus carota complex." *Israel Journal of Botany* 32: 51–65.

Hidber, Basilius. 1858. *Der ehemalige sogenannte äussere Stand der Stadt und Republik Bern.* Bern: Huber.

Hochstrasser, Julie Berger. 2000. "Feasting the eye: Painting and reality in the seventeenth-century 'Bancketje.'" In *Still-life paintings from the Netherlands 1550–1720,* ed. Alan Chong and Walter Kloek. Zwolle: Waanders.

Hochstrasser, Julie Berger. 2007. *Still life and trade in the Dutch golden age.* New Haven: Yale University Press.

Hoerner, Ludwig. 1999. *Marktwesen und Gastgewerbe im alten Hannover.* Hannover: Hahn.

Honig, Elizabeth. 1998a. *Painting and the market in early modern Antwerp.* New Haven: Yale University Press.

Honig, Elizabeth. 1998b. "Making sense of things: On the motives of Dutch still life." *RES: Anthropology and Aesthetics* 34: 166–83.

Honig, Elizabeth. 2001. "Desire and domestic economy." *Art Bulletin* 83 (2): 294–315.

Hoppitt, Julian. 2000. *A land of liberty? England 1689–1727.* Oxford: Oxford University Press.

Houston, R. A. 2001. "Colonies, enterprises, and wealth: The economies of Europe and the wider world in the seventeenth century." In *Early modern Europe: An Oxford history,* ed. Euan Cameron, 137–70. Oxford: Oxford University Press.

Howell, Martha. 2010. *Commerce before capitalism in Europe 1300–1600.* Cambridge: Cambridge University Press.

Hsia, R. Po-chia. 1989. *Social discipline in the Reformation: Central Europe 1550–1750.* London: Routledge.

Hunt, Margaret. 1992. "Wife beating, domesticity and women's independence in eighteenth century London." *Gender and History* 4 (1): 10–33.

Hunter, Lynette. 2002. "Books for daily life: Household, husbandry, behaviour." In *The history of the book in Britain: Vol. 4 1557–1695,* ed. John Barnard and D. F. McKenzie, with the assistance of Maureen Bell, 514–32. Cambridge: Cambridge University Press.

Hyman, Philip, and Mary Hyman. 2000. "Printing the kitchen: French cookbooks, 1480–1800." In *Food: A culinary history,* ed. Jean-Louis Flandrin and Massimo Montanari. New York: Penguin.

Hyman, Philip, and Mary Hyman. 2001. "Les livres de cuisine imprimés en France: du règne de Charles VIII á la fin de l'Ancien régime." In *Livres en bouche: cinq siècles d'art culinaire français,* 55–73. Paris: Bibliothèque nationale de France/Hermann.

Ishige, Naomichi. 2001. *The history and culture of Japanese food.* London and New York: Kegan Paul.

Jacobs, Marc, and Peter Scholliers, eds. 2003. *Eating out in Europe: Picnics, gourmet dining and snacks since the late eighteenth century.* Oxford: Berg.

Jahier, Hugues. 1998. "L'origine coloniale anglaise dans les activités économiques et la consommation domestique suisses au XVIIIe siècle." In *Prodotti e tecniche d'Oltremare nelle economie europee,* ed. Simonetta Cavaciocchi, 793–805. Florence: Le Monnier.

Jansen, Guido. 1999. "'On the lowest level': The status of the still life in Netherlandish art literature of the seventeenth century." In *Still-life paintings from the Netherlands 1550–1720,* ed. Alan Chong and Wouter Kloek. Zwolle: Waanders.

Janssens, Paul, and Siger Zeischka, eds. 2008. *The dining nobility. From the Burgundian dukes to the Belgian royalty/La nobless à table. Des ducs de Bourgogne aux rois des Belges.* Brussels: VUBPress.

Jenisch, Bertram. 1995. "Das Gasthaus 'Zu der Mohrin' in Villingen/Schwarzwald." *Jahrbuch für Hausforschung* 43: 267–78.

Johns, Adrian. 2002. "How to acknowledge a revolution." *American Historical Review* 107 (1): 106–25.

Jones, A., L. Montanarella, and R. Jones, eds. 2006. *Soil atlas of Europe.* Luxembourg: Office for Official Publications of the European Communities.

Jones, Jennifer. 2004. *Sexing la mode: Gender, fashion and commercial culture in old regime France.* Oxford: Berg.

Jones, Peter M. 1998. *The peasantry in the French revolution.* Cambridge: Cambridge University Press.

Kaemena, Bettina. 1999. *Studien zum Wirtshaus in der deutschen Literatur.* Frankfurt: Lang.

Kahl, William F. 1961. *The cooks' company in the eighteenth century.* London: Corporation.

Kamen, Henry. 2000. *Early modern European society.* London: Routledge.

Kaplan, Benjamin J. 2007. *Divided by faith: Religious conflict and the practice of toleration in early modern Europe.* Cambridge, Mass.: Harvard University Press.

Kaplan, Steven Laurence. 1976. *Bread, politics and political economy in the age of Louis XV.* 2 vols. Ithaca: Cornell University Press.

Kaplan, Steven Laurence. 1988. *Les ventres de Paris: pouvoir et approvisionnement dans la France d'Ancien Régime.* Paris: Fayard.

Kellenbenz, Hermann. 1983. "Pilgerhospitäler, albergues und ventas in Spanien." In *Gastfreundschaft, Taverne und Gasthaus im Mittelalter,* ed. Hans-Conrad Peyer, 137–52. Munich: Oldenbourg.

Kelly, Ian. 2003. *Cooking for kings: The life of Antonin Carême, the first celebrity chef.* London: Short Books.

Kerridge, Eric. 1951. "Ridge and furrow and agrarian history." *The Economic History Review* 4 (1): 14–36.

King, Lester. 1970. *The road to medical enlightenment, 1650–1695.* London: Macdonald.

Komecoğlu, Uğur. 2005. "The publicness and sociabilities of Ottoman coffeehouse." *The Public* 12 (2): 5–22.

Kriedte, Peter. 1983. *Peasants, landlords and merchant capitalists: Europe and the world economy, 1500–1800.* Cambridge: Cambridge University Press.

Kroener, Bernhard R. 1987. "Conditions de vie et origine sociale du personnel militaire subalterne au cours de la guerre de Trente Ans." *Francia* 15: 321–50.

Krug-Richter, Barbara. 1994. *Zwischen Fasten und Festmahl. Hospitalverpflegung in Münster 1540–1650.* Stuttgart: Franz Steiner.

Krugman, Paul R. 1997. *Development, geography, and economic theory.* Cambridge, MA and London: MIT Press.

Kümin, Beat. 2003a. "Eat in or take away: Food and drink in central European public houses around 1800." In *The landscape of food. The food relationship of town and country in modern times,* ed. Marjatta Hietala and Tanja Vahtikari, 73–82. Helsinki: Finnish Literature Society.

Kümin, Beat. 2003b. "Eating out before the restaurant: Dining cultures in early modern inns." In *Eating out in Europe: Picnics, gourmet dining and snacks since the late eighteenth century,* ed. M. Jacobs and P. Scholliers, 71–87. Oxford: Berg.

Kümin, Beat. 2003c. "Vormodernes Gastgewerbe und früher Tourismus in den bernischen Alpen." In *Tourismus und Entwicklung im Alpenraum 18.–20. Jh,* ed. Andrea Leonardi and Hans Heiss, 281–300. Innsbruck: StudienVerlag.

Kümin, Beat. 2007. *Drinking matters: Public houses and social exchange in early modern central Europe.* Basingstoke: Palgrave Macmillan.

Kümin, Beat, ed. 2009. *The European world 1500–1800: An introduction to early modern history.* London: Routledge.

Kümin, Beat, and B. Ann Tlusty, eds. 2002. *The world of the tavern: Public houses in early modern Europe.* Aldershot: Ashgate.

Kurlansky, Mark. 1997. *Cod.* New York: Walker Publishing Company.

*L'Art de la Cuisine Française au XVIIe Siècle.* 1995. Paris: Payot.

Lamb, H. H. 1985. *Climatic history and the future.* Princeton: Princeton University Press.

Langford, Paul. 1989. *A polite and commercial people: England 1727–83.* Oxford: Oxford University Press.

Laslett, Peter. 1965. *The world we have lost.* London: Methuen.

Latham, Robert, and W. Matthews, eds. [1970] 1983. "Taverns, inns and eating-houses." In *Diary of Samuel Pepys, Vol. 10: Companion,* 416–28. London: Bell.

Laudan, Rachel, and Jeffrey M. Pilcher. 1999. "Chiles, chocolate and race in new Spain: Glancing backward to Spain or looking forward to Mexico?" *Eighteenth-Century Life* 23 (2): 59–70.

Laurioux, Bruno. 2006. *Gastronomie, Humanisme et société à Rome au milieu du XVe siècle: Autour du De Honesta Voluptate de Platina.* Florence: Sismel.

Lawson, Peter. 1986. "Property crime and hard times in England, 1559–1624." *Law & History Review* 4: 95–127.

Le Roux, Thomas. 1996. *Le commerce intérieur de la France à la fin du XVIIIe siècle. Les contrastes économiques régionaux de l'espace français à travers les archives du maximum.* Paris: Nathan.

Le Roy Ladurie, Emmanuel. 1972. *Times of feast, times of famine: A history of climate since the year 1000.* London: Allen and Unwin.

Lee, R. D. 1981. "Short-term variations: Vital rates, prices and weather." In *The population history of England, 1541–1871: A reconstruction,* ed. E. A. Wrigley and R. S. Schofield, 356–401. London: Edward Arnold.

Lehmann, Gilly. 1999. "Politics in the kitchen." *Eighteenth-Century Life* 23 (2): 71–83.

Lehmann, Gilly. 2003. *The British housewife: Cookery books, cooking and society in eighteenth-century Britain.* Totnes: Prospect Books.

Li, Lillian M., and Alison Dray-Novey. 1999. "Guarding Beijing's food security in the Qing dynasty: State, market and police." *The Journal of Asian Studies* 58 (4): 992–1032.

Livi-Bacci, Massimo. 1990. *Population and nutrition: An essay on European demographic history.* Cambridge: Cambridge University Press.

Livi-Bacci, Massimo. 1991. *Population and nutrition: An essay on European demographic history.* Cambridge: Cambridge University Press.

Livi-Bacci, Massimo. 1999. *The population of Europe: A history.* Oxford: Blackwell.

Llopis, Manuel Martínez. 1995. *Historia de la Gastronomía española.* Huesca: Ministerio de Agricultura, Pesca y Alimentación.

Long, W. Harwood. 1979. "The low yields of corn in medieval England." *The Economic History Review* N.S. 32 (4): 459–69.

Ludington, Charles C. 2004. "'Be sometimes to your country true': The politics of wine in England, 1660–1714." In *A pleasing sinne: Drink and conviviality in seventeenth-century England,* ed. A. Smyth, 89–106. Cambridge: D. S. Brewer.

Lunn, Peter G. 1989. "Nutrition, immunity, and infection." In *Famine, disease and the social order in early modern society,* ed. John Walter and Roger Schofield. Cambridge: Cambridge University Press.

MacKenney, Richard. 1987. *Tradesmen and traders: The world of the guilds in Venice and Europe, c. 1250–c.1650.* London: Croom Helm.

Mączak, Antoni. 1995. *Travel in early modern Europe.* Cambridge: Polity Press.

Magagna, Victor V. 1991. *Communities of grain: Rural rebellion in comparative perspective.* Ithaca and London: Cornell University Press.

Malaguzzi, Silvia. 2008. *Food and feasting in art,* trans. Brian Phillips. Los Angeles: Getty.

Malthus, Thomas R. [1798] 1970. *An essay on the principle of population,* ed. Anthony Flew. Reprint, Harmondsworth: Penguin Books.

Mann, Charles C. 2005. *1491: New revelations of the Americas before Columbus.* New York: Alfred A. Knopf.

Marfany, Joan-Lluis. 1997. "Debate. The invention of leisure in early modern Europe." *Past and Present* 156: 174–91.

Margairaz, Dominique. 1988. *Foires et marchés dans la France préindustrielle.* Paris: EHESS.

Martin, A. Lynn. 2001. *Alcohol, sex and gender in late medieval and early modern Europe.* Basingstoke: Palgrave.

Martin, Laura C. 2007. *Tea: The drink that changed the world.* Rutland, VT: Tuttle Publishing.

Mattmüller, Markus. 1987. *Bevölkerungsgeschichte der Schweiz.* Basle: Helbing and Lichtenhahn.

McCann, James. 2005. *Maize and grace.* Harvard, MA: Harvard University Press.

McCusker, John J., and Russell R. Menard. 1991. *The economy of British America 1607–1789.* Chapel Hill: University of North Carolina Press.

McEvedy, Colin, and Richard Jones. 1978. *Atlas of world population history.* London: Allen Lane.

McKeon, Michael. [1987] 2003. *The origins of the English novel, 1600–1740.* Reprint, Baltimore: Johns Hopkins University Press.

McKeon, Michael. 2005. *The secret history of domesticity: Public, private, and the division of knowledge.* Baltimore: Johns Hopkins University Press.

McKeown, Thomas. 1976. *The modern rise of population.* London: Edward Arnold.

McTighe, Sheila. 2004. "Foods and the body in Italian genre paintings, about 1580: Campi, Passarotti, Carracci." *Art Bulletin* 86 (2): 301–23.

McTighe, Sheila. Forthcoming. *The imaginary everyday: Genre painting and prints in Italy and France 1580–1670.* Pittsburgh: The Bownes Library.

Meijer, Berthe. 1982. "Dutch cookbooks printed in the sixteenth and seventeenth centuries." *Petits Propos Culinaires* 11: 47–55.

Meldrum, Tim. 2000. *Domestic service and gender, 1650–1750.* Harlow: Pearson.

Melton, Edgar. 1998. "The Russian peasantries, 1450–1860." In *The peasantries of Europe: From the fourteenth to the eighteenth centuries,* ed. Tom Scott, 227–65. London: Addison Lesley Longman.

Mennell, Stephen. 1987. "Eten in Nederland." *De Gids* 2 (3): 198–207.

Mennell, Stephen. [1985] 1996. *All manners of food: Eating and taste in England and France from the Middle Ages to the present.* 2nd ed. Urbana: University of Illinois Press. [1st edn. Oxford: Blackwell.]

Mennell, Stephen. 2003. "Eating in the public sphere in the nineteenth and twentieth centuries." In *Eating out in Europe: Picnics, gourmet dining and snacks since the late eighteenth century,* ed. M. Jacobs and P. Scholliers, 245–60. Oxford: Berg.

Messent, Michael. 2001. *A short history of the worshipful company of cooks.* London: Worshipful Company of Cooks. Available at: http://www.cookslivery.org.uk/history.asp. Accessed September 27, 2009.

Meuvret, Jean. 1946. "Les crises de subsistances et la démographie de la France d'Ancien Régime." *Population* 1 (4): 643–50.

Meuvret, Jean. 1965. "Demographic crisis in France from the sixteenth to the eighteenth century." In *Population in History,* ed. David V. Glass and D.E.C. Eversley. London: Edward Arnold.

Meuvret, Jean. 1977–88. *Le Problème des subsistences pendant l'époque de Louis XIV.* 6 vols. Paris: Mouton.

Meyzie, Philippe. 2010. *L'alimentation en Europe à l'époque moderne.* Paris: Armand Colin.

Michel, Dominique. 1999. *Vatel et la naissance de la gastronomie.* Paris: Fayard.

Michel, Guy-Jean. 1993. "La distillation du kirsch à Fougerolles des origines à la première guerre mondiale." *Bulletin de la SALSA de la Haute-Saône* N.S. 25: 127–202.

Mikkeli, Heikki. 1999. *Hygiene in the early modern medical tradition.* Helsinki: Finnish Academy of Science and Letters.

Miller, Henry H. 1988. "An archaeological perspective on the evolution of diet in the colonial Chesapeake 1620–1745." In *Colonial Chesapeake society,* ed. Lois Green Carr, Philip D. Morgan, and Jean B. Russo, 176–99. Chapel Hill: University of North Carolina Press.

Milton, Giles. 1999. *Nathaniel's nutmeg.* London: Sceptre.

Mintz, Sidney W. 1986. *Sweetness and power: The place of sugar in modern history.* New York: Penguin.

Mintz, Sidney W. 1996. *Tasting food, tasting freedom.* Boston: Beacon Press.

Mitchell, A. R. 1977. "The European fisheries in early modern history." In *The Cambridge economic history of Europe. Vol. 5: The economic organization of early modern Europe,* ed. E. E. Rich and C. H. Wilson, 132–84. Cambridge: Cambridge University Press.

Mitchell, David. 2001. "The clerk's view." In *British cutlery,* ed. Peter Brown, 19–30. London: Philip Wilson.

Montanari, Massimo. 2006. *Food is culture.* New York: Columbia University Press.

Montenach, Anne. 2009. *L'économie du quotidien. Espaces et pratiques du commerce alimentaire à Lyon au XVIIe siècle.* Grenoble: Presses Universitaires de Grenoble.

Moriceau, Jean-Marc. 1994. *Les fermiers de l'Ile de France. L'ascension d'un patronat agricole (XVe–XVIIIe siècle).* Paris: Fayard.

Murphey, Rhoads. 1988. "Provisioning Istanbul: The state and subsistence in the early Middle East." *Food and Foodways* 2 (3): 217–63.

Musgrave, Peter. 1999. *The early modern European economy.* Basingstoke: Macmillan.

Nadal, Jordi. 1988. "La populación española durante los siglos XVI, XVII y XVIII: un balance a escala regional." In *Demografía histórica en España,* ed. Vicente Pérez Moreda and David Reher. Madrid: Ediciones El Arquero.

Netting, Robert McC. 1993. *Smallholders, householders: Farm families and the ecology of intensive, sustainable agriculture.* Stanford: Stanford University Press.

Nishiyama, Matsunosuke, and Gerald Groemer. 1997. *Edo culture: Daily life and diversions in urban Japan, 1600–1868.* Honolulu: University of Hawaii Press.

North, Michael. 2008. *Material delight and the joy of living: Cultural consumption in the age of enlightenment in Germany,* trans. Pamela Selwyn. Aldershot: Ashgate.

O'Brien, Patrick K. 1996. "Path dependency, or why Britain became an industrialized and urbanized economy long before France." *Economic History Review* 49 (2): 213–49.

O'Brien, Patrick K., and Gianni Toniolo. 1991. "The poverty of Italy and the backwardness of its agriculture before 1914." In *Land, labour and livestock: Historical studies in European agricultural productivity,* ed. B.M.S. Campbell and M. Overton, 385–409. Manchester: Manchester University Press.

O'Brien, Patrick K., and Leandro Prados de la Escosura. 1992. "Agricultural productivity and European industrialization, 1890–1980." *Economic History Review* 45 (3): 514–36.

O'Callaghan, Michelle. 2004. "Tavern societies, the Inns of Court, and the culture of conviviality in early seventeenth-century London." In *A Pleasing sinne: Drink and conviviality in seventeenth-century England,* ed. A. Smyth, 37–51. Cambridge: D.S. Brewer.

O'Callaghan, Michelle. 2007. *The English wits: Literature and sociability in early modern England.* Cambridge: Cambridge University Press.

O'Connell, Sheila. 1999. *The popular print in England.* London: British Museum Press.

Oberpenning, Hannelore. 1996. *Migration und Fernhandel im "Tödden-System." Wanderhändler aus dem nördlichen Münsterland im mittleren und nördlichen Europa des 18. und 19. Jahrhunderts.* Osnabrück: Rasch.

Ogilvie, Sheilagh. 2003. *A bitter living: Women, markets and social capital in early modern Germany.* Oxford: Oxford University Press.

Ogilvie, Sheilagh, and Markus Cerman, eds. 1996. *European proto-industrialization.* 2nd ed. Cambridge: Cambridge University Press.

Ogilvie, Sheilagh, Markus Küpfer, and Janine Maegraith. 2009. "Women and the material culture of food in early modern Germany." *Early Modern Women: An Interdisciplinary Journal* 4: 149–59.

Ogot, B. A., ed. 1999. *Africa from the sixteenth to the eighteenth century.* Paris: UNESCO.

Ohnuki-Tierney, Emiko. 1994. *Rice as self: Japanese identities through time.* Princeton: Princeton University Press.

Orlin, Lena Cowen, ed. 2000. *Material London c. 1600.* Philadelphia: University of Pennsylvania Press.

Orrman, Eljas. 2003. "Rural conditions." In *The Cambridge history of Scandinavia, Vol. 1: Prehistory to 1520,* ed. Knut Helle, 250–311. Cambridge: Cambridge University Press.

Outram, Dorinda. 1995. *The Enlightenment.* Cambridge: Cambridge University Press.

Overton, Mark. 1991. "The determinants of crop yields in early modern England." In *Land, labour and livestock: Historical studies in European agricultural productivity,* ed. B.M.S. Campbell and M. Overton, 284–322. Manchester: Manchester University Press.

Overton, Mark. 2001. "The integration of agricultural markets in England 1200–1800." In *Fiere e mercati nella integrazione delle economie europee,* ed. Simonetta Cavaciocchi, 299–308. Florence: Le Monnier.

Overton, Mark, Jane Whittle, Darron Dean, and Andrew Hann. 2004. *Production and consumption in English households 1600–1750.* London: Routledge.

*Oxford Dictionary of National Biography.* [2004] 2008. Available at: http://www.oxforddnb.com. Accessed November 4, 2010. [Print ed.: Ed. H.C.G. Matthew and Brian Harrison. Oxford: Oxford University Press].

Özveren, Eyüp. 2003. "Black Sea and the grain provisioning of Istanbul in the longue durée." In *Nourrir les cités de Méditerranée: antiquité–temps modernes,* ed. Brigitte Marin and Catherine Virlouvet, 223–50. Paris: Maisonneuve and Larose.

Pagel, Walter. 1982. *Joan Baptista van Helmont: Reformer of science and medicine.* Cambridge: Cambridge University Press.

Paliaga, Franco. 1997. *Vincenzo Campi.* Soncino: Edizioni dei Soncino.

Palmer, Richard. 1991. "Health, hygiene and longevity in medieval and renaissance Europe." In *History of hygiene,* ed. Y. Kawakita, S. Sakai, and Y. Ostuka, 75–98. Tokyo: Ishiyaku.

Parasecoli, Fabio. 2004. *Food culture in Italy.* Westport, CT: Greenwood Press.

Pardailhé-Galabrun, Annik. 1988. *La naissance de l'intime: 3000 foyers parisiens XVIIe–XVIIIe siècles.* Paris: Presses universitaires de France.

Parker, Geoffrey. 2008. "Crisis and catastrophe: The global crisis of the seventeenth century reconsidered." *American Historical Review* 113 (4): 1053–79.

Parthasarathi, Prasannan. 1998. "Rethinking wages and competitiveness in the eighteenth century: Britain and South India." *Past and Present* 158: 79–109.

Paulson, Ronald. 1993. *Hogarth, volume 3: Art and politics, 1750–1764.* New Brunswick: Rutgers University Press.

Pelet, Paul-Louis. 1962. "La Feuille d'Avis, miroir de l'économie vaudoise: 1762–1850." In *Deux cents ans de vie et d'histoire vaudoise: la Feuille d'Avis de Lausanne, 1762–1961,* 98–226. Lausanne: Payot.

Pendergrast, Mark. 1999. *Uncommon grounds: The history of coffee and how it transformed our world.* New York: Basic Books.

Pennell, Sara. 1997. "The material culture of food in early modern England, c. 1650–1750." D. Phil, University of Oxford.

Pennell, Sara. 1998. "'Pots and pans history': The material culture of the kitchen in early modern England." *Journal of Design History* 11 (3): 201–16.

Pennell, Sara. 2000. "'Great quantities of gooseberry pie and baked clod of beef': Victualling and eating out in early modern London." In *Londinopolis: Essays in the cultural and social history of early modern London,* ed. P. Griffiths and M.S.R. Jenner, 228–49. Manchester: Manchester University Press.

Pennell, Sara. 2002. "Four hundred years of keeping food hot." In *Elegant eating: Four hundred years of dining in style,* ed. Philippa Glanville and Hilary Young, 68–71. London: V&A Publications.

Pennell, Sara. 2004. "Perfecting practice? Women, manuscript recipes and knowledge in early modern England." In *Early modern women's manuscript writing,* ed. Victoria Burke and Jonathan Gibson, 237–58. Aldershot: Ashgate.

Pennell, Sara. 2010. "All but the kitchen sink: Household sales and the circulation of secondhand goods in early modern England." In *Modernity and the second-hand trade: European consumption cultures and practices 1700–1900,* ed. J. Stobart and I. Van Damme, 37–56. London: Palgrave.

Perrenoud, Alfred. 1997. "La mortalité." In *Histoire des populations de l'Europe,* ed. Jean-Pierre Bardet and Jacques Dupâquier. Vol. 1. Paris: Fayard.

Peterson, T. Sarah. 1994. *Acquired taste: The French origins of modern cooking.* Ithaca, NY: Cornell University Press.

Peterson, T. Sarah. 2006. *The cookbook that changed the world: The origins of modern cuisine.* Stroud: Tempus.

Pettid, Michael. 2008. *Korean cuisine: An illustrated history.* London: Reaktion Books.

Peyer, Hans-Conrad, ed. 1983. *Gastfreundschaft, Taverne und Gasthaus im Mittelalter.* Munich: Oldenbourg.

Pfister, Christian. 1997. "L'Allemagne: du XVIᵉ au XVIIIᵉ siècle." In *Histoire des populations de l'Europe,* ed. Jean-Pierre Bardet and Jacques Dupâquier. Vol. 1. Paris: Fayard.

Phillips, F.T. 1966. *A second history of the worshipful company of cooks, London.* London: privately printed.

Pickl, Othmar. 1993. "Die einstige Sprachinsel Gottschee/Kocevje (Slowenien) und ihre Wanderhändler." *In Wanderhandel in Europa,* ed. Wilfried Reininghaus, 93–99. Dortmund: Gesellschaft für Westfälische Wirtschaftsgeschichte.

Pignatti, Terisio. 1979. *The golden century of Venetian painting.* New York: George Braziller.

Pilcher, Jeffrey M. 2006. *Food in world history.* New York: Routledge.

Pinkard, Susan. 2009. *A revolution in taste: The rise of French cuisine 1650–1800.* Cambridge: Cambridge University Press.

Pleij, Herman. 2001. *Dreaming of Cockagine: Medieval fantasies of the perfect life,* trans. Diane Webb. New York: Columbia University Press.

Pomeranz, Kenneth. 2000. *The great divergence: Europe, China and the making of the modern world economy.* Princeton: Princeton University Press.

Pomeranz, Kenneth. 2002. "Beyond the East–West binary: Resituating development paths in the eighteenth-century world." *Journal of Asian Studies* 61 (2): 539–90.

Pomeranz, Kenneth, and Steven Topik. 1999. *The world that trade created: Society, culture and the world economy 1400 to the present.* Armonk, NY: M. E. Sharpe.

Post, John D. 1977. *The last great subsistence crisis in the Western world.* Baltimore: The Johns Hopkins University Press.

Potter, David. 1999. "Mrs Eells' 'Unique Receipts.'" *Petits Propos Culinaires* 61: 16–19.

Potter, David. 2000. "Some notes on Edward Kidder." *Petits Propos Culinaires* 65: 9–27.

Potter, David. 2006. "The household receipt book of Ann, Lady Fanshawe." *Petits Propos Culinaires* 80: 19–32.

Pounds, N.J.G. 1979. *An historical geography of Europe, 1500–1840.* Cambridge: Cambridge University Press.

Pounds, N.J.G. 1994. *An economic history of medieval Europe.* 2nd ed. London: Longman.

Poynter, F.N.L. 1962. *A bibliography of Gervase Markham, 1568?–1637.* Oxford Bibliographical Society Publications, N.S. 11. Oxford: Oxford University Press.

Prest, John. 1981. *The Garden of Eden: The botanic garden and the re-creation of paradise.* New Haven: Yale University Press.

Pullan, Brian. 1985. "The roles of the state and the town in the general crisis of the 1590s." In *The European crisis of the 1590s,* ed. Peter Clark. London: Allen and Unwin.

Pulz, Waltraud. 2007. *Nüchternes Kalkül—Verzehrende Leidenschaft. Nahrungsabstinenz im 16. Jahrhundert.* Cologne: Böhlau Verlag.

Quellier, Florent. 2003. *Des fruits et des hommes. L'arboriculture fruitière en Ile-de-France (vers 1600–vers 1800).* Rennes: PUR.

Quellier, Florent. 2007. *La table des Français, une histoire culturelle (XV^e–début XIX^e siècle).* Rennes: PUR.

Radeff, Anne. 1993. "Le réseau des auberges vaudoises au XVIIIe siècle." *Revue historique vaudoise* 101: 125–37.

Radeff, Anne. 1996. *Du café dans le chaudron. Economie globale d'Ancien Régime (Suisse occidentale, Franche-Comté et Savoie).* Lausanne: Société d'histoire de la Suisse romande.

Radeff, Anne. 2007a. "Centralités et décentralités alpines au XVIIIe siècle. Entre l'Alsace et le Milanais." In *Les fruits de la récolte. Etudes offertes à Jean-Michel Boehler,* ed. Jean-François Chauvard and Isabelle Laboulais, 421–36. Strasbourg: Presses universitaires.

Radeff, Anne. 2007b. "Centres et périphéries ou centralités et décentralités?" In *Per vie di terra. Movimenti di uomini e di cose nelle società di antico regime,* ed. Angelo Torre, 21–32. Milan: Franco Angeli.

Raeff, Marc. 1983. *The well-ordered police state: Social and institutional change through law in the Germanies and Russia, 1600–1800.* New Haven: Yale University Press.

Rageth-Fritz, Margrit. 1987. *Der Goldene Falken: Der berühmteste Gasthof im alten Bern.* Bern: Francke.

Rankin, Alisha. 2007. "Becoming an expert practitioner: Court experimentalism and the medical skills of Anna of Saxony (1532–85)." *Isis: Journal of the History of Science Society* 98: 23–53.

Raven, James. 1993. "Selling books across Europe, c. 1450–1800: An overview." *Publishing History* 34: 5–19.

Rebora, Giovanni. 2001. *Culture of the fork: A brief history of food in Europe,* trans. Albert Sonnenfeld. New York: Columbia University Press.

Reed, Michael. 1996. "London and its hinterland 1600–1800: The view from the provinces." In *Capital cities and their hinterlands in early modern Europe,* ed. Peter Clark and Bernard Lepetit, 51–83. Aldershot: Scolar Press.

Reininghaus, Wilfried, ed. 1993. *Wanderhandel in Europa.* Dortmund: Gesellschaft für Westfälische Wirtschaftsgeschichte.

Reis, Jaime. 2000. "How poor was the European periphery before 1850? The Mediterranean vs. Scandinavia." In *The Mediterranean response to globalization before 1950,* ed. Sevket Pamuk and Jeffrey G. Williamson. London: Routledge.

Richards, Sarah. 1999. *Eighteenth-century ceramics: Products for a civilised society.* Manchester: Manchester University Press.

Ringrose, David R. 1983. *Madrid and the Spanish economy, 1560–1850.* Berkeley and Los Angeles: University of California Press.

Roche, Daniel. 1983. "Cuisine et alimentation populaire à Paris." *Dix-huitième siècle* 15: 7–18.

Roche, Daniel. 1997. *Histoire des choses banales. Naissance de la société de consommation, XVIIIe-XIXe siècle.* Paris: Fayard.

Roche, Daniel. 1998a. *Le peuple de Paris. Essai sur la culture populaire au XVIIIe siècle.* Paris: Fayard.

Roche, Daniel. 1998b. *France in the Enlightenment.* Cambridge, MA: Harvard University Press.

Rogers, Ben. 2003. *Beef and liberty: Roast beef, John Bull and the English nation.* London: Chatto and Windus.

Rogers, Clifford J., ed. 1995. *The military revolution debate: Readings on the military transformation of early modern Europe.* Oxford: Westview.

Root, H. 1994. *The fountains of privilege.* Berkeley: University of California Press.

Rose, Peter G. 1989. *The sensible cook: Dutch foodways in the old and the new world.* Syracuse: Syracuse University Press.

Rosenberg, Charles. 1992. "Medical text and social context: Explaining William Buchan's *Domestic Medicine.*" In *Explaining epidemics and other studies in the history of medicine,* 32–56. Cambridge: Cambridge University Press.

Rosseaux, Ulrich. 2007. *Freiräume: Unterhaltung, Vergnügen und Erholung in Dresden, 1694–1830.* Cologne: Böhlau.

Roth-Lochner, Barbara. 1991. "Les repas du graveur Fournier à l'auberge de Grange-Canal (1778–83)." *Revue du Vieux-Genève* 21: 42–51.

Roux, Jean-Paul. 1984. *L'Histoire des Turcs.* Paris: Librerie Arthème Fayard.

Rugea, Sandra. 2009. "Hospitality and politics at the Lord Mayor's Day feasts of 1673 and 1714." MA Dissertation, Roehampton University.

Sabean, David Warren. 1984. *Power in the blood: Popular culture and village discourse in early modern Germany.* Cambridge: Cambridge University Press.

Sabean, David Warren. 1990. *Property, production and family in Neckarhausen 1700–1870.* Cambridge: Cambridge University Press.

Sabean, David Warren. 1998. *Kinship in Neckarhausen 1700–1870.* Cambridge: Cambridge University Press.

Sacks, David Harris. 2000. "London's dominion: The metropolis, the market economy, and the state." In *Material London c. 1600,* ed. L. C. Orlin, 20–54. Philadelphia: University of Pennsylvania Press.

Salaman, Redcliffe. [1949] 1985. *The history and social influence of the potato.* Reprint, Cambridge: Cambridge University Press.

Salinger, Sharon V. 2002. *Taverns and drinking in colonial America.* Baltimore: The Johns Hopkins University Press.

Sarti, Raffaella. 2002. *Europe at home: Family and material culture 1500–1800.* London/New Haven: Yale University Press.

Saupin, Guy. 2006. "Pratiques publicitaires dans les métiers du luxe dans trois villes provinciales de l'Ouest de la France dans la seconde moitié du XVIIIe siècle." In *Retailers and consumer changes in early modern Europe. England, France, Italy and the Low Countries,* ed. Bruno Blondé, Eugénie Briot, Natacha Coquery, and Laura Van Aert. Tours: PUFR.

Schama, Simon. [1987] 1988. *The embarrassment of riches: An interpretation of Dutch culture in the golden age.* Pbk. ed. Reprint, London: Fontana.

Schneider, Jürgen. 1998. "Die neuen Getränke: Schokolade, Kaffee und Tee (16.–18. Jahrhundert)." In *Prodotti e tecniche d'Oltremare nelle economie europee,* ed. Simonetta Cavaciocchi, 541–590. Florence: Le Monnier.

Schneider, Norbert. 2003. *Still life.* Köln: Taschen.

Schulz, Knut. 1983. "Gesellentrinkstuben und Gesellenherbergen im 14./15. und 16. Jahrhundert." In *Gastfreundschaft, Taverne und Gasthaus im Mittelalter,* ed. Hans-Conrad Peyer, 221–42. Munich: Oldenbourg.

Scott, Tom, ed. 1998. *The peasantries of Europe from the fourteenth to the eighteenth centuries.* London: Longman.

Seavoy, Ronald E. 1986. *Famine in peasant society.* New York: Greenwood Press.

Semple, Ellen Churchill. 1928. "Ancient Mediterranean agriculture: Part 1." *Agricultural History Review* 2 (2): 61–98.

Sen, Amartya. 1981. *Poverty and famines: An essay on entitlement and deprivation.* Oxford: Oxford University Press.

Shapin, Steven. 2003a. "How to eat like a gentleman: Dietetics and ethics in early modern England." In *Right living: An Anglo-American tradition of self-help medicine and hygiene,* ed. Charles Rosenberg, 21–58. Baltimore and London: Johns Hopkins University Press.

Shapin, Steven. 2003b. "Trusting George Cheyne: Scientific expertise, common sense, and moral authority in early eighteenth-century dietetic medicine." *The Bulletin of the History of Medicine* 77: 270–97.

Sheehan, James J. 1989. *German history 1770–1866.* Oxford: Oxford University Press.

Sheller, Mimi. 2003. *Consuming the Caribbean.* New York: Routledge.

Shiel, Robert S. 1991. "Improving soil productivity in the pre-fertiliser era." In *Land, labour and livestock: Historical studies in European agricultural productivity,* ed. B.M.S. Campbell and M. Overton, 51–77. Manchester: Manchester University Press.

Simonton, Deborah. 1991. "Apprenticeship, gender and training in eighteenth-century England." In *Markets and manufacture in early industrial Europe,* ed. Maxine Berg, 227–58. London: Routledge.

Simpson, James 2004. "European farmers and the British 'agricultural revolution.'" In *Exceptionalism and industrialization: Britain and its European rivals, 1688–1815,* ed. Leandro Prados de la Escosura, 69–85. Cambridge: Cambridge University Press.

Singer, Amy. 2002. *Constructing Ottoman beneficence: An Imperial soup kitchen in Jerusalem.* Albany: State University of New York Press.

Slicher van Bath, B. H. 1963. *The agrarian history of Western Europe, A.D. 500–1850.* London: Edward Arnold.

Slicher van Bath, B. H. 1977. "Agriculture in the vital revolution." In *The Cambridge economic history of Europe. Vol. 5: The economic organization of early modern Europe,* ed. E. E. Rich and C. H. Wilson, 42–132. Cambridge: Cambridge University Press.

Smith, Colin. 2002. "The wholesale and retail markets of London, 1660–1840." *Economic History Review* 55: 31–50.

Smyth, Adam, ed. 2004. *A pleasing sinne: Drink and conviviality in seventeenth-century England.* Woodbridge: Boydell and Brewer.

Souden, David. 1985. "Demographic crisis and Europe in the 1590s." In *The European crisis of the 1590s,* ed. Peter Clark. London: Allen and Unwin.

Spang, Rebecca. 2000. *The invention of the restaurant: Paris and modern gastronomic culture.* Cambridge, MA: Harvard UP.

Spary, Emma, and Paul White. 2004. "Food of paradise: Tahitian breadfruit and the autocritique of European consumption." *Endeavour* 28 (2): 75–80.

Starn, Randolph. 2002. "The early modern muddle." *Journal of Early Modern History* 6: 296–307.

Steedman, Carolyn. 2009. *Labours lost: Domestic service and the making of modern England.* Cambridge: Cambridge University Press.

Steinberger, Michael. 2009. *Au revoir to all that: Food, wine, and the end of France.* New York: Bloomsbury.

Stobart, J., and I. Van Damme, eds. 2010. "Modernity and the second-hand trade: Themes, topics and debates." In *Modernity and the second-hand trade: European consumption cultures and practices 1700–1900*. London: Palgrave.

Stoichita, Victor. 1997. *The self-aware image: An insight into early modern metapainting*, trans. Anne-Marie Glasheen. Cambridge: Cambridge University Press.

Strauss, Gerald. 1989. *Law, resistance and the state: The opposition to Roman law in Reformation Germany*. Princeton: Princeton University Press.

Tanzer, Gerhard. 1992. *"Spectacle müssen seyn." Die Freizeit der Wiener im 18. Jahrhundert*. Vienna: Böhlau.

Targett, Peter. 1989. "Edward Kidder: His book and his schools." *Petits Propos Culinaires* 32: 35–44.

Taylor, Charles. 2007. *A secular age*. Cambridge, MA: Harvard University Press.

Te Brake, Wayne. 1998. *Shaping history: Ordinary people in European politics, 1500–1700*. Berkeley: University of California Press.

Teply, Karl. 1980. *Die Einführung des Kaffees in Wien. Georg Franz Koltschitzky, Johannes Diodato, Isaak de Luca*. Vienna: Jugend und Volk.

Teuteberg, Hans-Jürgen. 1997. "Homo edens. Reflexionen zu einer neuen Kulturgeschichte des Essens." *Historische Zeitschrift* 265: 1–28.

Teuteberg, Hans-Jürgen. 2003. "The rising popularity of dining out in German restaurants in the aftermath of modern urbanization." In *Eating out in Europe: Picnics, gourmet dining and snacks since the late eighteenth century*, ed. M. Jacobs and P. Scholliers, 281–99. Oxford: Berg.

Thirsk, Joan. 1978. *Economic policy and projects: The development of a consumer society in early modern England*. Oxford: Clarendon Press.

Thirsk, Joan. 2000. "England's provinces: Did they serve or drive material London?" In *Material London c. 1600*, ed. L. C. Orlin, 97–108. Philadelphia: University of Pennsylvania Press.

Thirsk, Joan. 2007. *Food in early modern England: Phases, fads, fashions 1500–1760*. London: Hambledon Continuum.

This, Hervé, and Pierre Gagnaire. 2008. *Cooking: The quintessential art*, trans. Malcolm DeBevoise. Berkeley: University of California Press.

Thompson, F. P. 1971. "The moral economy of the English crowd in the eighteenth century." *Past and Present* 50: 76–136.

Thompson, E. P. 1991. "Rough music." In *Customs in common*, 467–568. Harmondsworth: Penguin.

Thornton, John. 1998. *African and Africans in the making of the Atlantic world, 1400–1800*. Cambridge: Cambridge University Press.

Tilly, Louise. 1971. "The food riot as a form of political conflict in France." *Journal of Interdisciplinary History* 2: 23–58.

Tlusty, B. Ann. 1998. "Water of life, water of death: The controversy over brandy and gin in early modern Augsburg." *Central European History* 31: 1–30.

Tlusty, B. Ann. 2001. *Bacchus and civic order: The culture of drink in early modern Germany*. Charlottesville: University of Virginia Press.

Tlusty, B. Ann. 2002. "The public house, defence and military culture in early modern Germany." In *The World of the Tavern: Public Houses in Early Modern Europe*, ed. B. Kümin and B.A. Tlusty, 136–56. Aldershot: Ashgate.

Tomasik, T. J., and J. M. Vitullo, eds. 2007. *At the table: Metaphorical and material cultures of food in medieval and early modern Europe*. Turnhout: Brepols.

Toussaint-Samat, Maguelonne. 2009. *A history of food*. New expanded ed. Oxford: Wiley-Blackwell.

Turner, Nicholas. 1986. *Florentine drawings of the sixteenth century*. Cambridge: Cambridge University Press.

Van Bavel, Bas J. P., and Eric Thoen, eds. 1999. *Land productivity and agrosystems in the North Sea area: Middle Ages–twentieth century, elements for comparison*. Turnhout: Brepols.

Van den Heuvel, Danielle. 2008. "Partners in marriage and business? Guilds and the family economy in urban food trades in the Dutch Republic." *Continuity and Change* 23: 217–36.

Van der Woude, Ad. 1991. "The volume and value of paintings in Holland at the time of the Dutch Republic." In *Art in history/history in art: Studies in seventeenth-century Dutch culture,* ed. David Freedberg and Jan de Vries. Santa Monica: Getty Center.

Van Koolbergen, Hans. 1997. "De materiele cultuur van Weesp en Weesperkarspel in de zeventiende en achttiende eeuw." In *Aards Geluk: de Nederlanders en Hun Spullen van 1550 tot 1850,* ed. Anton Schuurman, Jan de Vries, and Ad van der Woude, 121–60. Amsterdam: Uitgeverij Balans.

Van Zanden, J. L. 1991. "The first green revolution: The growth of production and productivity in European agriculture, 1870–1914." *Economic History Review* N.S. 44 (2): 215–39.

Varey, Simon. 1991. "New light on Edward Kidder's receipts." *Petits Propos Culinaire* 39: 46–51.

Varriano, John. 2009. *Tastes and temptations: Food and art in Renaissance Italy*. Berkeley: University of California Press.

Vertecchi, Giulia. 2009. *Il "masser ai formenti in terra nova." Il ruolo delle scorte granarie à Venezia nel XVIII secolo*. Roma: CROMA.

Viazzo, Pier Paolo. 1989. *Upland communities: Environment, population and social structure in the Alps since the sixteenth century*. Cambridge: Cambridge University Press.

Viazzo, Pier Paolo. 2003. "What's so special about the Mediterranean? Thirty years of research on household and family in Italy." *Continuity and Change* 18 (1): 111–37.

Villiers, John. 1981. "Trade and society in the Banda Islands in the sixteenth century." *Modern Asian Studies* 15 (4): 723–50.

Vogt, Jean. 1987. "Quelques aspects du grand commerce des bœufs et de l'approvisionnement de Strasbourg et de Paris." *Francia* 15: 281–97.

Vogt, Jean. 1992. "A propos du commerce des moutons dans la région d'Ingwiller." *Pays d'Alsace* 159–160: 93.

Voth, Hans-Joachim. 2000. *Time and work in England, 1750–1830.* Oxford: Clarendon Press.

Waley, Arthur. 1958. *Yuan Mei, eighteenth century Chinese poet.* Stanford, CA: Stanford University Press.

Waley-Cohen, Johanna. 2007. "The quest for perfect balance: Taste and gastronomy in Imperial China." In *Food: The history of taste,* ed. Paul Freedman, 99–132. Berkeley: University of California Press.

Wall, Wendy. 2002. *Staging domesticity: Household work and English identity in early modern drama.* Cambridge: Cambridge University Press.

Walter, John. 1989. "The social economy of dearth in early modern England." In *Famine, disease and the social order in early modern society,* ed. John Walter and Roger Schofield. Cambridge: Cambridge University Press.

Walter, John, and Roger Schofield, eds. 1989. "Famine, disease and crisis mortality in early modern society." In *Famine, disease and the social order in early modern society.* Cambridge: Cambridge University Press.

Watt, Ian. 1957. *The rise of the novel: Studies in Defoe, Richardson and Fielding.* Berkeley: University of California Press.

Weatherill, Lorna. 1988. *Consumer behaviour and material culture in Britain 1660–1760.* London: Routledge.

Weir, David R. 1984. "Life under pressure: France and England, 1670–1870." *The Journal of Economic History* 44 (1): 17–47.

Weiss Adamson, Melitta, ed. 2002. "Medieval Germany." In *Regional cuisines of medieval Europe: A book of essays.* London: Routledge.

Westermann, Ekkehard, ed. 1979. *Internationaler Ochsenhandel (1350–1750). Akten des 7th International Economic History Congress, Edinburgh, 1978.* Stuttgart: Klett-Cotta.

Westermann, Mariët. 1996. *A worldly art: The Dutch Republic 1585–1718.* New York: Abrams.

Wheaton, Barbara Ketcham. 1983. *Savoring the past: The French kitchen and table from 1300 to 1789.* Philadelphia: University of Pennsylvania Press.

White, Florence. 1951. *Good things in England.* London: Jonathan Cape.

Whittle, Jane, and Elizabeth Griffiths. Forthcoming. *Consumption and gender in the early-seventeenth-century household: The world of Alice Le Strange.* Oxford: Oxford University Press.

Wild, Antony. 2005. *Coffee: A dark history.* New York: W. W. Norton and Company.

Will, Pierre-Étienne, and R. Bin Wong. 1991. *Nourish the people: The state civilian granary system in China 1650–1850.* Ann Arbor: University of Michigan Center for Chinese Studies.

Willesme, Jean-Pierre. 1996. *Enseignes du Musée Carnavalet—Histoire de Paris: Catalogue raisonné.* Paris: Paris musées.

Wilson, Peter. 2010. *Europe's tragedy: A new history of the Thirty Years' War.* London: Penguin.

Wong, Roy Bin. 1997. *China transformed: Historical change and the limits of European experience.* Ithaca, NY: Cornell University Press.

Wrigley, E. Anthony. 1967. "A simple model of London's importance in changing English society and economy, 1650–1750." *Past and Present* 37: 44–70.

Wrigley, E. Anthony. 1991. "Energy availability and agricultural productivity." In *Land, labour and livestock: Historical studies in European agricultural productivity,* ed. B.M.S. Campbell and M. Overton, 326–30. Manchester: Manchester University Press.

Wrigley, E. Anthony, Rosalind S. Davies, James E. Oeppen, and Roger S. Schofield. 1997. *English population from family reconstitution 1580–1837.* Cambridge: Cambridge University Press.

Wrigley, E. Anthony, and Roger S. Schofield. 1981. *The population history of England, 1541–1871.* London: Edward Arnold.

Yerasimos, Marianna. 2005. *500 years of Ottoman cuisine.* Istanbul: Boyut.

Young, Hilary. 2002. "Porcelain for the dessert." In *Elegant eating: Four hundred years of dining in style,* ed. Philippa Glanville and Hilary Young, 90–91. London: V&A Publications.

Yuan, Mei. 2000. *Suiyuan Shidan.* Shanghai: Shanghai guji chubanshe.

Zahedieh, Nuala. 2001. "New international marketing. London and colonial commodities in the late seventeenth century." In *Fieri e mercati nella integrazione delle economie europee,* ed. S. Cavaciocchi, 359–70. Florence: Le Monnier.

Zanetti, Dante. 1963. "Contribution à l'étude des structures économiques: l'approvisionnement de Pavie au XVIᵉ siècle." *Annales E.S.C.* 18 (1): 44–62.

## WEB RESOURCES

British Museum, London, prints and drawings. Online collection database available at: http://www.britishmuseum.org/research/search_the_collection_database.aspx. Accessed November 7, 2010.

Coutts, Howard, and Ivan Day. 2008. "Sugar sculpture, porcelain and table layout, 1530–1830." Paper given at Henry Moore Institute, Leeds, October 8. Available at: http://www.henry-moore.org/hmi-journal/homepage/view-occasional-papers/sugar-sculptire/intro. Accessed April 1, 2010.

Gloning, Thomas. 2000. "Monumenta Culinaria et Diaetetica Historica: Corpus of culinary and dietetic texts of Europe from the Middle Ages to 1800." Available at: http://www.uni-giessen.de/gloning/kobu.htm. Accessed March 19, 2010.

Messent, Michael. 2001. *A short history of the worshipful company of cooks.* London: Worshipful company of cooks. Available at: http://www.cookslivery.org.uk/history.asp. Accessed September 27, 2009.

*Oxford Dictionary of National Biography.* 2008. Ed. H.C.G. Matthew and Brian Harrison. Available at: http://www.oxforddnb.com. Accessed November 4, 2010.

Radeff, Anne. 2000. "Historiens et modèles géographiques: des lieux centraux aux décentralités." In *Colloque Géoponts 2000 de Sion, Institut universitaire Kurt Bösch.* Available at: http://www.cyberato.org/. Accessed September 24, 2010.

Shaw-Taylor, Leigh, and E. A. Wrigley. 2008. "The occupational structure of England, c. 1750–1871: A preliminary report." Available at: www.geog.cam. ac.uk/research/projects/occupations/abstracts/. Accessed September 23, 2010.

Victoria and Albert Museum, London. "Collections." Available at: http://collections. vam.ac.uk/. Accessed June 11, 2011.

Waddesdon Manor: The Rothschild collection, "Trade cards and ephemera online." Available at: http://www.waddesdon.org.uk/searchthecollection/trade_cards_index.html. Accessed September 25, 2010.

# CONTRIBUTORS

**Brian Cowan** holds the Canada Research Chair in Early Modern British History at McGill University. He edits the *Journal of British Studies* with Elizabeth Elbourne, and his research focuses on the intersection between the early modern history of ideas and their social, cultural, and political contexts. He has published extensively on the history of the British coffee-house, amongst many other topics. Some publications include: *The Social Life of Coffee: The Emergence of the British Coffeehouse* (2005), *The State Trial of Doctor Henry Sacheverell* (2012), and "Publicity and Privacy in the Early Modern World," a forthcoming special issue of the journal *History Compass*.

**David Gentilcore** is professor of early modern history at the University of Leicester, where he also teaches in the medical faculty. He has published widely in the social and cultural history of early modern Italy, including, most recently, *Pomodoro! A History of the Tomato in Italy* (2010) with an Italian translation (2010). His *Medical Charlatanism in Early Modern Italy* (2006) was awarded the Royal Society of Canada's Jason A. Hannah medal.

**Beat Kümin** is professor of early modern European history at the University of Warwick. His research interests focus on the social and cultural history of German-speaking Europe and England (c. 1400–1800), especially social centres such as parish churches and public houses. Publications include *Drinking Matters: Public Houses and Social Exchange in Early Modern Central Europe*

(2007), and the (co-)edited collections *The World of the Tavern: Public Houses in Early Modern Europe* (2002), *The European World: An Introduction to Early Modern History* (2009), and "Brewing Cultures in Early Modern Towns" (special issue of the journal *Brewery History,* 135/2010).

**Victor Magagna** is associate professor of political science at the University of California San Diego. His research examines the cultural foundations of politics in pre-modern and early modern societies as diverse as nineteenth-century Spain, Tokugawa Japan, and Mayan civilization. He has published *Communities of Grain: Rural Rebellion in Comparative Perspective* (1991), which finds the sources of peasant rebellion not in class conflict, but in the structure of rural communities. Magagna is now completing two book manuscripts: *Revaluing the Republic: The Social Radicalism of Democratic Politics in Comparative Perspective* and a study of domestic politics in the ancient world.

**Fabio Parasecoli** is associate professor of food studies at the New School in New York City. His research focuses on the intersections among food, media, and politics. He is program advisor at Gustolab, a center for food and culture in Rome, and collaborates with other institutions, among which are the Universitat Oberta de Catalunya in Barcelona and the University of Gastronomic Sciences in Pollenzo, Italy. Among his recent publications are *Food Culture in Italy* (2004), the introduction to *Culinary Cultures in Europe* (The Council of Europe, 2005), and *Bite Me! Food and Pop Culture* (2008).

**Sara Pennell** is senior lecturer in the Humanities Department at Roehampton University, London. She teaches and researches subjects as various as Renaissance and early modern food practices; domestic knowledge and its manifestations; and consumption and everyday material culture in the period c. 1600–1800. Her most recent publications include book chapters on second-hand circulation in early modern England, and the meanings of broken china in early eighteenth-century England, and she is currently co-editing (with Michelle DiMeo) a book of essays entitled *Reading and Writing Recipes, circa 1600–1800,* which will be published with Manchester University Press in 2012.

**Anne Radeff** is *Professeur honoraire des Universités* (in France) and *Privatdozent* at the University of Bern (Switzerland). She chairs the inter-disciplinary science association Cyberato (www.cyberato.org) and is an expert advisor for the *Historical Dictionary of Switzerland* (www.dhs.ch). Her research examines sixteenth- to twenty-first-century Europe from two perspectives: the dialectical—economic, commercial, social, and political—relations of centrality–decentrality between different locations on the one hand, and global economy and spatial mobilities on the other. Her pub-lications include *Du café dans le chaudron: Economie globale d'Ancien Régime* (1996) and "Centres et périphéries ou centralités et décentralités?" in Angelo Torre (ed.), *Per vie di terra* (2007).

**Govind Sreenivasan** is associate professor of history at Brandeis University in Waltham, Massachusetts. His research centers on the peasantry of early modern Germany (c. 1400–1800), especially on the role of law and legal institutions in rural life. He also works on the legal history of the early modern world, and in particular on the comparative development of the European, Islamic, and East Asian legal traditions. Recent publications in-clude *The Peasants of Ottobeuren, 1487–1726: A Rural Society in Early Modern Europe* (2004).

**Pier Paolo Viazzo** is professor of social anthropology at the University of Turin. He has worked extensively, among other things, on European social, demographic, and environmental history, with special reference to the Alps and other mountain areas. His publications include *Upland Communities: Environment, Population and Social Structure in the Alps since the Sixteenth Century* (1989), the co-edited volume *The Decline of Infant and Child Mortality: The European Experience, 1750–1990* (1997), and the chapter on "Mortality, Fertility, and Family" in D. I. Kertzer and M. Barbagli (eds.), *Family Life in Early Modern Times, 1500–1789* (2001).

# INDEX

Individual victuals are grouped together under headings like "meat," "fruit," "grain," and "vegetables." In terms of names and places, the focus lies on entries deemed to be of particular significance by the contributors. Extra-European locations are subsumed under the respective Continents.

www.ingramcontent.com/pod-product-compliance
Lightning Source LLC
Chambersburg PA
CBHW081431270326
41932CB00019B/3158